Natural Language Processing with PyTorch

Build Intelligent Language Applications Using Deep Learning

Delip Rao and Brian McMahan

Beijing · Boston · Farnham · Sebastopol · Tokyo

Natural Language Processing with PyTorch

by Delip Rao and Brian McMahan

Published by O'Reilly Media, Inc., 1005 Gravenstein Highway North, Sebastopol, CA 95472.

O'Reilly books may be purchased for educational, business, or sales promotional use. Online editions are also available for most titles (*http://oreilly.com/safari*). For more information, contact our corporate/institutional sales department: 800-998-9938 or *corporate@oreilly.com*.

Acquisition Editor: Rachel Roumeliotis
Production Editor: Nan Barber
Proofreader: Rachel Head
Interior Designer: David Futato
Illustrator: Rebecca Demarest

Development Editor: Jeff Bleiel
Copyeditor: Octal Publishing, LLC
Indexer: Judy McConville
Cover Designer: Karen Montgomery

February 2019:   First Edition

Revision History for the First Edition
2019-01-16:   First Release

See *http://oreilly.com/catalog/errata.csp?isbn=9781491978238* for release details.

978-1-491-97823-8

[LSI]

Table of Contents

Preface

This book aims to bring newcomers to natural language processing (NLP) and deep learning to a tasting table covering important topics in both areas. Both of these subject areas are growing exponentially. As it introduces both deep learning and NLP with an emphasis on implementation, this book occupies an important middle ground. While writing the book, we had to make difficult, and sometimes uncomfortable, choices on what material to leave out. For a beginner reader, we hope the book will provide a strong foundation in the basics and a glimpse of what is possible. Machine learning, and deep learning in particular, is an experiential discipline, as opposed to an intellectual science. The generous end-to-end code examples in each chapter invite you to partake in that experience.

When we began working on the book, we started with PyTorch 0.2. The examples were revised with each PyTorch update from 0.2 to 0.4. PyTorch 1.0 (*https://pytorch.org/2018/05/02/road-to-1.0.html*) is due to release around when this book comes out. The code examples in the book are PyTorch 0.4–compliant and should work as they are with the upcoming PyTorch 1.0 release.[1]

A note regarding the style of the book. We have intentionally avoided mathematics in most places, not because deep learning math is particularly difficult (it is not), but because it is a distraction in many situations from the main goal of this book—to empower the beginner learner. Likewise, in many cases, both in code and text, we have favored exposition over succinctness. Advanced readers and experienced programmers will likely see ways to tighten up the code and so on, but our choice was to be as explicit as possible so as to reach the broadest of the audience that we want to reach.

---

1 See *https://pytorch.org/2018/05/02/road-to-1.0.html*

Conventions Used in This Book

The following typographical conventions are used in this book:

Italic
> Indicates new terms, URLs, email addresses, filenames, and file extensions.

`Constant width`
> Used for program listings, as well as within paragraphs to refer to program elements such as variable or function names, databases, data types, environment variables, statements, and keywords.

`Constant width bold`
> Shows commands or other text that should be typed literally by the user.

`Constant width italic`
> Shows text that should be replaced with user-supplied values or by values determined by context.

> This element signifies a tip or suggestion.

> This element signifies a general note.

> This element indicates a warning or caution.

Using Code Examples

Supplemental material (code examples, exercises, etc.) is available for download at *https://nlproc.info/PyTorchNLPBook/repo/*.

This book is here to help you get your job done. In general, if example code is offered with this book, you may use it in your programs and documentation. You do not need to contact us for permission unless you're reproducing a significant portion of the code. For example, writing a program that uses several chunks of code from this book does not require permission. Selling or distributing a CD-ROM of examples from O'Reilly books does require permission. Answering a question by citing this book and quoting example code does not require permission. Incorporating a significant amount of example code from this book into your product's documentation does require permission.

We appreciate, but do not require, attribution. An attribution usually includes the title, author, publisher, and ISBN. For example: "*Natural Language Processing with PyTorch* by Delip Rao and Brian McMahan (O'Reilly). Copyright 2019, Delip Rao and Brian McMahan, 978-1-491-97823-8."

If you feel your use of code examples falls outside fair use or the permission given above, feel free to contact us at *permissions@oreilly.com*.

O'Reilly Safari

 *Safari* (formerly Safari Books Online) is a membership-based training and reference platform for enterprise, government, educators, and individuals.

Members have access to thousands of books, training videos, Learning Paths, interactive tutorials, and curated playlists from over 250 publishers, including O'Reilly Media, Harvard Business Review, Prentice Hall Professional, Addison-Wesley Professional, Microsoft Press, Sams, Que, Peachpit Press, Adobe, Focal Press, Cisco Press, John Wiley & Sons, Syngress, Morgan Kaufmann, IBM Redbooks, Packt, Adobe Press, FT Press, Apress, Manning, New Riders, McGraw-Hill, Jones & Bartlett, and Course Technology, among others.

For more information, please visit *http://oreilly.com/safari*.

How to Contact Us

Please address comments and questions concerning this book to the publisher:

O'Reilly Media, Inc.
1005 Gravenstein Highway North
Sebastopol, CA 95472
800-998-9938 (in the United States or Canada)
707-829-0515 (international or local)
707-829-0104 (fax)

We have a web page for this book, where we list errata, examples, and any additional information. You can access this page at *http://bit.ly/nlprocbk*.

To comment or ask technical questions about this book, send email to *bookquestions@oreilly.com.*

For more information about our books, courses, conferences, and news, see our website at *http://www.oreilly.com.*

Find us on Facebook: *http://facebook.com/oreilly*

Follow us on Twitter: *http://twitter.com/oreillymedia*

Watch us on YouTube: *http://www.youtube.com/oreillymedia*

Acknowledgments

This book has gone through an evolution of sorts, with each version of the book looking unlike the version before. Different folks (and even different DL frameworks) were involved in each version.

The authors want to thank Goku Mohandas for his initial involvement in the book. Goku brought a lot of energy to the project before he had to leave for work reasons. Goku's enthusiasm for PyTorch and his positivity are unmatched, and the authors missed his presence. We expect great things coming from him!

The book would not be in top technical form if it not for the kind yet high-quality feedback from our technical reviewers, Liling Tan and Debasish Gosh. Liling contributed his expertise in developing products with state-of-the-art NLP, while Debasish gave highly valuable feedback from the perspective of the developer audience. We are also grateful for the encouragement from Alfredo Canziani, Soumith Chintala, and the many other amazing folks on the PyTorch Developer Forums. We also benefited from the daily rich NLP conversations among the Twitter #nlproc crowd. Many of this book's insights are as much attributable to that community as to our personal practice.

We would be remiss in our duties if we did not express gratitude to Jeff Bleiel for his excellent support as our editor. Without his direction, this book would not have made the light of the day. Bob Russell's copy edits and Nan Barber's production support turned this manuscript from a rough draft into a printable book. We also want to thank Shannon Cutt for her support in the book's early stages.

Much of the material in the book evolved from the 2-day NLP training the authors offered at O'Reilly's AI and Strata conferences. We want to thank Ben Lorica, Jason Perdue, and Sophia DeMartini for working with us on the trainings.

Delip is grateful to have Brian McMahan as a coauthor. Brian went out of his way to support the development of the book. It was a trip to share the joy and pains of development with Brian! Delip also wishes to thank Ben Lorica at O'Reilly for originally insisting he write a book on NLP.

Brian wishes to thank Sara Manuel for her endless support and Delip Rao for being the engine that drove this book to completion. Without Delip's unending persistence and grit, this book would not have been possible.

## CHAPTER 1

Introduction

Household names like Echo (Alexa), Siri, and Google Translate have at least one thing in common. They are all products derived from the application of *natural language processing* (NLP), one of the two main subject matters of this book. NLP refers to a set of techniques involving the application of statistical methods, with or without insights from linguistics, to understand text for the sake of solving real-world tasks. This "understanding" of text is mainly derived by transforming texts to useable computational *representations*, which are discrete or continuous combinatorial structures such as vectors or tensors, graphs, and trees.

The learning of representations suitable for a task from data (text in this case) is the subject of *machine learning*. The application of machine learning to textual data has more than three decades of history, but in the last 10 years[1] a set of machine learning techniques known as *deep learning* have continued to evolve and begun to prove highly effective for various artificial intelligence (AI) tasks in NLP, speech, and computer vision. Deep learning is another main subject that we cover; thus, this book is a study of NLP and deep learning.

 References are listed at the end of each chapter in this book.

Put simply, deep learning enables one to efficiently learn representations from data using an abstraction called the *computational graph* and numerical optimization

---

1 While the history of neural networks and NLP is long and rich, Collobert and Weston (2008) are often credited with pioneering the adoption of modern-style application deep learning to NLP.

techniques. Such is the success of deep learning and computational graphs that major tech companies such as Google, Facebook, and Amazon have published implementations of computational graph frameworks and libraries built on them to capture the mindshare of researchers and engineers. In this book, we consider *PyTorch*, an increasingly popular Python-based computational graph framework to implement deep learning algorithms. In this chapter, we explain what computational graphs are and our choice of using PyTorch as the framework.

The field of machine learning and deep learning is vast. In this chapter, and for most of this book, we mostly consider what's called *supervised learning*; that is, learning with labeled training examples. We explain the supervised learning paradigm that will become the foundation for the book. If you are not familiar with many of these terms so far, you're in the right place. This chapter, along with future chapters, not only clarifies but also dives deeper into them. If you are already familiar with some of the terminology and concepts mentioned here, we still encourage you to follow along, for two reasons: to establish a shared vocabulary for rest of the book, and to fill any gaps needed to understand the future chapters.

The goals for this chapter are to:

- Develop a clear understanding of the supervised learning paradigm, understand terminology, and develop a conceptual framework to approach learning tasks for future chapters.
- Learn how to encode inputs for the learning tasks.
- Understand what computational graphs are.
- Master the basics of PyTorch.

Let's get started!

The Supervised Learning Paradigm

Supervision in machine learning, or *supervised learning*, refers to cases where the ground truth for the *targets* (what's being predicted) is available for the *observations*. For example, in document classification, the target is a categorical label,[2] and the observation is a document. In machine translation, the observation is a sentence in one language and the target is a sentence in another language. With this understanding of the input data, we illustrate the supervised learning paradigm in Figure 1-1.

---

2 A categorical variable is one that takes one of a fixed set of values; for example, {TRUE, FALSE}, {VERB, NOUN, ADJECTIVE, ...}, and so on.

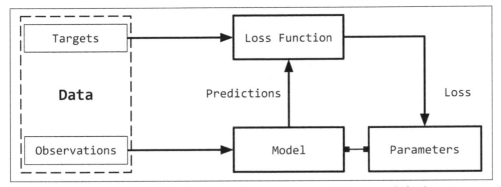

Figure 1-1. The supervised learning paradigm, a conceptual framework for learning from labeled input data.

We can break down the supervised learning paradigm, as illustrated in Figure 1-1, to six main concepts:

Observations
Observations are items about which we want to predict something. We denote observations using x. We sometimes refer to the observations as *inputs*.

Targets
Targets are labels corresponding to an observation. These are usually the things being predicted. Following standard notations in machine learning/deep learning, we use y to refer to these. Sometimes, these labels known as the *ground truth*.

Model
A model is a mathematical expression or a function that takes an observation, x, and predicts the value of its target label.

Parameters
Sometimes also called *weights*, these parameterize the model. It is standard to use the notation w (for weights) or $\hat{w}$.

Predictions
Predictions, also called *estimates*, are the values of the targets guessed by the model, given the observations. We denote these using a "hat" notation. So, the prediction of a target y is denoted as $\hat{y}$.

Loss function
A loss function is a function that compares how far off a prediction is from its target for observations in the training data. Given a target and its prediction, the loss function assigns a scalar real value called the *loss*. The lower the value of the loss, the better the model is at predicting the target. We use L to denote the loss function.

Although it is not strictly necessary to be mathematically formal to be productive in NLP/deep learning modeling or to write this book, we will formally restate the supervised learning paradigm to equip readers who are new to the area with the standard terminology so that they have some familiarity with the notations and style of writing in the research papers they may encounter on arXiv.

Consider a dataset $D = \{X_i, y_i\}_{i=1}^{n}$ with n examples. Given this dataset, we want to learn a function (a model) f parameterized by weights w. That is, we make an assumption about the structure of f, and given that structure, the learned values of the weights w will fully characterize the model. For a given input X, the model predicts $\hat{y}$ as the target:

$$\hat{y} = f(X, w)$$

In supervised learning, for training examples, we know the true target y for an observation. The loss for this instance will then be $L(y, \hat{y})$. Supervised learning then becomes a process of finding the optimal parameters/weights w that will minimize the cumulative loss for all the n examples.

Training Using (Stochastic) Gradient Descent

The goal of supervised learning is to pick values of the parameters that minimize the loss function for a given dataset. In other words, this is equivalent to finding roots in an equation. We know that *gradient descent* is a common technique to find roots of an equation. Recall that in traditional gradient descent, we guess some initial values for the roots (parameters) and update the parameters iteratively until the objective function (loss function) evaluates to a value below an acceptable threshold (aka convergence criterion). For large datasets, implementation of traditional gradient descent over the entire dataset is usually impossible due to memory constraints, and very slow due to the computational expense. Instead, an approximation for gradient descent called *stochastic gradient descent* (SGD) is usually employed. In the stochastic case, a data point or a subset of data points are picked at random, and the gradient is computed for that subset. When a single data point is used, the approach is called pure SGD, and when a subset of (more than one) data points are used, we refer to it as *minibatch SGD*. Often the words "pure" and "minibatch" are dropped when the approach being used is clear based on the context. In practice, pure SGD is rarely used because it results in very slow convergence due to noisy updates. There are different variants of the general SGD algorithm, all aiming for faster convergence. In later chapters, we explore some of these variants along with how the gradients are used in updating the parameters. This process of iteratively updating the parameters is called *backpropagation*. Each step (aka epoch) of backpropagation consists of a *forward pass* and a *backward pass*. The forward pass evaluates the inputs with the cur-

---

rent values of the parameters and computes the loss function. The backward pass updates the parameters using the gradient of the loss.

Observe that until now, nothing here is specific to deep learning or neural networks.[3] The directions of the arrows in Figure 1-1 indicate the "flow" of data while training the system. We will have more to say about training and on the concept of "flow" in "Computational Graphs" on page 10, but first, let's take a look at how we can represent our inputs and targets in NLP problems numerically so that we can train models and predict outcomes.

Observation and Target Encoding

We will need to represent the observations (text) numerically to use them in conjunction with machine learning algorithms. Figure 1-2 presents a visual depiction.

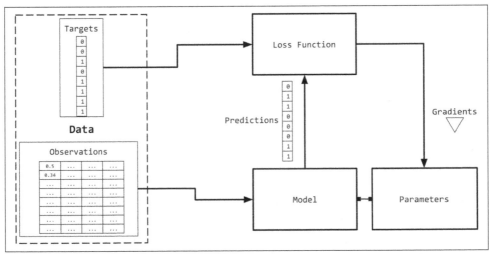

Figure 1-2. Observation and target encoding: The targets and observations from Figure 1-1 are represented numerically as vectors, or tensors. This is collectively known as input "encoding."

A simple way to represent text is as a numerical vector. There are innumerable ways to perform this mapping/representation. In fact, much of this book is dedicated to learning such representations for a task from data. However, we begin with some simple count-based representations that are based on heuristics. Though simple, they

---

3 Deep learning is distinguished from traditional neural networks as discussed in the literature before 2006 in that it refers to a growing collection of techniques that enabled reliability by adding more layers in the network. We study why this is important in Chapters 3 and 4.

are incredibly powerful as they are and can serve as a starting point for richer representation learning. All of these count-based representations start with a vector of fixed dimension.

One-Hot Representation

The *one-hot representation*, as the name suggests, starts with a zero vector, and sets as 1 the corresponding entry in the vector if the word is present in the sentence or document. Consider the following two sentences:

```
Time flies like an arrow.
Fruit flies like a banana.
```

Tokenizing the sentences, ignoring punctuation, and treating everything as lowercase, will yield a vocabulary of size 8: {time, fruit, flies, like, a, an, arrow, banana}. So, we can represent each word with an eight-dimensional one-hot vector. In this book, we use 1_w to mean one-hot representation for a token/word w.

The collapsed one-hot representation for a phrase, sentence, or a document is simply a logical OR of the one-hot representations of its constituent words. Using the encoding shown in Figure 1-3, the one-hot representation for the phrase "like a banana" will be a 3×8 matrix, where the columns are the eight-dimensional one-hot vectors. It is also common to see a "collapsed" or a binary encoding where the text/phrase is represented by a vector the length of the vocabulary, with 0s and 1s to indicate absence or presence of a word. The binary encoding for "like a banana" would then be: [0, 0, 0, 1, 1, 0, 0, 1].

	time	fruit	flies	like	a	an	arrow	banana
1_{time}	1	0	0	0	0	0	0	0
1_{fruit}	0	1	0	0	0	0	0	0
1_{flies}	0	0	1	0	0	0	0	0
1_{like}	0	0	0	1	0	0	0	0
1_{a}	0	0	0	0	1	0	0	0
1_{an}	0	0	0	0	0	1	0	0
1_{arrow}	0	0	0	0	0	0	1	0
1_{banana}	0	0	0	0	0	0	0	1

Figure 1-3. One-hot representation for encoding the sentences "Time flies like an arrow" and "Fruit flies like a banana."

At this point, if you are cringing that we collapsed the two different meanings (or senses) of "flies," congratulations, astute reader! Language is full of ambiguity, but we can still build useful solutions by making horribly simplifying assumptions. It is possible to learn sense-specific representations, but we are getting ahead of ourselves now.

Although we will rarely use anything other than a one-hot representation for the inputs in this book, we will now introduce the *Term-Frequency* (TF) and *Term-Frequency-Inverse-Document-Frequency* (TF-IDF) representations. This is done because of their popularity in NLP, for historical reasons, and for the sake of completeness. These representations have a long history in information retrieval (IR) and are actively used even today in production NLP systems.

TF Representation

The TF representation of a phrase, sentence, or document is simply the sum of the one-hot representations of its constituent words. To continue with our silly examples, using the aforementioned one-hot encoding, the sentence "Fruit flies like time flies a fruit" has the following TF representation: [1, 2, 2, 1, 1, 0, 0, 0]. Notice that each entry is a count of the number of times the corresponding word appears in the sentence (corpus). We denote the TF of a word *w* by *TF(w)*.

Example 1-1. Generating a "collapsed" one-hot or binary representation using scikit-learn

```
from sklearn.feature_extraction.text import CountVectorizer
import seaborn as sns

corpus = ['Time flies flies like an arrow.',
          'Fruit flies like a banana.']
one_hot_vectorizer = CountVectorizer(binary=True)
one_hot = one_hot_vectorizer.fit_transform(corpus).toarray()
sns.heatmap(one_hot, annot=True,
            cbar=False, xticklabels=vocab,
            yticklabels=['Sentence 2'])
```

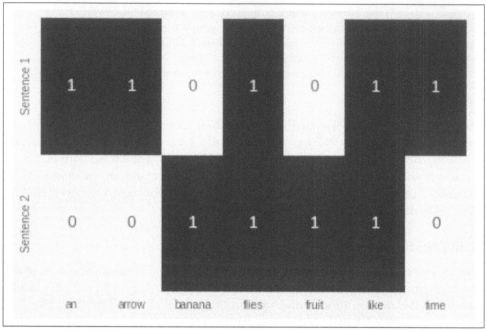

Figure 1-4. The collapsed one-hot representation generated by Example 1-1.

TF-IDF Representation

Consider a collection of patent documents. You would expect most of them to contain words like *claim, system, method, procedure,* and so on, often repeated multiple times. The TF representation weights words proportionally to their frequency. However, common words such as "claim" do not add anything to our understanding of a specific patent. Conversely, if a rare word (such as "tetrafluoroethylene") occurs less frequently but is quite likely to be indicative of the nature of the patent document, we would want to give it a larger weight in our representation. The Inverse-Document-Frequency (IDF) is a heuristic to do exactly that.

The IDF representation penalizes common tokens and rewards rare tokens in the vector representation. The *IDF(w)* of a token *w* is defined with respect to a corpus as:

$$IDF(w) = \log \frac{N}{n_w}$$

where n_w is the number of documents containing the word *w* and *N* is the total number of documents. The TF-IDF score is simply the product *TF(w) * IDF(w)*. First, notice how if there is a very common word that occurs in all documents (i.e., $n_w = N$), *IDF(w)* is 0 and the TF-IDF score is 0, thereby completely penalizing that term. Second, if a term occurs very rarely, perhaps in only one document, the IDF will be the maximum possible value, log N. Example 1-2 shows how to generate a TF-IDF representation of a list of English sentences using scikit-learn.

Example 1-2. Generating a TF-IDF representation using scikit-learn

```
from sklearn.feature_extraction.text import TfidfVectorizer
import seaborn as sns

tfidf_vectorizer = TfidfVectorizer()
tfidf = tfidf_vectorizer.fit_transform(corpus).toarray()
sns.heatmap(tfidf, annot=True, cbar=False, xticklabels=vocab,
            yticklabels= ['Sentence 1', 'Sentence 2'])
```

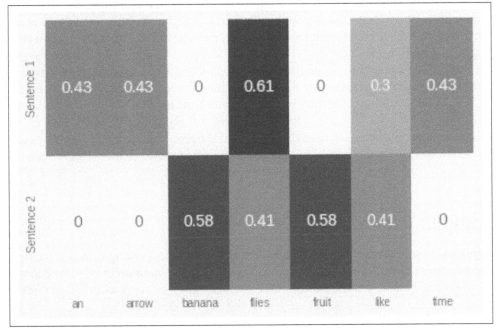

Figure 1-5. The TF-IDF representation generated by Example 1-2.

In deep learning, it is rare to see inputs encoded using heuristic representations like TF-IDF because the goal is to learn a representation. Often, we start with a one-hot encoding using integer indices and a special "embedding lookup" layer to construct inputs to the neural network. In later chapters, we present several examples of doing this.

Target Encoding

As noted in the "The Supervised Learning Paradigm" on page 2, the exact nature of the target variable can depend on the NLP task being solved. For example, in cases of machine translation, summarization, and question answering, the target is also text and is encoded using approaches such as the previously described one-hot encoding.

Many NLP tasks actually use categorical labels, wherein the model must predict one of a fixed set of labels. A common way to encode this is to use a unique index per label, but this simple representation can become problematic when the number of output labels is simply too large. An example of this is the *language modeling* problem, in which the task is to predict the next word, given the words seen in the past. The label space is the entire vocabulary of a language, which can easily grow to several hundred thousand, including special characters, names, and so on. We revisit this problem in later chapters and see how to address it.

Some NLP problems involve predicting a numerical value from a given text. For example, given an English essay, we might need to assign a numeric grade or a readability score. Given a restaurant review snippet, we might need to predict a numerical star rating up to the first decimal. Given a user's tweets, we might be required to predict the user's age group. Several approaches exist to encode numerical targets, but simply placing the targets into categorical "bins"—for example, "0-18," "19-25," "25-30," and so on—and treating it as an ordinal classification problem is a reasonable approach.[4] The binning can be uniform or nonuniform and data-driven. Although a detailed discussion of this is beyond the scope of this book, we draw your attention to these issues because target encoding affects performance dramatically in such cases, and we encourage you to see Dougherty et al. (1995) and the references therein.

Computational Graphs

Figure 1-1 summarized the supervised learning (training) paradigm as a data flow architecture where the inputs are transformed by the model (a mathematical expression) to obtain predictions, and the loss function (another expression) to provide a feedback signal to adjust the parameters of the model. This data flow can be conveniently implemented using the computational graph data structure.[5] Technically, a computational graph is an abstraction that models mathematical expressions. In the context of deep learning, the implementations of the computational graph (such as Theano, TensorFlow, and PyTorch) do additional bookkeeping to implement automatic differentiation needed to obtain gradients of parameters during training in the supervised learning paradigm. We explore this further in "PyTorch Basics" on page 11.

---

4 An "ordinal" classification is a multiclass classification problem in which there exists a partial order between the labels. In our age example, the category "0–18" comes before "19–25," and so on.

5 Seppo Linnainmaa (*http://bit.ly/2Rnmdao*) first introduced the idea of automatic differentiation on computational graphs as a part of his 1970 masters' thesis! Variants of that became the foundation for modern deep learning frameworks like Theano, TensorFlow, and PyTorch.

Inference (or prediction) is simply expression evaluation (a forward flow on a computational graph). Let's see how the computational graph models expressions. Consider the expression:

$$y = wx + b$$

This can be written as two subexpressions, $z = wx$ and $y = z + b$. We can then represent the original expression using a directed acyclic graph (DAG) in which the nodes are the mathematical operations, like multiplication and addition. The inputs to the operations are the incoming edges to the nodes and the output of each operation is the outgoing edge. So, for the expression $y = wx + b$, the computational graph is as illustrated in Figure 1-6. In the following section, we see how PyTorch allows us to create computational graphs in a straightforward manner and how it enables us to calculate the gradients without concerning ourselves with any bookkeeping.

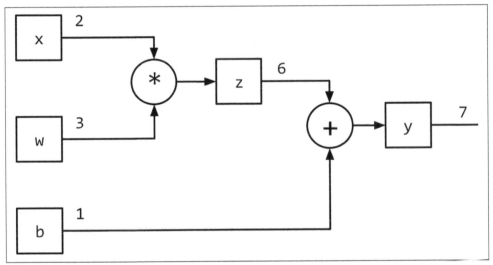

Figure 1-6. Representing $y = wx + b$ using a computational graph.

PyTorch Basics

In this book, we extensively use PyTorch for implementing our deep learning models. PyTorch is an open source, community-driven deep learning framework. Unlike Theano, Caffe, and TensorFlow, PyTorch implements a tape-based automatic differentiation (*http://bit.ly/2Jrntq1*) method that allows us to define and execute computational graphs dynamically. This is extremely helpful for debugging and also for constructing sophisticated models with minimal effort.

> ## Dynamic Versus Static Computational Graphs
>
> Static frameworks like Theano, Caffe, and TensorFlow require the computational graph to be first declared, compiled, and then executed.[6] Although this leads to extremely efficient implementations (useful in production and mobile settings), it can become quite cumbersome during research and development. Modern frameworks like Chainer, DyNet, and PyTorch implement dynamic computational graphs to allow for a more flexible, imperative style of development, without needing to compile the models before every execution. Dynamic computational graphs are especially useful in modeling NLP tasks for which each input could potentially result in a different graph structure.

PyTorch is an optimized tensor manipulation library that offers an array of packages for deep learning. At the core of the library is the *tensor*, which is a mathematical object holding some multidimensional data. A tensor of order zero is just a number, or a *scalar*. A tensor of order one (1st-order tensor) is an array of numbers, or a *vector*. Similarly, a 2nd-order tensor is an array of vectors, or a *matrix*. Therefore, a tensor can be generalized as an *n*-dimensional array of scalars, as illustrated in Figure 1-7.

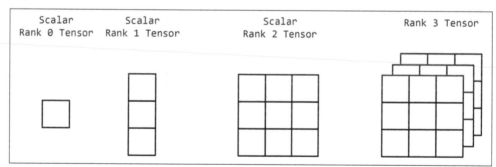

Figure 1-7. Tensors as a generalization of multidimensional arrays.

In this section, we take our first steps with PyTorch to familiarize you with various PyTorch operations. These include:

- Creating tensors

---

6 As of v1.7, TensorFlow has an "eager mode" that makes it unnecessary to compile the graph before execution, but static graphs are still the mainstay of TensorFlow.

- Operations with tensors
- Indexing, slicing, and joining with tensors
- Computing gradients with tensors
- Using CUDA tensors with GPUs

We recommend that at this point you have a Python 3.5+ notebook ready with PyTorch installed, as described next, and that you follow along with the examples.[7] We also recommend working through the exercises later in the chapter.

Installing PyTorch

The first step is to install PyTorch on your machines by choosing your system preferences at *pytorch.org* (*http://bit.ly/2DqhmCv*). Choose your operating system and then the package manager (we recommend Conda or Pip), followed by the version of Python that you are using (we recommend 3.5+). This will generate the command for you to execute to install PyTorch. As of this writing, the install command for the Conda environment, for example, is as follows:

```
conda install pytorch torchvision -c pytorch
```

If you have a CUDA-enabled graphics processor unit (GPU), you should also choose the appropriate version of CUDA. For additional details, follow the installation instructions on *pytorch.org* (*http://bit.ly/2DqhmCv*).

Creating Tensors

First, we define a helper function, describe(x), that will summarize various properties of a tensor *x*, such as the type of the tensor, the dimensions of the tensor, and the contents of the tensor:

Input[0]	`def describe(x):`
	`    print("Type: {}".format(x.type()))`
	`    print("Shape/size: {}".format(x.shape))`
	`    print("Values: \n{}".format(x))`

---

7 You can find the code for this section under */chapters/chapter_1/PyTorch_Basics.ipynb* in this book's GitHub repo (*https://nlproc.info/PyTorchNLPBook/repo/*).

PyTorch allows us to create tensors in many different ways using the torch package. One way to create a tensor is to initialize a random one by specifying its dimensions, as shown in Example 1-3.

Example 1-3. Creating a tensor in PyTorch with torch.Tensor

Input[0]
```
import torch
describe(torch.Tensor(2, 3))
```

Output[0]
```
Type: torch.FloatTensor
Shape/size: torch.Size([2, 3])
Values:
tensor([[ 3.2018e-05,  4.5747e-41,  2.5058e+25],
        [ 3.0813e-41,  4.4842e-44,  0.0000e+00]])
```

We can also create a tensor by randomly initializing it with values from a uniform distribution on the interval [0, 1) or the standard normal distribution[8] as illustrated in Example 1-4. Randomly initialized tensors, say from the uniform distribution, are important, as you will see in Chapters 3 and 4.

Example 1-4. Creating a randomly initialized tensor

Input[0]
```
import torch
describe(torch.rand(2, 3))   # uniform random
describe(torch.randn(2, 3))  # random normal
```

Output[0]
```
Type:   torch.FloatTensor
Shape/size:   torch.Size([2, 3])
Values:
 tensor([[ 0.0242,  0.6630,  0.9787],
         [ 0.1037,  0.3920,  0.6084]])

Type: torch.FloatTensor
Shape/size: torch.Size([2, 3])
Values:
tensor([[-0.1330, -2.9222, -1.3649],
        [ 2.3648,  1.1561,  1.5042]])
```

We can also create tensors all filled with the same scalar. For creating a tensor of zeros or ones, we have built-in functions, and for filling it with specific values, we can use the fill_() method. Any PyTorch method with an underscore (_) refers to an

---

8 The standard normal distribution is a normal distribution with mean=0 and variance=1,

in-place operation; that is, it modifies the content in place without creating a new object, as shown in Example 1-5.

Example 1-5. Creating a filled tensor

Input[0]
```
import torch
describe(torch.zeros(2, 3))
x = torch.ones(2, 3)
describe(x)
x.fill_(5)
describe(x)
```

Output[0]
```
Type: torch.FloatTensor
Shape/size: torch.Size([2, 3])
Values:
tensor([[ 0.,   0.,   0.],
        [ 0.,   0.,   0.]])

Type: torch.FloatTensor
Shape/size: torch.Size([2, 3])
Values:
tensor([[ 1.,   1.,   1.],
        [ 1.,   1.,   1.]])

Type: torch.FloatTensor
Shape/size: torch.Size([2, 3])
Values:
tensor([[ 5.,   5.,   5.],
        [ 5.,   5.,   5.]])
```

Example 1-6 demonstrates how we can also create a tensor declaratively by using Python lists.

Example 1-6. Creating and initializing a tensor from lists

Input[0]
```
x = torch.Tensor([[1, 2, 3],
                  [4, 5, 6]])
describe(x)
```

Output[0]
```
Type: torch.FloatTensor
Shape/size: torch.Size([2, 3])
Values:
tensor([[ 1.,   2.,   3.],
        [ 4.,   5.,   6.]])
```

The values can either come from a list, as in the preceding example, or from a NumPy array. And, of course, we can always go from a PyTorch tensor to a NumPy array, as well. Notice that the type of the tensor is DoubleTensor instead of the default FloatTensor (see the next section). This corresponds with the data type of the NumPy random matrix, a float64, as presented in Example 1-7.

Example 1-7. Creating and initializing a tensor from NumPy

| Input[0] | ```
import torch
import numpy as np
npy = np.random.rand(2, 3)
describe(torch.from_numpy(npy))
``` |
| Output[0] | ```
Type: torch.DoubleTensor
Shape/size: torch.Size([2, 3])
Values:
tensor([[ 0.8360,  0.8836,  0.0545],
        [ 0.6928,  0.2333,  0.7984]], dtype=torch.float64)
``` |

The ability to convert between NumPy arrays and PyTorch tensors becomes important when working with legacy libraries that use NumPy-formatted numerical values.

Tensor Types and Size

Each tensor has an associated type and size. The default tensor type when you use the torch.Tensor constructor is torch.FloatTensor. However, you can convert a tensor to a different type (float, long, double, etc.) by specifying it at initialization or later using one of the typecasting methods. There are two ways to specify the initialization type: either by directly calling the constructor of a specific tensor type, such as Float Tensor or LongTensor, or using a special method, torch.tensor(), and providing the dtype, as shown in Example 1-8.

Example 1-8. Tensor properties

| Input[0] | ```
x = torch.FloatTensor([[1, 2, 3],
                       [4, 5, 6]])
describe(x)
``` |
| Output[0] | ```
Type: torch.FloatTensor
Shape/size: torch.Size([2, 3])
Values:
tensor([[ 1.,  2.,  3.],
        [ 4.,  5.,  6.]])
``` |
| Input[1] | ```
x = x.long()
describe(x)
``` |
```

| Output[1] | ```
Type: torch.LongTensor
Shape/size: torch.Size([2, 3])
Values:
tensor([[ 1,  2,  3],
        [ 4,  5,  6]])
``` |

| Input[2] | ```
x = torch.tensor([[1, 2, 3],
                  [4, 5, 6]], dtype=torch.int64)
describe(x)
``` |

| Output[2] | ```
Type: torch.LongTensor
Shape/size: torch.Size([2, 3])
Values:
tensor([[ 1,  2,  3],
        [ 4,  5,  6]])
``` |

| Input[3] | ```
x = x.float()
describe(x)
``` |

| Output[3] | ```
Type: torch.FloatTensor
Shape/size: torch.Size([2, 3])
Values:
tensor([[ 1.,  2.,  3.],
        [ 4.,  5.,  6.]])
``` |

We use the shape property and size() method of a tensor object to access the measurements of its dimensions. The two ways of accessing these measurements are mostly synonymous. Inspecting the shape of the tensor is an indispensable tool in debugging PyTorch code.

Tensor Operations

After you have created your tensors, you can operate on them like you would do with traditional programming language types, like +, -, *, /. Instead of the operators, you can also use functions like .add(), as shown in Example 1-9, that correspond to the symbolic operators.

Example 1-9. Tensor operations: addition

| Input[0] | ```
import torch
x = torch.randn(2, 3)
describe(x)
``` |

```
Output[0]    Type: torch.FloatTensor
             Shape/size: torch.Size([2, 3])
             Values:
             tensor([[ 0.0461,  0.4024, -1.0115],
                     [ 0.2167, -0.6123,  0.5036]])
```

```
Input[1]     describe(torch.add(x, x))
```

```
Output[1]    Type: torch.FloatTensor
             Shape/size: torch.Size([2, 3])
             Values:
             tensor([[ 0.0923,  0.8048, -2.0231],
                     [ 0.4335, -1.2245,  1.0072]])
```

```
Input[2]     describe(x + x)
```

```
Output[2]    Type: torch.FloatTensor
             Shape/size: torch.Size([2, 3])
             Values:
             tensor([[ 0.0923,  0.8048, -2.0231],
                     [ 0.4335, -1.2245,  1.0072]])
```

There are also operations that you can apply to a specific dimension of a tensor. As you might have already noticed, for a 2D tensor we represent rows as the dimension 0 and columns as dimension 1, as illustrated in Example 1-10.

Example 1-10. Dimension-based tensor operations

```
Input[0]     import torch
             x = torch.arange(6)
             describe(x)
```

```
Output[0]    Type: torch.FloatTensor
             Shape/size: torch.Size([6])
             Values:
             tensor([ 0.,  1.,  2.,  3.,  4.,  5.])
```

```
Input[1]     x = x.view(2, 3)
             describe(x)
```

```
Output[1]    Type: torch.FloatTensor
             Shape/size: torch.Size([2, 3])
             Values:
             tensor([[ 0.,  1.,  2.],
                     [ 3.,  4.,  5.]])
```

<table>
<tr><td>Input[2]</td><td>

```
describe(torch.sum(x, dim=0))
```

</td></tr>
<tr><td>Output[2]</td><td>

```
Type: torch.FloatTensor
Shape/size: torch.Size([3])
Values:
tensor([ 3.,   5.,   7.])
```

</td></tr>
<tr><td>Input[3]</td><td>

```
describe(torch.sum(x, dim=1))
```

</td></tr>
<tr><td>Output[3]</td><td>

```
Type: torch.FloatTensor
Shape/size: torch.Size([2])
Values:
tensor([  3.,  12.])
```

</td></tr>
<tr><td>Input[4]</td><td>

```
describe(torch.transpose(x, 0, 1))
```

</td></tr>
<tr><td>Output[4]</td><td>

```
Type: torch.FloatTensor
Shape/size: torch.Size([3, 2])
Values:
tensor([[ 0.,   3.],
        [ 1.,   4.],
        [ 2.,   5.]])
```

</td></tr>
</table>

Often, we need to do more complex operations that involve a combination of indexing, slicing, joining, and mutations. Like NumPy and other numeric libraries, PyTorch has built-in functions to make such tensor manipulations very simple.

Indexing, Slicing, and Joining

If you are a NumPy user, PyTorch's indexing and slicing scheme, shown in Example 1-11, might be very familiar to you.

Example 1-11. Slicing and indexing a tensor

<table>
<tr><td>Input[0]</td><td>

```
import torch
x = torch.arange(6).view(2, 3)
describe(x)
```

</td></tr>
<tr><td>Output[0]</td><td>

```
Type: torch.FloatTensor
Shape/size: torch.Size([2, 3])
Values:
tensor([[ 0.,   1.,   2.],
        [ 3.,   4.,   5.]])
```

</td></tr>
<tr><td>Input[1]</td><td>

```
describe(x[:1, :2])
```

</td></tr>
</table>

```
Output[1]    Type: torch.FloatTensor
             Shape/size: torch.Size([1, 2])
             Values:
             tensor([[ 0.,  1.]])


Input[2]     describe(x[0, 1])


Output[2]    Type: torch.FloatTensor
             Shape/size: torch.Size([])
             Values:
             1.0
```

Example 1-12 demonstrates that PyTorch also has functions for complex indexing and slicing operations, where you might be interested in accessing noncontiguous locations of a tensor efficiently.

Example 1-12. Complex indexing: noncontiguous indexing of a tensor

```
Input[0]     indices = torch.LongTensor([0, 2])
             describe(torch.index_select(x, dim=1, index=indices))


Output[0]    Type: torch.FloatTensor
             Shape/size: torch.Size([2, 2])
             Values:
             tensor([[ 0.,  2.],
                     [ 3.,  5.]])


Input[1]     indices = torch.LongTensor([0, 0])
             describe(torch.index_select(x, dim=0, index=indices))


Output[1]    Type: torch.FloatTensor
             Shape/size: torch.Size([2, 3])
             Values:
             tensor([[ 0.,  1.,  2.],
                     [ 0.,  1.,  2.]])


Input[2]     row_indices = torch.arange(2).long()
             col_indices = torch.LongTensor([0, 1])
             describe(x[row_indices, col_indices])


Output[2]    Type: torch.FloatTensor
             Shape/size: torch.Size([2])
             Values:
             tensor([ 0.,  4.])
```

Notice that the indices are a `LongTensor`; this is a requirement for indexing using PyTorch functions. We can also join tensors using built-in concatenation functions, as shown in Example 1-13, by specifying the tensors and dimension.

Example 1-13. Concatenating tensors

Input[0]
```
import torch
x = torch.arange(6).view(2,3)
describe(x)
```

Output[0]
```
Type: torch.FloatTensor
Shape/size: torch.Size([2, 3])
Values:
tensor([[ 0.,   1.,   2.],
        [ 3.,   4.,   5.]])
```

Input[1]
```
describe(torch.cat([x, x], dim=0))
```

Output[1]
```
Type: torch.FloatTensor
Shape/size: torch.Size([4, 3])
Values:
tensor([[ 0.,   1.,   2.],
        [ 3.,   4.,   5.],
        [ 0.,   1.,   2.],
        [ 3.,   4.,   5.]])
```

Input[2]
```
describe(torch.cat([x, x], dim=1))
```

Output[2]
```
Type: torch.FloatTensor
Shape/size: torch.Size([2, 6])
Values:
tensor([[ 0.,   1.,   2.,   0.,   1.,   2.],
        [ 3.,   4.,   5.,   3.,   4.,   5.]])
```

Input[3]
```
describe(torch.stack([x, x]))
```

Output[3]
```
Type: torch.FloatTensor
Shape/size: torch.Size([2, 2, 3])
Values:
tensor([[[ 0.,   1.,   2.],
         [ 3.,   4.,   5.]],

        [[ 0.,   1.,   2.],
         [ 3.,   4.,   5.]]])
```

PyTorch also implements highly efficient linear algebra operations on tensors, such as multiplication, inverse, and trace, as you can see in Example 1-14.

Example 1-14. Linear algebra on tensors: multiplication

| Input[0] | ```
import torch
x1 = torch.arange(6).view(2, 3)
describe(x1)
``` |
|---|---|

| Output[0] | ```
Type: torch.FloatTensor
Shape/size: torch.Size([2, 3])
Values:
tensor([[ 0.,   1.,   2.],
        [ 3.,   4.,   5.]])
``` |
|---|---|

| Input[1] | ```
x2 = torch.ones(3, 2)
x2[:, 1] += 1
describe(x2)
``` |
|---|---|

| Output[1] | ```
Type: torch.FloatTensor
Shape/size: torch.Size([3, 2])
Values:
tensor([[ 1.,   2.],
        [ 1.,   2.],
        [ 1.,   2.]])
``` |
|---|---|

| Input[2] | ```
describe(torch.mm(x1, x2))
``` |
|---|---|

| Output[2] | ```
Type: torch.FloatTensor
Shape/size: torch.Size([2, 2])
Values:
tensor([[ 3.,    6.],
        [ 12.,   24.]])
``` |
|---|---|

So far, we have looked at ways to create and manipulate constant PyTorch tensor objects. Just as a programming language (such as Python) has variables that encapsulate a piece of data and has additional information about that data (like the memory address where it is stored, for example), PyTorch tensors handle the bookkeeping needed for building computational graphs for machine learning simply by enabling a Boolean flag at instantiation time.

Tensors and Computational Graphs

PyTorch tensor class encapsulates the data (the tensor itself) and a range of operations, such as algebraic operations, indexing, and reshaping operations. However, as shown in Example 1-15, when the `requires_grad` Boolean flag is set to `True` on a tensor, bookkeeping operations are enabled that can track the gradient at the tensor as well as the gradient function, both of which are needed to facilitate the gradient-based learning discussed in "The Supervised Learning Paradigm" on page 2.

Example 1-15. Creating tensors for gradient bookkeeping

```
Input[0]    import torch
            x = torch.ones(2, 2, requires_grad=True)
            describe(x)
            print(x.grad is None)
```

```
Output[0]   Type: torch.FloatTensor
            Shape/size: torch.Size([2, 2])
            Values:
            tensor([[ 1.,   1.],
                    [ 1.,   1.]])
            True
```

```
Input[1]    y = (x + 2) * (x + 5) + 3
            describe(y)
            print(x.grad is None)
```

```
Output[1]   Type: torch.FloatTensor
            Shape/size: torch.Size([2, 2])
            Values:
            tensor([[ 21.,   21.],
                    [ 21.,   21.]])
            True
```

```
Input[2]    z = y.mean()
            describe(z)
            z.backward()
            print(x.grad is None)
```

```
Output[2]   Type: torch.FloatTensor
            Shape/size: torch.Size([])
            Values:
            21.0
            False
```

When you create a tensor with `requires_grad=True`, you are requiring PyTorch to manage bookkeeping information that computes gradients. First, PyTorch will keep track of the values of the forward pass. Then, at the end of the computations, a single scalar is used to compute a backward pass. The backward pass is initiated by using the `backward()` method on a tensor resulting from the evaluation of a loss function. The backward pass computes a gradient value for a tensor object that participated in the forward pass.

In general, the gradient is a value that represents the slope of a function output with respect to the function input. In the computational graph setting, gradients exist for each parameter in the model and can be thought of as the parameter's contribution to the error signal. In PyTorch, you can access the gradients for the nodes in the computational graph by using the `.grad` member variable. Optimizers use the `.grad` variable to update the values of the parameters.

CUDA Tensors

So far, we have been allocating our tensors on the CPU memory. When doing linear algebra operations, it might make sense to utilize a GPU, if you have one. To use a GPU, you need to first allocate the tensor on the GPU's memory. Access to the GPUs is via a specialized API called CUDA. The CUDA API was created by NVIDIA and is limited to use on only NVIDIA GPUs.[9] PyTorch offers CUDA tensor objects that are indistinguishable in use from the regular CPU-bound tensors except for the way they are allocated internally.

PyTorch makes it very easy to create these CUDA tensors, transfering the tensor from the CPU to the GPU while maintaining its underlying type. The preferred method in PyTorch is to be *device agnostic* and write code that works whether it's on the GPU or the CPU. In Example 1-16, we first check whether a GPU is available by using `torch.cuda.is_available()`, and retrieve the device name with `torch.device()`. Then, all future tensors are instantiated and moved to the target device by using the `.to(device)` method.

Example 1-16. Creating CUDA tensors

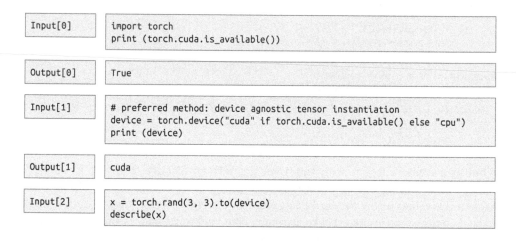

| Input[0] | ```
import torch
print (torch.cuda.is_available())
``` |
|---|---|
| Output[0] | `True` |
| Input[1] | ```
# preferred method: device agnostic tensor instantiation
device = torch.device("cuda" if torch.cuda.is_available() else "cpu")
print (device)
``` |
| Output[1] | `cuda` |
| Input[2] | ```
x = torch.rand(3, 3).to(device)
describe(x)
``` |

9 This means if you have a non-NVIDIA GPU, say AMD or ARM, you're out of luck as of this writing (of course, you can still use PyTorch in CPU mode). However, this might change in the future (*http://bit.ly/ 2JpSafj*).
```

```
Output[2]    Type: torch.cuda.FloatTensor
             Shape/size: torch.Size([3, 3])
             Values:
             tensor([[ 0.9149,  0.3993,  0.1100],
                     [ 0.2541,  0.4333,  0.4451],
                     [ 0.4966,  0.7865,  0.6604]], device='cuda:0')
```

To operate on CUDA and non-CUDA objects, we need to ensure that they are on the same device. If we don't, the computations will break, as shown in Example 1-17. This situation arises when computing monitoring metrics that aren't part of the computational graph, for instance. When operating on two tensor objects, make sure they're both on the same device.

Example 1-17. Mixing CUDA tensors with CPU-bound tensors

```
Input[0]     y = torch.rand(3, 3)
             x + y
```

```
Output[0]    ---------------------------------------------------------------------
             RuntimeError                           Traceback (most recent call last)
                   1 y = torch.rand(3, 3)
             ----> 2 x + y

             RuntimeError: Expected object of type
             torch.cuda.FloatTensor but found type torch.FloatTensor for argument #3 'other'
```

```
Input[1]     cpu_device = torch.device("cpu")
             y = y.to(cpu_device)
             x = x.to(cpu_device)
             x + y
```

```
Output[1]    tensor([[ 0.7159,  1.0685,  1.3509],
                     [ 0.3912,  0.2838,  1.3202],
                     [ 0.2967,  0.0420,  0.6559]])
```

Keep in mind that it is expensive to move data back and forth from the GPU. Therefore, the typical procedure involves doing many of the parallelizable computations on the GPU and then transferring just the final result back to the CPU. This will allow you to fully utilize the GPUs. If you have several CUDA-visible devices (i.e., multiple GPUs), the best practice is to use the CUDA_VISIBLE_DEVICES environment variable when executing the program, as shown here:

```
CUDA_VISIBLE_DEVICES=0,1,2,3 python main.py
```

We do not cover parallelism and multi-GPU training as a part of this book, but they are essential in scaling experiments and sometimes even to train large models. We recommend that you refer to the PyTorch documentation and discussion forums (*http://bit.ly/2PqdsPF*) for additional help and support on this topic.

Exercises

The best way to master a topic is to solve problems. Here are some warm-up exercises. Many of the problems will require going through the official documentation (*http://bit.ly/2F6PSU8*) and finding helpful functions.

1. Create a 2D tensor and then add a dimension of size 1 inserted at dimension 0.

2. Remove the extra dimension you just added to the previous tensor.

3. Create a random tensor of shape 5x3 in the interval [3, 7)

4. Create a tensor with values from a normal distribution (mean=0, std=1).

5. Retrieve the indexes of all the nonzero elements in the tensor torch.Tensor([1, 1, 1, 0, 1]).

6. Create a random tensor of size (3,1) and then horizontally stack four copies together.

7. Return the batch matrix-matrix product of two three-dimensional matrices (a=torch.rand(3,4,5), b=torch.rand(3,5,4)).

8. Return the batch matrix-matrix product of a 3D matrix and a 2D matrix (a=torch.rand(3,4,5), b=torch.rand(5,4)).

Solutions

1. ```
   a = torch.rand(3, 3)
   a.unsqueeze(0)
   ```

2. ```
   a.squeeze(0)
   ```

3. ```
   3 + torch.rand(5, 3) * (7 - 3)
   ```

4. ```
   a = torch.rand(3, 3)
   a.normal_()
   ```

5. ```
   a = torch.Tensor([1, 1, 1, 0, 1])
   torch.nonzero(a)
   ```

6. ```
   a = torch.rand(3, 1)
   a.expand(3, 4)
   ```

7. ```
   a = torch.rand(3, 4, 5)
   ```
   ```

```
   b = torch.rand(3, 5, 4)
   torch.bmm(a, b)
8. a = torch.rand(3, 4, 5)
   b = torch.rand(5, 4)
   torch.bmm(a, b.unsqueeze(0).expand(a.size(0), *b.size()))
```

Summary

In this chapter, we introduced the main topics of this book—natural language processing, or NLP, and deep learning—and developed a detailed understanding of the supervised learning paradigm. You should now be familiar with, or at least aware of, various relevant terms such as observations, targets, models, parameters, predictions, loss functions, representations, learning/training, and inference. You also saw how to encode inputs (observations and targets) for learning tasks using one-hot encoding, and we also examined count-based representations like TF and TF-IDF. We began our journey into PyTorch by first exploring what computational graphs are, then considering static versus dynamic computational graphs and taking a tour of PyTorch's tensor manipulation operations. In Chapter 2, we provide an overview of traditional NLP. These two chapters should lay down the necessary foundation for you if you're new to the book's subject matter and prepare for you for the rest of the chapters.

References

1. PyTorch official API documentation. (*http://bit.ly/2RjBxVw*)

2. Dougherty, James, Ron Kohavi, and Mehran Sahami. (1995). "Supervised and Unsupervised Discretization of Continuous Features." *Proceedings of the 12th International Conference on Machine Learning.*

3. Collobert, Ronan, and Jason Weston. (2008). "A Unified Architecture for Natural Language Processing: Deep Neural Networks with Multitask Learning." *Proceedings of the 25th International Conference on Machine Learning.*

A Quick Tour of Traditional NLP

Natural language processing (NLP, introduced in the previous chapter) and *computational linguistics* (CL) are two areas of computational study of human language. NLP aims to develop methods for solving practical problems involving language, such as information extraction, automatic speech recognition, machine translation, sentiment analysis, question answering, and summarization. CL, on the other hand, employs computational methods to understand properties of human language. How do we understand language? How do we produce language? How do we learn languages? What relationships do languages have with one another?

In literature, it is common to see a crossover of methods and researchers, from CL to NLP and vice versa. Lessons from CL about language can be used to inform priors in NLP, and statistical and machine learning methods from NLP can be applied to answer questions CL seeks to answer. In fact, some of these questions have ballooned into disciplines of their own, like phonology, morphology, syntax, semantics, and pragmatics.

In this book, we concern ourselves with only NLP, but we borrow ideas routinely from CL as needed. Before we fully vest ourselves into neural network methods for NLP—the focus of the rest of this book—it is worthwhile to review some traditional NLP concepts and methods. That is the goal of this chapter.

If you have some background in NLP, you can skip this chapter, but you might as well stick around for nostalgia and to establish a shared vocabulary for the future.

Corpora, Tokens, and Types

All NLP methods, be they classic or modern, begin with a text dataset, also called a *corpus* (plural: *corpora*). A corpus usually contains raw text (in ASCII or UTF-8) and any metadata associated with the text. The raw text is a sequence of characters (bytes), but most times it is useful to group those characters into contiguous units called *tokens*. In English, tokens correspond to words and numeric sequences separated by white-space characters or punctuation.

The metadata could be any auxiliary piece of information associated with the text, like identifiers, labels, and timestamps. In machine learning parlance, the text along with its metadata is called an *instance* or *data point*. The corpus (Figure 2-1), a collection of instances, is also known as a *dataset*. Given the heavy machine learning focus of this book, we freely interchange the terms corpus and dataset throughout.

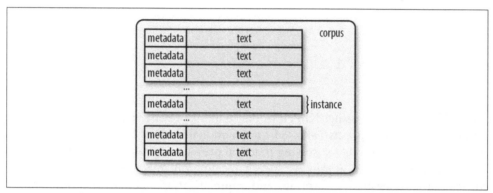

Figure 2-1. The corpus: the starting point of NLP tasks.

The process of breaking a text down into tokens is called *tokenization*. For example, there are six tokens in the Esperanto sentence "Maria frapis la verda sorĉistino."[1] Tokenization can become more complicated than simply splitting text based on non-alphanumeric characters, as is demonstrated in Figure 2-2. For agglutinative languages like Turkish, splitting on whitespace and punctuation might not be sufficient, and more specialized techniques might be warranted. As you will see in Chapters 4 and 6, it may be possible to entirely circumvent the issue of tokenization in some neural network models by representing text as a stream of bytes; this becomes very important for agglutinative languages.

---

1 Translation: "Mary slapped the green witch." We use this sentence as a running example in this chapter. We acknowledge the example is rather violent, but our use is a hat-tip to the most famous artificial intelligence textbook of our times (Russell and Norvig, 2016), which also uses this sentence as a running example.

Turkish	English
kork(-mak)	(to) fear
korku	fear
korkusuz	fearless
korkusuzlaş (-mak)	(to) become fearless
korkusuzlaşmış	One who has become fearless
korkusuzlaştır(-mak)	(to) make one fearless
korkusuzlaştırıl(-mak)	(to) be made fearless
korkusuzlaştırılmış	One who has been made fearless
korkusuzlaştırılabil(-mek)	(to) be able to be made fearless
korkusuzlaştırılabilecek	One who will be able to be made fearless
korkusuzlaştırabileceklerimiz	Ones who we can make fearless
korkusuzlaştırabileceklerimizden	From the ones who we can make fearless
korkusuzlaştırabileceklerimizdenmiş	I gather that one is one of those we can make fearless
korkusuzlaştırabileceklerimizdenmişçesine	As if that one is one of those we can make fearless
korkusuzlaştırabileceklerimizdenmişçesineyken	when it seems like that one is one of those we can make fearless

Figure 2-2. Tokenization in languages like Turkish can become complicated quickly.

Finally, consider the following tweet:

Tokenizing tweets involves preserving hashtags and @handles, and segmenting smilies such as : -) and URLs as one unit. Should the hashtag #MakeAMovieCold be one token or four? Most research papers don't give much attention to these matters, and in fact, many of the tokenization decisions tend to be arbitrary—but those decisions can significantly affect accuracy in practice more than is acknowledged. Often considered the grunt work of preprocessing, most open source NLP packages provide reasonable support for tokenization to get you started. Example 2-1 shows examples from NLTK (*http://www.nltk.org/*) and spaCy (*https://spacy.io/*), two commonly used packages for text processing.

Example 2-1. Tokenizing text

```
Input[0]    import spacy
            nlp = spacy.load('en')
            text = "Mary, don't slap the green witch"
            print([str(token) for token >in nlp(text.lower())])
```

```
Output[0]   ['mary', ',', 'do', "n't", 'slap', 'the', 'green', 'witch', '.']
```

```
Input[1]    from nltk.tokenize import TweetTokenizer
            tweet=u"Snow White and the Seven Degrees
                #MakeAMovieCold@midnight:-)"
            tokenizer = TweetTokenizer()
            print(tokenizer.tokenize(tweet.lower()))
```

```
Output[1]   ['snow', 'white', 'and', 'the', 'seven', 'degrees',
             '#makeamoviecold', '@midnight', ':-)']
```

Types are unique tokens present in a corpus. The set of all types in a corpus is its *vocabulary* or *lexicon*. Words can be distinguished as *content words* and *stopwords*. Stopwords such as articles and prepositions serve mostly a grammatical purpose, like filler holding the content words.

Feature Engineering

This process of understanding the linguistics of a language and applying it to solving NLP problems is called *feature engineering*. This is something that we keep to a minimum here, for convenience and portability of models across languages. But when building and deploying real-world production systems, feature engineering is indispensable, despite recent claims to the contrary. For an introduction to feature engineering in general, consider reading the book by Zheng and Casari (2016).

Unigrams, Bigrams, Trigrams, . . . , N-grams

N-grams are fixed-length (*n*) consecutive token sequences occurring in the text. A bigram has two tokens, a unigram one. Generating *n*-grams from a text is straightforward enough, as illustrated in Example 2-2, but packages like spaCy and NLTK provide convenient methods.

Example 2-2. Generating n-grams from text

```
Input[0]    def n_grams(text, n):
                '''
                takes tokens or text, returns a list of n-grams
                '''
                return [text[i:i+n] for i in range(len(text)-n+1)]

            cleaned = ['mary', ',', "n't", 'slap', 'green', 'witch', '.']
            print(n_grams(cleaned, 3))
```

```
Output[0]   [['mary', ',', "n't"],
             [',', "n't", 'slap'],
             ["n't", 'slap', 'green'],
             ['slap', 'green', 'witch'],
             ['green', 'witch', '.']]
```

For some situations in which the subword information itself carries useful information, one might want to generate character *n*-grams. For example, the suffix "-ol" in "methanol" indicates it is a kind of alcohol; if your task involved classifying organic compound names, you can see how the subword information captured by *n*-grams can be useful. In such cases, you can reuse the same code, but treat every character *n*-gram as a token.[2]

Lemmas and Stems

Lemmas are root forms of words. Consider the verb *fly*. It can be *inflected* into many different words—*flow, flew, flies, flown, flowing,* and so on—and *fly* is the lemma for all of these seemingly different words. Sometimes, it might be useful to reduce the tokens to their lemmas to keep the dimensionality of the vector representation low. This reduction is called *lemmatization,* and you can see it in action in Example 2-3.

Example 2-3. Lemmatization: reducing words to their root forms

```
Input[0]    import spacy
            nlp = spacy.load('en')
            doc = nlp(u"he was running late")
            for token in doc:
                print('{} --> {}'.format(token, token.lemma_))
```

---

2 In Chapters 4 and 6, we look at deep learning models that implicitly capture this substructure efficiently.

```
Output[0]          he --> he
                   was --> be
                   running --> run
                   late --> late
```

spaCy, for example, uses a predefined dictionary, called WordNet, for extracting lemmas, but lemmatization can be framed as a machine learning problem requiring an understanding of the morphology of the language.

Stemming is the poor-man's lemmatization.[3] It involves the use of handcrafted rules to strip endings of words to reduce them to a common form called *stems*. Popular stemmers often implemented in open source packages include the Porter and Snowball stemmers. We leave it to you to find the right spaCy/NLTK APIs to perform stemming.

Categorizing Sentences and Documents

Categorizing or classifying documents is probably one of the earliest applications of NLP. The TF and TF-IDF representations we described in Chapter 1 are immediately useful for classifying and categorizing longer chunks of text such as documents or sentences. Problems such as assigning topic labels, predicting sentiment of reviews, filtering spam emails, language identification, and email triaging can be framed as supervised document classification problems. (Semi-supervised versions, in which only a small labeled dataset is used, are incredibly useful, but that topic is beyond the scope of this book.)

Categorizing Words: POS Tagging

We can extend the concept of labeling from documents to individual words or tokens. A common example of categorizing words is part-of-speech (POS) tagging, as demonstrated in Example 2-4.

Example 2-4. Part-of-speech tagging

```
Input[0]           import spacy
                   nlp = spacy.load('en')
                   doc = nlp(u"Mary slapped the green witch.")
                   for token in doc:
                       print('{} - {}'.format(token, token.pos_))
```

---

3 To understand the difference between stemming and lemmatization, consider the word "geese." Lemmatization produces "goose," whereas stemming produces "gees."

```
Output[0]        Mary - PROPN
                 slapped - VERB
                 the - DET
                 green - ADJ
                 witch - NOUN
                 . - PUNCT
```

Categorizing Spans: Chunking and Named Entity Recognition

Often, we need to label a span of text; that is, a contiguous multitoken boundary. For example, consider the sentence, "Mary slapped the green witch." We might want to identify the noun phrases (NP) and verb phrases (VP) in it, as shown here:

```
[NP Mary] [VP slapped] [the green witch].
```

This is called *chunking* or *shallow parsing*. Shallow parsing aims to derive higher-order units composed of the grammatical atoms, like nouns, verbs, adjectives, and so on. It is possible to write regular expressions over the part-of-speech tags to approximate shallow parsing if you do not have data to train models for shallow parsing. Fortunately, for English and most extensively spoken languages, such data and pretrained models exist. Example 2-5 presents an example of shallow parsing using spaCy.

Example 2-5. Noun Phrase (NP) chunking

```
Input[0]         import spacy
                 nlp = spacy.load('en')
                 doc  = nlp(u"Mary slapped the green witch.")
                 for chunk in doc.noun_chunks:
                     print ('{} - {}'.format(chunk, chunk.label_))
```

```
Output[0]        Mary - NP
                 the green witch - NP
```

Another type of span that's useful is the *named entity*. A named entity is a string mention of a real-world concept like a person, location, organization, drug name, and so on. Here's an example:

Structure of Sentences

Whereas shallow parsing identifies phrasal units, the task of identifying the relationship between them is called *parsing*. You might recall from elementary English class diagramming sentences like in the example shown in Figure 2-3.

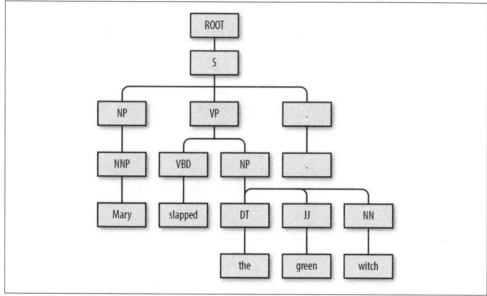

Figure 2-3. A constituent parse of the sentence "Mary slapped the green witch."

Parse trees indicate how different grammatical units in a sentence are related hierarchically. The parse tree in Figure 2-3 shows what's called a *constituent parse*. Another, possibly more useful, way to show relationships is using *dependency parsing*, depicted in Figure 2-4.

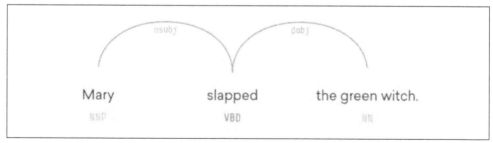

Figure 2-4. A dependency parse of the sentence "Mary slapped the green witch."

To learn more about traditional parsing, see the "References" section at the end of this chapter.

Word Senses and Semantics

Words have meanings, and often more than one. The different meanings of a word are called its *senses*. WordNet, a long-running lexical resource project from Princeton University, aims to catalog the senses of all (well, most) words in the English language, along with other lexical relationships.[4] For example, consider a word like "plane." Figure 2-5 shows the different senses in which this word could be used.

Word to search for: plane   Search WordNet

Display Options: (Select option to change) ⬛ Change
Key: "S:" = Show Synset (semantic) relations, "W:" = Show Word (lexical) relations
Display options for sense: (gloss) "an example sentence"

Noun

- S: (n) airplane, aeroplane, **plane** (an aircraft that has a fixed wing and is powered by propellers or jets) *"the flight was delayed due to trouble with the airplane"*
- S: (n) **plane**, sheet ((mathematics) an unbounded two–dimensional shape) *"we will refer to the plane of the graph as the X–Y plane"; "any line joining two points on a plane lies wholly on that plane"*
- S: (n) **plane** (a level of existence or development) *"he lived on a worldly plane"*
- S: (n) **plane**, planer, planing machine (a power tool for smoothing or shaping wood)
- S: (n) **plane**, carpenter's plane, woodworking plane (a carpenter's hand tool with an adjustable blade for smoothing or shaping wood) *"the cabinetmaker used a plane for the finish work"*

Verb

- S: (v) **plane**, shave (cut or remove with or as if with a plane) *"The machine shaved off fine layers from the piece of wood"*
- S: (v) **plane**, skim (travel on the surface of water)
- S: (v) **plane** (make even or smooth, with or as with a carpenter's plane) *"plane the top of the door"*

Adjective

- S: (adj) flat, level, **plane** (having a surface without slope, tilt in which no part is higher or lower than another) *"a flat desk"; "acres of level farmland"; "a plane surface"; "skirts sewn with fine flat seams"*

Figure 2-5. Senses for the word "plane" (courtesy of WordNet (http://bit.ly/2CQNVYX)).

---

4 Attempts to create multilingual versions of WordNet exist. See BabelNet (*http://babelnet.org*) as an example.

The decades of effort that have been put into projects like WordNet are worth availing yourself of, even in the presence of modern approaches. Later chapters in this book present examples of using existing linguistic resources in the context of neural networks and deep learning methods.

Word senses can also be induced from the context—automatic discovery of word senses from text was actually the first place semi-supervised learning was applied to NLP. Even though we don't cover that in this book, we encourage you to read Jurafsky and Martin (2014), Chapter 17, and Manning and Schütze (1999), Chapter 7.

Summary

In this chapter, we reviewed some basic terminology and ideas in NLP that should be handy in future chapters. This chapter covered only a smattering of what traditional NLP has to offer. We omitted significant aspects of traditional NLP because we want to allocate the bulk of this book to the use of deep learning for NLP. It is, however, important to know that there is a rich body of NLP research work that doesn't use neural networks, and yet is highly impactful (i.e., used extensively in building production systems). The neural network–based approaches should be considered, in many cases, as a supplement and not a replacement for traditional methods. Experienced practitioners often use the best of both worlds to build state-of-the-art systems. To learn more about the traditional approaches to NLP, we recommend the references listed in the following section.

References

1. Manning, Christopher D., and Hinrich Schütze. (1999). *Foundations of Statistical Natural Language Processing*. MIT press.

2. Bird, Steven, Ewan Klein, and Edward Loper. (2009). *Natural Language Processing with Python: Analyzing Text with the Natural Language Toolkit*. O'Reilly.

3. Smith, Noah A. (2011). *Linguistic Structure prediction*. Morgan and Claypool.

4. Jurafsky, Dan, and James H. Martin. (2014). *Speech and Language Processing*, Vol. 3. Pearson.

5. Russell, Stuart J., and Peter Norvig. (2016). *Artificial Intelligence: A Modern Approach*. Pearson.

6. Zheng, Alice, and Casari, Amanda. (2018). *Feature Engineering for Machine Learning: Principles and Techniques for Data Scientists*. O'Reilly.

Foundational Components of Neural Networks

This chapter sets the stage for later chapters by introducing the basic ideas involved in building neural networks, such as activation functions, loss functions, optimizers, and the supervised training setup. We begin by looking at the perceptron, a one-unit neural network, to tie together the various concepts. The perceptron itself is a building block in more complex neural networks. This is a common pattern that will repeat itself throughout the book—every architecture or network we discuss can be used either standalone or compositionally within other complex networks. This compositionality will become clear as we discuss computational graphs and the rest of this book.

The Perceptron: The Simplest Neural Network

The simplest neural network unit is a *perceptron*. The perceptron was historically and very loosely modeled after the biological neuron. As with a biological neuron, there is input and output, and "signals" flow from the inputs to the outputs, as illustrated in Figure 3-1.

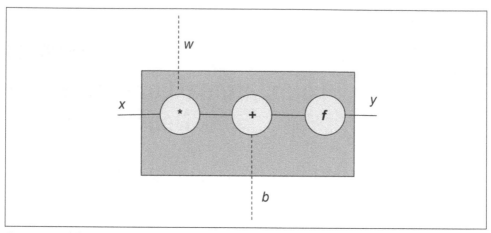

Figure 3-1. The computational graph for a perceptron with an input (x) and an output (y). The weights (w) and bias (b) constitute the parameters of the model.

Each perceptron unit has an input (x), an output (y), and three "knobs": a set of weights (w), a bias (b), and an activation function (f). The weights and the bias are learned from the data, and the activation function is handpicked depending on the network designer's intuition of the network and its target outputs. Mathematically, we can express this as follows:

$$y = f(wx + b)$$

It is usually the case that there is more than one input to the perceptron. We can represent this general case using vectors. That is, x, and w are vectors, and the product of w and x is replaced with a dot product:

$$y = f(wx + b)$$

The activation function, denoted here by f, is typically a nonlinear function. A linear function is one whose graph is a straight line. In this example, $wx+b$ is a linear function. So, essentially, a perceptron is a composition of a linear and a nonlinear function. The linear expression $wx+b$ is also known as an *affine transform*.

Example 3-1 presents a perceptron implementation in PyTorch that takes an arbitrary number of inputs, does the affine transform, applies an activation function, and produces a single output.

Example 3-1. Implementing a perceptron using PyTorch

```
import torch
import torch.nn as nn
```

```
class Perceptron(nn.Module):
    """ A perceptron is one linear layer """
    def __init__(self, input_dim):
        """
        Args:
            input_dim (int): size of the input features
        """
        super(Perceptron, self).__init__()
        self.fc1 = nn.Linear(input_dim, 1)

    def forward(self, x_in):
        """The forward pass of the perceptron

        Args:
            x_in (torch.Tensor): an input data tensor
                x_in.shape should be (batch, num_features)
        Returns:
            the resulting tensor. tensor.shape should be (batch,).
        """
        return torch.sigmoid(self.fc1(x_in)).squeeze()
```

PyTorch conveniently offers a `Linear` class in the `torch.nn` module that does the bookkeeping needed for the weights and biases, and does the needed affine transform.[1] In "Diving Deep into Supervised Training" on page 49, you'll see how to "learn" the values of the weights *w* and *b* from data. The activation function used in the preceding example is the *sigmoid function*. In the following section, we review some common activation functions, including this one.

Activation Functions

Activation functions are nonlinearities introduced in a neural network to capture complex relationships in data. In "Diving Deep into Supervised Training" on page 49 and "The Multilayer Perceptron" on page 82 we dive deeper into why nonlinearities are required in the learning, but first, let's look at a few commonly used activation functions.[2]

---

1 The weights and bias values are internally managed in the nn.Linear class. If, for some unlikely reason, you would like a model without the bias, you can explicitly set bias=False in the constructor of nn.Linear.

2 There are many types of activation functions—the PyTorch library itself has more than 20 predefined. When you are comfortable with this chapter, you can peruse the documentation (*http://bit.ly/2SuIQLm*) to learn more.

Sigmoid

The sigmoid is one of the earliest used activation functions in neural network history. It takes any real value and squashes it into the range between 0 and 1. Mathematically, the sigmoid function is expressed as follows:

$$f(x) = \frac{1}{1 + e^{-x}}$$

It is easy to see from the expression that the sigmoid is a smooth, differentiable function. torch implements the sigmoid as torch.sigmoid(), as shown in Example 3-2.

Example 3-2. Sigmoid activation

```
import torch
import matplotlib.pyplot as plt

x = torch.range(-5., 5., 0.1)
y = torch.sigmoid(x)
plt.plot(x.numpy(), y.numpy())
plt.show()
```

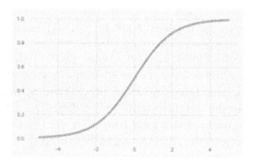

As you can observe from the plot, the sigmoid function saturates (i.e., produces extreme valued outputs) very quickly and for a majority of the inputs. This can become a problem because it can lead to the gradients becoming either zero or diverging to an overflowing floating-point value. These phenomena are also known as *vanishing gradient problem* and *exploding gradient problem*, respectively. As a consequence, it is rare to see sigmoid units used in neural networks other than at the output, where the squashing property allows one to interpret outputs as probabilities.

Tanh

The tanh activation function is a cosmetically different variant of the sigmoid. This becomes clear when you write down the expression for tanh:

$$f(x) = \tanh x = \frac{e^x - e^{-x}}{e^x + e^{-x}}$$

With a little bit of wrangling (which we leave for you as an exercise), you can convince yourself that tanh is simply a linear transform of the sigmoid function, as shown in Example 3-3. This is also evident when you write down the PyTorch code for `tanh()` and plot the curve. Notice that tanh, like the sigmoid, is also a "squashing" function, except that it maps the set of real values from (−∞, +∞) to the range [-1, +1].

Example 3-3. Tanh activation

```
import torch
import matplotlib.pyplot as plt

x = torch.range(-5., 5., 0.1)
y = torch.tanh(x)
plt.plot(x.numpy(), y.numpy())
plt.show()
```

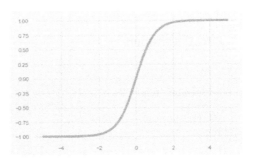

ReLU

ReLU (pronounced ray-luh) stands for *rectified linear unit*. This is arguably the most important of the activation functions. In fact, one could venture as far as to say that many of the recent innovations in deep learning would've been impossible without the use of ReLU. For something so fundamental, it's also surprisingly new as far as neural network activation functions go. And it's surprisingly simple in form:

$$f(x) = \max(0, x)$$

So, all a ReLU unit is doing is clipping the negative values to zero, as demonstrated in Example 3-4.

Example 3-4. ReLU activation

```
import torch
import matplotlib.pyplot as plt

relu = torch.nn.ReLU()
x = torch.range(-5., 5., 0.1)
y = relu(x)

plt.plot(x.numpy(), y.numpy())
plt.show()
```

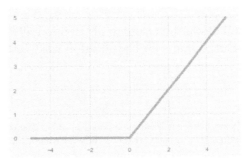

The clipping effect of ReLU that helps with the vanishing gradient problem can also become an issue, where over time certain outputs in the network can simply become zero and never revive again. This is called the "dying ReLU" problem. To mitigate that effect, variants such as the Leaky ReLU and Parametric ReLU (PReLU) activation functions have proposed, where the leak coefficient a is a learned parameter. Example 3-5 shows the result.

$$f(x) = \max(x,\ ax)$$

Example 3-5. PReLU activation

```
import torch
import matplotlib.pyplot as plt

prelu = torch.nn.PReLU(num_parameters=1)
x = torch.range(-5., 5., 0.1)
y = prelu(x)

plt.plot(x.numpy(), y.numpy())
plt.show()
```

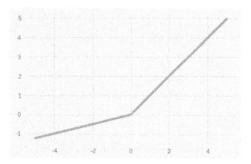

Softmax

Another choice for the activation function is the softmax. Like the sigmoid function, the softmax function squashes the output of each unit to be between 0 and 1, as shown in Example 3-6. However, the softmax operation also divides each output by the sum of all the outputs, which gives us a discrete probability distribution[3] over k possible classes:

$$softmax(x_i) = \frac{e^{x_i}}{\sum\limits_{j=1}^{k} e^{x_j}}$$

The probabilities in the resulting distribution all sum up to one. This is very useful for interpreting outputs for classification tasks, and so this transformation is usually

---

3 The words "probability" and "distribution" here must be taken with a grain of salt. By "probability," what we mean is that the value at outputs is bounded between 0 and 1. By "distribution," we mean the outputs sum to 1.

paired with a probabilistic training objective, such as categorical cross entropy, which is covered in "Diving Deep into Supervised Training" on page 49.

Example 3-6. Softmax activation

Input[0]	

```
import torch.nn as nn
import torch

softmax = nn.Softmax(dim=1)
x_input = torch.randn(1, 3)
y_output = softmax(x_input)
print(x_input)
print(y_output)
print(torch.sum(y_output, dim=1))
```

Output[0]	

```
tensor([[ 0.5836, -1.3749, -1.1229]])
tensor([[ 0.7561,  0.1067,  0.1372]])
tensor([ 1.])
```

In this section, we studied four important activation functions: sigmoid, tanh, ReLU, and softmax. These are but four of the many possible activations that you could use in building neural networks. As we progress through this book, it will become clear which activation functions should be used and where, but a general guide is to simply follow what has worked in the past.

Loss Functions

In Chapter 1, we saw the general supervised machine learning architecture and how loss functions or objective functions help guide the training algorithm to pick the right parameters by looking at the data. Recall that a loss function takes a truth (y) and a prediction ($\hat{y}$) as an input and produces a real-valued score. The higher this score, the worse the model's prediction is. PyTorch implements more loss functions in its nn package than we can cover here, but we will review some of the most commonly used loss functions.

Mean Squared Error Loss

For regression problems for which the network's output ($\hat{y}$) and the target (y) are continuous values, one common loss function is the mean squared error (MSE):

$$L_{MSE}(y, \hat{y}) = \frac{1}{n}\sum_{i=1}^{n}(y - \hat{y})^2$$

The MSE is simply the average of the squares of the difference between the predicted and target values. There are several other loss functions that you can use for regression problems, such as mean absolute error (MAE) and root mean squared error (RMSE), but they all involve computing a real-valued distance between the output and target. Example 3-7 shows how you can implement MSE loss using PyTorch.

Example 3-7. MSE loss

```
import torch
import torch.nn as nn

mse_loss = nn.MSELoss()
outputs = torch.randn(3, 5, requires_grad=True)
targets = torch.randn(3, 5)
loss = mse_loss(outputs, targets)
print(loss)
```

Input[0]

Output[0]
```
tensor(3.8618)
```

Categorical Cross-Entropy Loss

The categorical cross-entropy loss is typically used in a multiclass classification setting in which the outputs are interpreted as predictions of class membership probabilities. The target (y) is a vector of n elements that represents the true multinomial distribution[4] over all the classes. If only one class is correct, this vector is a one-hot vector. The network's output ($\hat{y}$) is also a vector of n elements but represents the network's prediction of the multinomial distribution. Categorical cross entropy will compare these two vectors ($y,\hat{y}$) to measure the loss:

$$L_{cross\_entropy}(y,\hat{y}) = -\sum_i y_i \log(\hat{y}_i)$$

Cross-entropy and the expression for it have origins in information theory, but for the purpose of this section it is helpful to consider this as a method to compute how different two distributions are. We want the probability of the correct class to be close to 1, whereas the other classes have a probability close to 0.

To correctly use PyTorch's `CrossEntropyLoss()` function, it is important to understand the relationship between the network's outputs, how the loss function is com-

---

4 Two properties are required for a multinomial distribution vector: the sum over elements in the vector should be one and every element in the vector should be nonnegative.

puted, and the kinds of computational constraints that stem from really representing floating-point numbers. Specifically, there are four pieces of information that determine the nuanced relationship between network output and loss function. First, there is a limit to how small or how large a number can be. Second, if input to the exponential function used in the softmax formula is a negative number, the resultant is an exponentially small number, and if it's a positive number, the resultant is an exponentially large number. Next, the network's output is assumed to be the vector just prior to applying the softmax function.[5] Finally, the *log* function is the inverse of the exponential function,[6] and *log(exp(x))* is just equal to *x*. Stemming from these four pieces of information, mathematical simplifications are made assuming the exponential function that is the core of the softmax function and the log function that is used in the cross-entropy computations in order to be more numerically stable and avoid really small or really large numbers. The consequences of these simplifications are that the network output without the use of a softmax function can be used in conjunction with PyTorch's CrossEntropyLoss() to optimize the probability distribution. Then, when the network has been trained, the softmax function can be used to create a probability distribution, as shown in Example 3-8.

Example 3-8. Cross-entropy loss

| Input[0] | ```
import torch
import torch.nn as nn

ce_loss = nn.CrossEntropyLoss()
outputs = torch.randn(3, 5, requires_grad=True)
targets = torch.tensor([1, 0, 3], dtype=torch.int64)
loss = ce_loss(outputs, targets)
print(loss)
``` |
|---|---|
| Output[0] | ```
tensor(2.7256)
``` |

In this code example, a vector of random values is first used to simulate network output. Then, the ground truth vector, called targets, is created as a vector of integers because PyTorch's implementation of CrossEntropyLoss() assumes that each input has one particular class, and each class has a unique index. This is why targets has three elements: an index representing the correct class for each input. From this

---

5 In PyTorch, there are actually two softmax functions: Softmax() and LogSoftmax(). LogSoftmax() produces log-probabilities, which preserve the relative ratios of any two numbers but aren't going to run into numerical problems.

6 This is true only when the *base* of the log function is the exponential constant *e*, which is the default base for PyTorch's *log*.

assumption, it performs the computationally more efficient operation of indexing into the model output.[7]

Binary Cross-Entropy Loss

The categorical cross-entropy loss function we saw in the previous section is very useful in classification problems when we have multiple classes. Sometimes, our task involves discriminating between two classes—also known as *binary classification*. For such situations, it is efficient to use the binary cross-entropy (BCE) loss. We look at this loss function in action in "Example: Classifying Sentiment of Restaurant Reviews" on page 56.

In Example 3-9, we create a binary probability output vector, *probabilities*, using the sigmoid activation function on a random vector that represents the output of the network. Next, the ground truth is instantiated as a vector of 0's and 1's.[8] Finally, we compute binary cross-entropy loss using the binary probability vector and the ground truth vector.

Example 3-9. Binary cross-entropy loss

Input[0]
```
bce_loss = nn.BCELoss()
sigmoid = nn.Sigmoid()
probabilities = sigmoid(torch.randn(4, 1, requires_grad=True))
targets = torch.tensor([1, 0, 1, 0], dtype=torch.float32).view(4, 1)
loss = bce_loss(probabilities, targets)
print(probabilities)
print(loss)
```

Output[0]
```
tensor([[ 0.1625],
        [ 0.5546],
        [ 0.6596],
        [ 0.4284]])
tensor(0.9003)
```

---

7 Using the one-hots in the cross-entropy formula means that all but one of the multiplications will result in a nonzero value. This is a large waste of computation.

8 Note that the code example shows the ground truth vector as being a float vector. Although binary cross entropy is nearly the same as categorical cross entropy (but with only two classes), its computations leverage the 0 and 1 values in the binary cross-entropy formula rather than using them as indexing indices, as was shown for categorical cross entropy.

Diving Deep into Supervised Training

Supervised learning is the problem of learning how to map *observations* to specified *targets* given labeled examples. In this section, we go into more detail. Specifically, we explicitly describe how to use model *predictions* and *a loss function* to do gradient-based optimization of a model's *parameters*. This is an important section because the rest of the book relies on it, so it is worth going through it in detail even if you are somewhat familiar with supervised learning.

Recall from Chapter 1 that supervised learning requires the following: a model, a loss function, training data, and an optimization algorithm. The training data for supervised learning is pairs of observations and targets; the model computes predictions from the observations, and the loss measures the error of the predictions as compared to the targets. The goal of the training is to use the gradient-based optimization algorithm to adjust the model's parameters so that the losses are as low as possible.

In the remainder of this section, we discuss a classic toy problem: classifying two-dimensional points into one of two classes. Intuitively, this means learning a single line, called a *decision boundary* or *hyperplane*, to discriminate the points of one class from the other. We step through and describe the data construction, choosing the model, selecting a loss function, setting up the optimization algorithm, and, finally, running it all together.

Constructing Toy Data

In machine learning, it is a common practice to create synthetic data with well-understood properties when trying to understand an algorithm. For this section, we use synthetic data for the task of classifying two-dimensional points into one of two classes. To construct the data, we sample[9] the points from two different parts of the xy-plane, creating an easy-to-learn situation for the model. Samples are shown in the plot depicted in Figure 3-2. The goal of the model is to classify the stars (★) as one class, and the circles (◯) as another class. This is visualized on the righthand side, where everything above the line is classified differently than everything below the line. The code for generating the data is in the function named `get_toy_data()` in the Python notebook that accompanies this chapter.

---

[9] We are sampling from two Gaussian distributions with unit variance. If you don't get what that means, just assume that the "shape" of the data looks like what's shown in the figure.

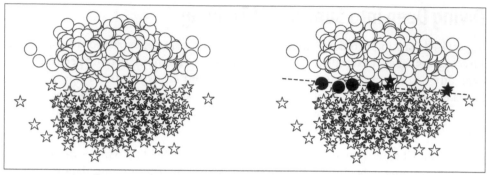

Figure 3-2. Creating a toy dataset that's linearly separable. The dataset is a sampling from two normal distributions, one for each class; the classification task becomes one of distinguishing whether a data point belongs to one distribution or the other.

Choosing a model

The model we use here is the one introduced at the beginning of the chapter: the perceptron. The perceptron is flexible in that it allows for any input size. In a typical modeling situation, the input size is determined by the task and data. In this toy example, the input size is 2 because we explicitly constructed the data to be in a two-dimensional plane. For this two-class problem, we assign a numeric indices to the classes: 0 and 1. The mapping of the string labels ⋆ and ○ to the class indexes is arbitrary as long as it is consistent throughout data preprocessing, training, evaluation, and testing. An important, additional property of this model is the nature of its output. Due to the perceptron's activation function being a sigmoid, the output of the perceptron is the probability of the data point (x) being class 1; that is, $P(y = 1 \mid x)$.

Converting the probabilities to discrete classes

For the binary classification problem, we can convert the output probability into two discrete classes by imposing a decision boundary, δ. If the predicted probability $P(y = 1 \mid x) > \delta$, the predicted class is 1, else the class is 0. Typically, this decision boundary is set to be 0.5, but in practice, you might need to tune this hyperparameter (using an evaluation dataset) to achieve a desired precision in classification.

Choosing a loss function

After you have prepared the data and selected a model architecture, there are two other vital components to choose in supervised training: a loss function and an optimizer. For situations in which the model's output is a probability, the most appropriate family of loss functions are cross entropy–based losses. For this toy data example, because the model is producing binary outcomes, we specifically use the BCE loss.

Choosing an optimizer

The final choice point in this simplified supervised training example is the optimizer. While the model produces predictions and the loss function measures the error between predictions and targets, the optimizer updates the weights of the model using the error signal. In its simplest form, there is a single hyperparameter that controls the update behavior of the optimizer. This hyperparameter, called a *learning rate*, controls how much impact the error signal has on updating the weights. Learning rate is a critical hyperparameter, and you should try several different learning rates and compare them. Large learning rates will cause bigger changes to the parameters and can affect convergence. Too-small learning rates can result in very little progress during training.

The PyTorch library offers several choices for an optimizer. Stochastic gradient descent (SGD) is a classic algorithm of choice, but for difficult optimization problems, SGD has convergence issues, often leading to poorer models. The current preferred alternative are adaptive optimizers, such as Adagrad or Adam, which use information about updates over time.[10] In the following example we use Adam, but it is always worth looking at several optimizers. With Adam, the default learning rate is 0.001. With hyperparameters such as learning rate, it's always recommended to use the default values first, unless you have a recipe from a paper calling for a specific value.

Example 3-10. Instantiating the Adam optimizer

```
Input[0]    import torch.nn as nn
            import torch.optim as optim

            input_dim = 2
            lr = 0.001

            perceptron = Perceptron(input_dim=input_dim)
            bce_loss = nn.BCELoss()
            optimizer = optim.Adam(params=perceptron.parameters(), lr=lr)
```

Putting It Together: Gradient-Based Supervised Learning

Learning begins with computing the loss; that is, how far off the model predictions are from the target. The gradient of the loss function, in turn, becomes a signal for "how much" the parameters should change. The gradient for each parameter represents instantaneous rate of change in the loss value given the parameter. Effectively,

---

10 There is a perpetual debate in the machine learning and optimization communities on the merits and demerits of SGD. We find that such discussions, although intellectually stimulating, get in the way of learning.

this means that you can know how much each parameter contributed to the loss function. Intuitively, this is a slope and you can imagine each parameter is standing on its own hill and wants to take a step up or down the hill. In its most minimal form, all that is involved with gradient-based model training is iteratively updating each parameter with the gradient of the loss function with respect to that parameter.

Let's take a look at how this gradient-stepping algorithm looks. First, any bookkeeping information, such as gradients, currently stored inside the model (`perceptron`) object is cleared with a function named `zero_grad()`. Then, the model computes outputs (`y_pred`) given the input data (`x_data`). Next, the loss is computed by comparing model outputs (`y_pred`) to intended targets (`y_target`). This is the supervised part of the supervised training signal. The PyTorch loss object (`criterion`) has a function named `backward()` that iteratively propagates the loss backward through the computational graph and notifies each parameter of its gradient. Finally, the optimizer (`opt`) instructs the parameters how to update their values knowing the gradient with a function named `step()`.

The entire training dataset is partitioned into *batches*. Each iteration of the gradient step is performed on a batch of data. A hyperparameter named `batch_size` specifies the size of the batches. Because the training dataset is fixed, increasing the batch size decreases the number of batches.

 In the literature, and also in this book, the term *minibatch* is used interchangeably with batch to highlight that each of the batches is significantly smaller than the size of the training data; for example, the training data size could be in the millions, whereas the minibatch could be just a few hundred in size.

After a number of batches (typically, the number of batches that are in a finite-sized dataset), the training loop has completed an *epoch*. An epoch is a complete training iteration. If the number of batches per epoch is the same as the number of batches in a dataset, then an epoch is a complete iteration over a dataset. Models are trained for a certain number of epochs. The number of epochs to train is not trivial to select, but there are methods for determining when to stop, which we discuss shortly. As Example 3-11 illustrates, the supervised training loop is thus a nested loop: an inner loop over a dataset or a set number of batches, and an outer loop, which repeats the inner loop over a fixed number of epochs or other termination criteria.

Example 3-11. A supervised training loop for a perceptron and binary classification

```
# each epoch is a complete pass over the training data
for epoch_i in range(n_epochs):
    # the inner loop is over the batches in the dataset
    for batch_i in range(n_batches):
```

```
# Step 0: Get the data
x_data, y_target = get_toy_data(batch_size)

# Step 1: Clear the gradients
perceptron.zero_grad()

# Step 2: Compute the forward pass of the model
y_pred = perceptron(x_data, apply_sigmoid=True)

# Step 3: Compute the loss value that we wish to optimize
loss = bce_loss(y_pred, y_target)

# Step 4: Propagate the loss signal backward
loss.backward()

# Step 5: Trigger the optimizer to perform one update
optimizer.step()
```

Auxiliary Training Concepts

The core idea of supervised gradient-based learning is simple: define a model, compute outputs, use a loss function to compute gradients, and apply an optimization algorithm to update model parameters with the gradient. However, there are several auxiliary concepts that are important to the training process. We cover a few of them in this section.

Correctly Measuring Model Performance: Evaluation Metrics

The most important component outside of the core supervised training loop is an objective measure of performance using data on which the model has never trained. Models are evaluated using one or more *evaluation metrics*. In natural language processing, there are multiple such metrics. The most common, and the one we will use in this chapter, is *accuracy*. Accuracy is simply the fraction of the predictions that were correct on a dataset unseen during training.

Correctly Measuring Model Performance: Splitting the Dataset

It is important to always keep in mind that the final goal is to *generalize* well to the true distribution of data. What do we mean by that? There exists a distribution of data that exists globally assuming we were able see an infinite amount of data ("*true/ unseen distribution*"). Obviously, we cannot do that. Instead, we make do with a finite sample that we call the training data. We observe a distribution of data in the finite sample that's an approximation or an incomplete picture of the true distribution. A model is said to have *generalized better* than another model if it not only reduces the error on samples seen in the training data, but also on the samples from the unseen distribution. As the model works toward lowering its loss on the training data, it can "overfit" and adapt to idiosyncrasies that aren't actually part of the true data distribution.

To accomplish this goal of generalizing well, it is standard practice to either split a dataset into three randomly sampled partitions (called the *training, validation,* and *test* datasets) or do *k-fold cross validation.* Splitting into three partitions is the simpler of the two methods because it only requires a single computation. You should take precautions to make sure the distribution of classes remains the same between each of the three splits, however. In other words, it is good practice to aggregate the dataset by class label and then randomly split each set separated by class label into the training, validation, and test datasets. A common split percentage is to reserve 70% for training, 15% for validation, and 15% for testing. This is not a hardcoded convention, though.

In some cases, a predefined training, validation, and test split might exist; this is common in datasets for benchmarking tasks. In such cases, it is important to use training data only for updating model parameters, use validation data for measuring model performance at the end of every epoch, and use test data only once, after all modeling choices are explored and the final results need to be reported. This last part is extremely important because the more the machine learning engineer peeks at the model performance on a test dataset, the more they are biased toward choices which perform better on the test set. When this happens, it is impossible to know how the model will perform on unseen data without gathering more data.

Model evaluation with k-fold cross validation is very similar to evaluation with predefined splits, but is preceded by an extra step of splitting the entire dataset into k equally sized "folds." One of the folds is reserved for evaluation, and the remaining *k-1* folds for training. This is iteratively repeated by swapping out the fold used for evaluation. Because there are k folds, each fold gets a chance to become an evaluation fold, resulting in k accuracy values. The final reported accuracy is simply the average with standard deviation. k–fold evaluation is computationally expensive but extremely necessary for smaller datasets, for which the wrong split can lead to either too much optimism (because the testing data wound up being too easy) or too much pessimism (because the testing data wound up being too hard).

Knowing When to Stop Training

The example earlier trained the model for a fixed number of epochs. Although this is the simplest approach, it is arbitrary and unnecessary. One key function of correctly measuring model performance is to use that measurement to determine when training should stop. The most common method is to use a heuristic called *early stopping.* Early stopping works by keeping track of the performance on the validation dataset from epoch to epoch and noticing when the performance no longer improves. Then, if the performance continues to not improve, the training is terminated. The number of epochs to wait before terminating the training is referred to as the *patience*. In general, the point at which a model stops improving on some dataset is said to be when the model has *converged*. In practice, we rarely wait for a model to completely converge because convergence is time-consuming, and it can lead to overfitting.

Finding the Right Hyperparameters

We learned earlier that a parameter (or weight) takes real values adjusted by an optimizer with respect to a fixed subset of training data called a minibatch. A *hyperparameter* is any model setting that affects the number of parameters in the model and values taken by the parameters. There are many different choices that go into determining how the model is trained. These include choosing a loss function; the optimizer; learning rate(s) for the optimizer, as layer sizes (covered in Chapter 4); patience for early stopping; and various regularization decisions (also covered in Chapter 4). It is important to be mindful that these decisions can have large effects on whether a model converges and its performance, and you should explore the various choice points systematically.

Regularization

One of the most important concepts in deep learning (and machine learning, in general) is *regularization*. The concept of regularization comes from numerical optimization theory. Recall that most machine learning algorithms are optimizing the loss function to find the most likely values of the parameters (or "the model") that explains the observations (i.e., produces the least amount of loss). For most datasets and tasks, there could be multiple solutions (possible models) to this optimization problem. So which one should we (or the optimizer) pick? To develop an intuitive understanding, consider Figure 3-3 for the task of fitting a curve through a set of points.

Both curves "fit" the points, but which one is an unlikely explanation? By appealing to Occam's razor, we intuit that the simpler explanation is better than the complex one. This smoothness constraint in machine learning is called *L2 regularization*. In PyTorch, you can control this by setting the `weight_decay` parameter in the optimizer. The larger the `weight_decay` value, the more likely it is that the optimizer will select the smoother explanation (that is, the stronger is the L2 regularization).

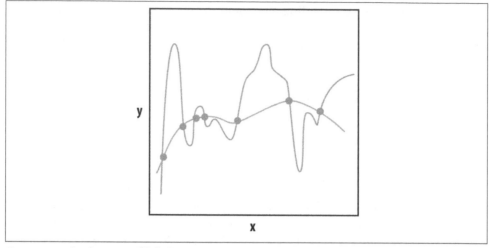

Figure 3-3. Both curves "fit" the points, but one of them seems more reasonable than the other—regularization helps us to select this more reasonable explanation (courtesy of Wikipedia (http://bit.ly/2qAU18y)).

In addition to L2, another popular regularization is *L1 regularization*. L1 is usually used to encourage sparser solutions; in other words, where most of the model parameter values are close to zero. In Chapter 4, we will look at another structural regularization technique, called *dropout*. The topic of model regularization is an active area of research and PyTorch is a flexible framework for implementing custom regularizers.

Example: Classifying Sentiment of Restaurant Reviews

In the previous section, we dove deep into supervised training with a toy example and illustrated many fundamental concepts. In this section we repeat that exercise, but this time with a real-world task and dataset: to classify whether restaurant reviews on Yelp are positive or negative using a perceptron and supervised training. Because this is the first full NLP example in this book, we will describe the assisting data structures and training routine in excruciating detail. The examples in later chapters will follow very similar patterns, so we encourage you to carefully follow along with this section and refer back to it as needed for a refresher.[11]

At the start of each example in this book, we describe the dataset that we are using. In this example we use the Yelp dataset, which pairs reviews with their sentiment labels

---

11 You can find the code for classifying the sentiment of Yelp reviews in this book's GitHub repository (*https://nlproc.info/pytorch/repo*).

(positive or negative). We additionally describe a couple of dataset manipulation steps we took to clean and partition it into training, validation, and test sets.

After understanding the dataset, you will see a pattern defining three assisting classes that is repeated throughout this book and is used to transform text data into a vectorized form: the Vocabulary, the Vectorizer, and PyTorch's DataLoader. The Vocabulary coordinates the integer-to-token mappings that we discussed in "Observation and Target Encoding" on page 5. We use a Vocabulary both for mapping the text tokens to integers and for mapping the class labels to integers. Next, the Vectorizer encapsulates the vocabularies and is responsible for ingesting string data, like a review's text, and converting it to numerical vectors that will be used in the training routine. We use the final assisting class, PyTorch's DataLoader, to group and collate the individual vectorized data points into minibatches.

The following section describes the perceptron classifier and its training routine. The training routine mostly remains the same for every example in this book, but we discuss it in more detail in this section, so again, we encourage you to use this example as a reference for future training routines. We conclude the example by discussing the results and taking a peek under the hood to see what the model learned.

The Yelp Review Dataset

In 2015, Yelp held a contest in which it asked participants to predict the rating of a restaurant given its review. Zhang, Zhao, and Lecun (2015) simplified the dataset by converting the 1- and 2-star ratings into a "negative" sentiment class and the 3- and 4-star ratings into a "positive" sentiment class, and split it into 560,000 training samples and 38,000 testing samples. In this example we use the simplified Yelp dataset, with two minor differences. In the remainder of this section, we describe the process by which we minimally clean the data and derive our final dataset. Then, we outline the implementation that utilizes PyTorch's Dataset class.

The first of the differences mentioned is that we use a "light" version of the dataset, which is derived by selecting 10% of the training samples as the full dataset.[12] This has two consequences. First, using a small dataset makes the training–testing loop fast, so we can experiment quickly. Second, it produces a model with lower accuracy than would be achieved by using all of the data. This low accuracy is usually not a major issue, because you can retrain with the entire dataset using the knowledge gained from the smaller subset. This is a very useful trick in training deep learning models, where the amount of training data in many situations can be enormous.

---

12 You can find the code for munging the "light" (*https://nlproc.info/pytorch/repo/chapters/chap ter_3/3_5_yelp_dataset_preprocessing_LITE.ipynb*) and "full" (*https://nlproc.info/pytorch/repo/chapters/chap ter_3/3_5_yelp_dataset_preprocessing_FULL.ipynb*) versions of Yelp review dataset on GitHub.

From this smaller subset, we split the dataset into three partitions: one for training, one for validation, and one for testing. Although the original dataset has only two partitions, it's important to have a validation set. In machine learning, you will often train a model on the training partition of a dataset and require a held-out partition for evaluating how well the model did. If model decisions are based on that held-out portion, the model will inevitably be biased toward performing better on the held-out portion. Because measuring incremental progress is vital, the solution to this problem is to have a third partition, which is used for evaluation as little as possible.

To summarize, you should use the training partition of a dataset to derive model parameters, the validation partition of a dataset for selecting among hyperparameters (making modeling decisions), and the testing partition of the dataset for final evaluation and reporting.[13] In Example 3-12, we show how we split the dataset. Note that the random seed is set to a static number and that we first aggregate by class label to guarantee the class distribution remains the same.

Example 3-12. Creating training, validation, and testing splits

```
# Split the subset by rating to create new train, val, and test splits
by_rating = collections.defaultdict(list)
for _, row in review_subset.iterrows():
    by_rating[row.rating].append(row.to_dict())

# Create split data
final_list = []
np.random.seed(args.seed)

for _, item_list in sorted(by_rating.items()):
    np.random.shuffle(item_list)

    n_total = len(item_list)
    n_train = int(args.train_proportion * n_total)
    n_val = int(args.val_proportion * n_total)
    n_test = int(args.test_proportion * n_total)

    # Give data point a split attribute
    for item in item_list[:n_train]:
        item['split'] = 'train'

    for item in item_list[n_train:n_train+n_val]:
        item['split'] = 'val'
```

---

13 This split of data into training, validation, and test sets works well with large datasets. Sometimes, when the training data is not large, we recommend using *k*-fold cross validation. How large is "large"? That depends on the network being trained, the complexity of the task being modeled, the size of input instances, and so on, but for many NLP tasks, this is usually when you have hundreds of thousands or millions of training examples.

```
    for item in item_list[n_train+n_val:n_train+n_val+n_test]:
        item['split'] = 'test'

    # Add to final list
    final_list.extend(item_list)

final_reviews = pd.DataFrame(final_list)
```

In addition to creating a subset that has three partitions for training, validation, and testing, we also minimally clean the data by adding whitespace around punctuation symbols and removing extraneous symbols that aren't punctuation for all the splits, as shown in Example 3-13.[14]

Example 3-13. Minimally cleaning the data

```
def preprocess_text(text):
    text = text.lower()
    text = re.sub(r"([.,!?])", r" \1 ", text)
    text = re.sub(r"[^a-zA-Z.,!?]+", r" ", text)
    return text

final_reviews.review = final_reviews.review.apply(preprocess_text)
```

Understanding PyTorch's Dataset Representation

The ReviewDataset class presented in Example 3-14 assumes that the dataset that has been minimally cleaned and split into three partitions. In particular, the dataset assumes that it can split reviews based on whitespace in order to get the list of tokens in a review.[15] Further, it assumes that the data has an annotation for which split it belongs to. It is important to notice that we indicate the entry point method for this dataset class using Python's classmethod decorator. We follow this pattern throughout the book.

PyTorch provides an abstraction for the dataset by providing a Dataset class. The Dataset class is an abstract iterator. When using PyTorch with a new dataset, you

---

14 Data cleaning or preprocessing is an important issue that's glossed over in many machine learning books (and even papers!). We have intentionally kept the concepts simple here to focus more on the modeling, but we highly recommend studying and using all available text preprocessing tools, including NLTK and spaCy. Preprocessing can either improve or hinder accuracy, depending on the data and the task. Use recommendations of what has worked in the past, and experiment often with small data subsets. When implementing a paper, if you find the preprocessing information is missing/unclear, ask the authors!

15 Recall from Chapter 2 that for some languages splitting on whitespace might not be ideal, but we are dealing with cleaned-up English reviews here. You might also want to review "Corpora, Tokens, and Types" on page 29 at this point.

must first subclass (or inherit from) the `Dataset` class and implement these `__geti` `tem__()` and `__len__()` methods. For this example, we create a `ReviewDataset` class that inherits from PyTorch's `Dataset` class and implements the two methods: `__geti` `tem__` and `__len__`. This creates a conceptual pact that allows various PyTorch utilities to work with our dataset. We cover one of these utilities, in particular the `DataLoader`, in the next section. The implementation that follows relies heavily on a class called `ReviewVectorizer`. We describe the `ReviewVectorizer` in the next section, but intuitively you can picture it as a class that handles the conversion from review text to a vector of numbers representing the review. Only through some vectorization step can a neural network interact with text data. The overall design pattern is to implement a dataset class that handles the vectorization logic for one data point. Then, PyTorch's `DataLoader` (also described in the next section) will create minibatches by sampling and collating from the dataset.

Example 3-14. A PyTorch Dataset class for the Yelp Review dataset

```
from torch.utils.data import Dataset

class ReviewDataset(Dataset):
    def __init__(self, review_df, vectorizer):
        """
        Args:
            review_df (pandas.DataFrame): the dataset
            vectorizer (ReviewVectorizer): vectorizer instantiated from dataset
        """
        self.review_df = review_df
        self._vectorizer = vectorizer

        self.train_df = self.review_df[self.review_df.split=='train']
        self.train_size = len(self.train_df)

        self.val_df = self.review_df[self.review_df.split=='val']
        self.validation_size = len(self.val_df)

        self.test_df = self.review_df[self.review_df.split=='test']
        self.test_size = len(self.test_df)

        self._lookup_dict = {'train': (self.train_df, self.train_size),
                             'val': (self.val_df, self.validation_size),
                             'test': (self.test_df, self.test_size)}

        self.set_split('train')

    @classmethod
    def load_dataset_and_make_vectorizer(cls, review_csv):
        """Load dataset and make a new vectorizer from scratch

        Args:
```

```python
        review_csv (str): location of the dataset
    Returns:
        an instance of ReviewDataset
    """
    review_df = pd.read_csv(review_csv)
    return cls(review_df, ReviewVectorizer.from_dataframe(review_df))

def get_vectorizer(self):
    """ returns the vectorizer """
    return self._vectorizer

def set_split(self, split="train"):
    """ selects the splits in the dataset using a column in the dataframe

    Args:
        split (str): one of "train", "val", or "test"
    """
    self._target_split = split
    self._target_df, self._target_size = self._lookup_dict[split]

def __len__(self):
    return self._target_size

def __getitem__(self, index):
    """"the primary entry point method for PyTorch datasets

    Args:
        index (int): the index to the data point
    Returns:
        a dict of the data point's features (x_data) and label (y_target)
    """
    row = self._target_df.iloc[index]

    review_vector = \
        self._vectorizer.vectorize(row.review)

    rating_index = \
        self._vectorizer.rating_vocab.lookup_token(row.rating)

    return {'x_data': review_vector,
            'y_target': rating_index}

def get_num_batches(self, batch_size):
    """"Given a batch size, return the number of batches in the dataset

    Args:
        batch_size (int)
    Returns:
        number of batches in the dataset
    """
    return len(self) // batch_size
```

The Vocabulary, the Vectorizer, and the DataLoader

The Vocabulary, the Vectorizer, and the DataLoader are three classes that we use in nearly every example in this book to perform a crucial pipeline: converting text inputs to vectorized minibatches. The pipeline starts with preprocessed text; each data point is a collection of tokens. In this example, the tokens happen to be words, but as you will see in Chapter 4 and Chapter 6, tokens can also be characters. The three classes presented in the following subsections are responsible for mapping each token to an integer, applying this mapping to each data point to create a vectorized form, and then grouping the vectorized data points into a minibatch for the model.

Vocabulary

The first stage in going from text to vectorized minibatch is to map each token to a numerical version of itself. The standard methodology is to have a bijection—a mapping that can be reversed—between the tokens and integers. In Python, this is simply two dictionaries. We encapsulate this bijection into a Vocabulary class, shown in Example 3-15. The Vocabulary class not only manages this bijection—allowing the user to add new tokens and have the index autoincrement—but also handles a special token called UNK,[16] which stands for "unknown." By using the UNK token, we can handle tokens at test time that were never seen in training (for instance, you might encounter words that were not encountered in the training dataset). As we will see in the Vectorizer next, we will even explicitly restrict infrequent tokens from our Vocabulary so that there are UNK tokens in our training routine. This is essential in limiting the memory used by the Vocabulary class.[17] The expected behavior is that add_token() is called to add new tokens to the Vocabulary, lookup_token() when retrieving the index for a token, and lookup_index() when retrieving the token corresponding to a specific index.

Example 3-15. The Vocabulary class maintains token to integer mapping needed for the rest of the machine learning pipeline

```
class Vocabulary(object):
    """Class to process text and extract Vocabulary for mapping"""

    def __init__(self, token_to_idx=None, add_unk=True, unk_token="<UNK>"):
        """
```

---

16 You will see more special tokens when we get to sequence models in Chapter 6

17 Words in any language follow a power law distribution. The number of unique words in the corpus can be on the order of a million, and the majority of these words appear only a few times in the training dataset. Although it is possible to consider them in the model's vocabulary, doing so will increase the memory requirement by an order of magnitude or more.

```
        Args:
            token_to_idx (dict): a pre-existing map of tokens to indices
            add_unk (bool): a flag that indicates whether to add the UNK token
            unk_token (str): the UNK token to add into the Vocabulary
        """

        if token_to_idx is None:
            token_to_idx = {}
        self._token_to_idx = token_to_idx

        self._idx_to_token = {idx: token
                              for token, idx in self._token_to_idx.items()}

        self._add_unk = add_unk
        self._unk_token = unk_token

        self.unk_index = -1
        if add_unk:
            self.unk_index = self.add_token(unk_token)


    def to_serializable(self):
        """ returns a dictionary that can be serialized """
        return {'token_to_idx': self._token_to_idx,
                'add_unk': self._add_unk,
                'unk_token': self._unk_token}

    @classmethod
    def from_serializable(cls, contents):
        """ instantiates the Vocabulary from a serialized dictionary """
        return cls(**contents)

    def add_token(self, token):
        """Update mapping dicts based on the token.

        Args:
            token (str): the item to add into the Vocabulary
        Returns:
            index (int): the integer corresponding to the token
        """
        if token in self._token_to_idx:
            index = self._token_to_idx[token]
        else:
            index = len(self._token_to_idx)
            self._token_to_idx[token] = index
            self._idx_to_token[index] = token
        return index

    def lookup_token(self, token):
        """Retrieve the index associated with the token
           or the UNK index if token isn't present.
```

```
        Args:
            token (str): the token to look up
        Returns:
            index (int): the index corresponding to the token
        Notes:
            `unk_index` needs to be >=0 (having been added into the Vocabulary)
                for the UNK functionality
        """
        if self.add_unk:
            return self._token_to_idx.get(token, self.unk_index)
        else:
            return self._token_to_idx[token]

    def lookup_index(self, index):
        """Return the token associated with the index

        Args:
            index (int): the index to look up
        Returns:
            token (str): the token corresponding to the index
        Raises:
            KeyError: if the index is not in the Vocabulary
        """
        if index not in self._idx_to_token:
            raise KeyError("the index (%d) is not in the Vocabulary" % index)
        return self._idx_to_token[index]

    def __str__(self):
        return "<Vocabulary(size=%d)>" % len(self)

    def __len__(self):
        return len(self._token_to_idx)
```

Vectorizer

The second stage of going from a text dataset to a vectorized minibatch is to iterate through the tokens of an input data point and convert each token to its integer form. The result of this iteration should be a vector. Because this vector will be combined with vectors from other data points, there is a constraint that the vectors produced by the Vectorizer should always have the same length.

To accomplish these goals, the Vectorizer class encapsulates the review Vocabulary, which maps words in the review to integers. In Example 3-16, the Vectorizer utilizes Python's @classmethod decorator for the method from_dataframe() to indicate an entry point to instantiating the Vectorizer. The method from_dataframe() iterates over the rows of a Pandas DataFrame with two goals. The first goal is to count the frequency of all tokens present in the dataset. The second goal is to create a Vocabulary that only uses tokens that are as frequent as a provided keyword argument to the method, cutoff. Effectively, this method is finding all words that occur at least cutoff times and adding them to the Vocabulary. Because the UNK token is also added to the Vocabulary, any words that are not added will have the unk_index when the Vocabulary's lookup_token() method is called.

The method vectorize() encapsulates the core functionality of the Vectorizer. It takes as an argument a string representing a review and returns a vectorized representation of the review. In this example, we use the collapsed one-hot representation that we introduced in Chapter 1. This representation creates a binary vector—a vector of 1s and 0s—that has a length equal to the size of the Vocabulary. The binary vector has 1 in the locations that correspond to the words in the review. Note that this representation has some limitations. The first is that it is sparse—the number of unique words in the review will always be far less than the number of unique words in the Vocabulary. The second is that it discards the order in which the words appeared in the review (the "bag of words" approach). In the subsequent chapters, you will see other methods that don't have these limitations.

Example 3-16. The Vectorizer class converts text to numeric vectors

```python
class ReviewVectorizer(object):
    """ The Vectorizer which coordinates the Vocabularies and puts them to use"""
    def __init__(self, review_vocab, rating_vocab):
        """
        Args:
            review_vocab (Vocabulary): maps words to integers
            rating_vocab (Vocabulary): maps class labels to integers
        """
        self.review_vocab = review_vocab
        self.rating_vocab = rating_vocab

    def vectorize(self, review):
        """Create a collapsed one-hit vector for the review

        Args:
            review (str): the review
        Returns:
            one_hot (np.ndarray): the collapsed one-hot encoding
        """
        one_hot = np.zeros(len(self.review_vocab), dtype=np.float32)

        for token in review.split(" "):
            if token not in string.punctuation:
                one_hot[self.review_vocab.lookup_token(token)] = 1

        return one_hot

    @classmethod
    def from_dataframe(cls, review_df, cutoff=25):
        """Instantiate the vectorizer from the dataset dataframe
```

```
        Args:
            review_df (pandas.DataFrame): the review dataset
            cutoff (int): the parameter for frequency-based filtering
        Returns:
            an instance of the ReviewVectorizer
        """
        review_vocab = Vocabulary(add_unk=True)
        rating_vocab = Vocabulary(add_unk=False)

        # Add ratings
        for rating in sorted(set(review_df.rating)):
            rating_vocab.add_token(rating)

        # Add top words if count > provided count
        word_counts = Counter()
        for review in review_df.review:
            for word in review.split(" "):
                if word not in string.punctuation:
                    word_counts[word] += 1

        for word, count in word_counts.items():
            if count > cutoff:
                review_vocab.add_token(word)

        return cls(review_vocab, rating_vocab)

    @classmethod
    def from_serializable(cls, contents):
        """Intantiate a ReviewVectorizer from a serializable dictionary

        Args:
            contents (dict): the serializable dictionary
        Returns:
            an instance of the ReviewVectorizer class
        """
        review_vocab = Vocabulary.from_serializable(contents['review_vocab'])
        rating_vocab =  Vocabulary.from_serializable(contents['rating_vocab'])

        return cls(review_vocab=review_vocab, rating_vocab=rating_vocab)

    def to_serializable(self):
        """Create the serializable dictionary for caching

        Returns:
            contents (dict): the serializable dictionary
        """
        return {'review_vocab': self.review_vocab.to_serializable(),
                'rating_vocab': self.rating_vocab.to_serializable()}
```

DataLoader

The final stage of the text-to-vectorized-minibatch pipeline is to actually group the vectorized data points. Because grouping into minibatches is a vital part of training neural networks, PyTorch provides a built-in class called `DataLoader` for coordinating the process. The `DataLoader` class is instantiated by providing a PyTorch `Dataset` (such as the `ReviewDataset` defined for this example), a `batch_size`, and a handful of other keyword arguments. The resulting object is a Python iterator that groups and collates the data points provided in the `Dataset`.[18] In Example 3-17, we wrap the `DataLoader` in a `generate_batches()` function, which is a generator to conveniently switch the data between the CPU and the GPU.

Example 3-17. Generating minibatches from a dataset

```
def generate_batches(dataset, batch_size, shuffle=True,
                     drop_last=True, device="cpu"):
    """
    A generator function which wraps the PyTorch DataLoader. It will
      ensure each tensor is on the write device location.
    """

    dataloader = DataLoader(dataset=dataset, batch_size=batch_size,
                            shuffle=shuffle, drop_last=drop_last)

    for data_dict in dataloader:
        out_data_dict = {}
        for name, tensor in data_dict.items():
            out_data_dict[name] = data_dict[name].to(device)
        yield out_data_dict
```

A Perceptron Classifier

The model we use in this example is a reimplementation of the `Perceptron` classifier we showed at the beginning of the chapter. The `ReviewClassifier` inherits from PyTorch's `Module` and creates a single `Linear` layer with a single output. Because this is a binary classification setting (negative or positive review), this is an appropriate setup. The sigmoid function is used as the final nonlinearity.

We parameterize the `forward()` method to allow for the sigmoid function to be optionally applied. To understand why, it is important to first point out that in a binary classification task, binary cross-entropy loss (`torch.nn.BCELoss()`) is the most appropriate loss function. It is mathematically formulated for binary probabili-

---

18 Recall that in order to subclass PyTorch's `Dataset` class, the programmer must implement the `__getitem__()` and `__len__()` methods. This allows the `DataLoader` class to iterate over the dataset by iterating over the indices in the dataset.

ties. However, there are numerical stability issues with applying a sigmoid and then using this loss function. To provide its users with shortcuts that are more numerically stable, PyTorch provides BCEWithLogitsLoss(). To use this loss function, the output should not have the sigmoid function applied. Therefore, by default, we do not apply the sigmoid. However, in the case that the user of the classifier would like a probability value, the sigmoid is required, and it is left as an option. We see an example of it being used in this way in the results section in Example 3-18.

Example 3-18. A perceptron classifier for classifying Yelp reviews

```python
import torch.nn as nn
import torch.nn.functional as F

class ReviewClassifier(nn.Module):
    """ a simple perceptron-based classifier """
    def __init__(self, num_features):
        """
        Args:
            num_features (int): the size of the input feature vector
        """
        super(ReviewClassifier, self).__init__()
        self.fc1 = nn.Linear(in_features=num_features,
                             out_features=1)

    def forward(self, x_in, apply_sigmoid=False):
        """The forward pass of the classifier

        Args:
            x_in (torch.Tensor): an input data tensor
                x_in.shape should be (batch, num_features)
            apply_sigmoid (bool): a flag for the sigmoid activation
                should be false if used with the cross-entropy losses
        Returns:
            the resulting tensor. tensor.shape should be (batch,).
        """
        y_out = self.fc1(x_in).squeeze()
        if apply_sigmoid:
            y_out = F.sigmoid(y_out)
        return y_out
```

The Training Routine

In this section, we outline the components of the training routine and how they come together with the dataset and model to adjust the model parameters and increase its performance. At its core, the training routine is responsible for instantiating the model, iterating over the dataset, computing the output of the model when given the data as input, computing the loss (how wrong the model is), and updating the model proportional to the loss. Although this may seem like a lot of details to manage, there are not many places to change the training routine, and as such it will become habitual in your deep learning development process. To aid in management of the higher-level decisions, we make use of an `args` object to centrally coordinate all decision points, which you can see in Example 3-19.[19]

Example 3-19. Hyperparameters and program options for the perceptron-based Yelp review classifier

```
from argparse import Namespace

args = Namespace(
    # Data and path information
    frequency_cutoff=25,
    model_state_file='model.pth',
    review_csv='data/yelp/reviews_with_splits_lite.csv',
    save_dir='model_storage/ch3/yelp/',
    vectorizer_file='vectorizer.json',
    # No model hyperparameters
    # Training hyperparameters
    batch_size=128,
    early_stopping_criteria=5,
    learning_rate=0.001,
    num_epochs=100,
    seed=1337,
    # Runtime options omitted for space
)
```

In the remainder of this section, we first describe the *training state*, a small dictionary that we use to track information about the training process. This dictionary will grow as you track more details about the training routine, and you can systematize it if you choose to do so, but the dictionary presented in our next example is the basic set of information you will be tracking in during model training. After describing the training state, we outline the set of objects that are instantiated for model training to be executed. This includes the model itself, the dataset, the optimizer, and the loss function. In other examples and in the supplementary material, we include additional components, but we do not list them in the text for simplicity. Finally, we wrap up this section with the training loop itself and demonstrate the standard PyTorch optimization pattern.

---

19 We use the Namespace class from the built-in `argparse` package because it nicely encapsulates a property dictionary and works well with static analyzers. Additionally, if you build out command line–based model training routines, you can switch to using the `ArgumentParser` from the `argparse` package without changing the rest of your code.

Setting the stage for the training to begin

Example 3-20 shows the training components that we instantiate for this example. The first item is the initial training state. The function accepts the `args` object as an argument so that the training state can handle complex information, but in the text in this book, we do not show any of these complexities. We refer you to the supplementary material to see what additional things you can use in the training state. The minimal set shown here includes the epoch index and lists for the training loss, training accuracy, validation loss, and validation accuracy. It also includes two fields for the test loss and test accuracy.

The next two items to be instantiated are the dataset and the model. In this example, and in the examples in the remainder of the book, we design the datasets to be responsible for instantiating the vectorizers. In the supplementary material, the dataset instantiation is nested in an `if` statement that allows either the loading of previously instantiated vectorizers or a new instantiation that will also save the vectorizer to disk. The model is importantly moved to the correct device by coordinating with the wishes of the user (through `args.cuda`) and a conditional that checks whether a GPU device is indeed available. The target device is used in the `generate_batches()` function call in the core training loop so that the data and model will be in the same device location.

The last two items in the initial instantiation are the loss function and the optimizer. The loss function used in this example is `BCEWithLogitsLoss()`. (As mentioned in "A Perceptron Classifier" on page 67, the most appropriate loss function for binary classification is binary cross-entropy loss, and it is more numerically stable to pair the `BCEWithLogitsLoss()` function with a model that doesn't apply the sigmoid function to the output than to pair the `BCELoss()` function with a model that does apply the sigmoid function to the output.) The optimizer we use is the Adam optimizer. In general, Adam is highly competitive with other optimizers, and as of this writing there is no compelling evidence to use any other optimizer over Adam. We do encourage you to verify this for yourself by trying other optimizers and noting the performance.

Example 3-20. Instantiating the dataset, model, loss, optimizer, and training state

```
import torch.optim as optim

def make_train_state(args):
    return {'epoch_index': 0,
            'train_loss': [],
            'train_acc': [],
            'val_loss': [],
            'val_acc': [],
            'test_loss': -1,
            'test_acc': -1}
```

```
train_state = make_train_state(args)

if not torch.cuda.is_available():
    args.cuda = False
args.device = torch.device("cuda" if args.cuda else "cpu")

# dataset and vectorizer
dataset = ReviewDataset.load_dataset_and_make_vectorizer(args.review_csv)
vectorizer = dataset.get_vectorizer()

# model
classifier = ReviewClassifier(num_features=len(vectorizer.review_vocab))
classifier = classifier.to(args.device)

# loss and optimizer
loss_func = nn.BCEWithLogitsLoss()
optimizer = optim.Adam(classifier.parameters(), lr=args.learning_rate)
```

The training loop

The training loop uses the objects from the initial instantiation to update the model parameters so that it improves over time. More specifically, the training loop is composed of two loops: an inner loop over minibatches in the dataset, and an outer loop, which repeats the inner loop a number of times. In the inner loop, losses are computed for each minibatch, and the optimizer is used to update the model parameters. Example 3-21 presents the code; a more thorough walkthrough of what's going on follows.

Example 3-21. A bare-bones training loop

```
for epoch_index in range(args.num_epochs):
    train_state['epoch_index'] = epoch_index

    # Iterate over training dataset

    # setup: batch generator, set loss and acc to 0, set train mode on
    dataset.set_split('train')
    batch_generator = generate_batches(dataset,
                                       batch_size=args.batch_size,
                                       device=args.device)
    running_loss = 0.0
    running_acc = 0.0
    classifier.train()

    for batch_index, batch_dict in enumerate(batch_generator):
        # the training routine is 5 steps:

        # step 1. zero the gradients
        optimizer.zero_grad()
```

```
    # step 2. compute the output
    y_pred = classifier(x_in=batch_dict['x_data'].float())

    # step 3. compute the loss
    loss = loss_func(y_pred, batch_dict['y_target'].float())
    loss_batch = loss.item()
    running_loss += (loss_batch - running_loss) / (batch_index + 1)

    # step 4. use loss to produce gradients
    loss.backward()

    # step 5. use optimizer to take gradient step
    optimizer.step()

    # -----------------------------------------
    # compute the accuracy
    acc_batch = compute_accuracy(y_pred, batch_dict['y_target'])
    running_acc += (acc_batch - running_acc) / (batch_index + 1)

train_state['train_loss'].append(running_loss)
train_state['train_acc'].append(running_acc)

# Iterate over val dataset

# setup: batch generator, set loss and acc to 0, set eval mode on
dataset.set_split('val')
batch_generator = generate_batches(dataset,
                                   batch_size=args.batch_size,
                                   device=args.device)
running_loss = 0.
running_acc = 0.
classifier.eval()

for batch_index, batch_dict in enumerate(batch_generator):

    # step 1. compute the output
    y_pred = classifier(x_in=batch_dict['x_data'].float())

    # step 2. compute the loss
    loss = loss_func(y_pred, batch_dict['y_target'].float())
    loss_batch = loss.item()
    running_loss += (loss_batch - running_loss) / (batch_index + 1)

    # step 3. compute the accuracy
    acc_batch = compute_accuracy(y_pred, batch_dict['y_target'])
    running_acc += (acc_batch - running_acc) / (batch_index + 1)

train_state['val_loss'].append(running_loss)
train_state['val_acc'].append(running_acc)
```

In the first line, we use a for loop, which ranges over the epochs. The number of epochs is a hyperparameter that you can set. It controls how many passes over the dataset the training routine should do. In practice, you should use something like an early stopping criterion to terminate this loop before it reaches the end. In the supplementary material, we show how you can do this.

At the top of the `for` loop, several routine definitions and instantiations take place. First, the training state's epoch index is set. Then, the split of the dataset is set (to `'train'` at first, then to `'val'` later when we want to measure model performance at the end of the epoch, and finally to `'test'` when we want to evaluate the model's final performance). Given how we've constructed our dataset, the split should always be set before `generate_batches()` is called. After the `batch_generator` is created, two floats are instantiated for tracking the loss and accuracy from batch to batch. For more details about the "running mean formula" we use here, we refer you to the "moving average" (*http://bit.ly/2Ezb9DP*) Wikipedia page. Finally, we call the classifier's `.train()` method to indicate that the model is in "training mode" and the model parameters are mutable. This also enables regularization mechanisms like dropout (see "Regularizing MLPs: Weight Regularization and Structural Regularization (or Dropout)" on page 99).

The next portion of the training loop iterates over the training batches in `batch_gen erator` and performs the essential operations that update the model parameters. Inside each batch iteration, the optimizer's gradients are first reset using the `opti mizer.zero_grad()` method. Then, the outputs are computed from the model. Next, the loss function is used to compute the loss between the model outputs and the supervision target (the true class labels). Following this, the `loss.backward()` method is called on the loss object (not the loss function object), resulting in gradients being propagated to each parameter. Finally, the optimizer uses these propagated gradients to perform parameter updates using the `optimizer.step()` method. These five steps are the essential steps for gradient descent. Beyond this, there are a couple of additional operations for bookkeeping and tracking. Specifically, the loss and accuracy values (stored as regular Python variables) are computed and then used to update the running loss and running accuracy variables.

After the inner loop over the training split batches, there are a few more bookkeeping and instantiation operations. The training state is first updated with the final loss and accuracy values. Then, a new batch generator, running loss, and running accuracy are created. The loop over the validation data is almost identical to the training data, and so the same variables are reused. There is a major difference, though: the classifier's `.eval()` method is called, which performs the inverse operation to the classifier's `.train()` method. The `.eval()` method makes the model parameters immutable and disables dropout. The eval mode also disables computation of the loss and propagation of gradients back to the parameters. This is important because we do not want the model adjusting its parameters relative to validation data. Instead, we want this data to serve as a measure of how well the model is performing. If there is a large divergence between its measured performance on the training data versus the measured performance on the validation data, it is likely that the model is overfitting to the training data, and we should make adjustments to the model or to the training routine (such as setting up early stopping, which we use in the supplementary notebook for this example).

After iterating over the validation data and saving the resulting validation loss and accuracy values, the outer for loop is complete. Every training routine we implement in this book will follow a very similar design pattern. In fact, all gradient descent algorithms follow similar design patterns. After you have grown accustomed to writing this loop from scratch, you will have learned what it means to perform gradient descent.

Evaluation, Inference, and Inspection

After you have a trained model, the next steps are to either evaluate how it did against some held-out portion of the data, use it to do inference on new data, or inspect the model weights to see what it is has learned. In this section, we will show you all three steps.

Evaluating on test data

To evaluate the data on the held-out test set, the code is exactly the same as the validation loop in the training routine we saw in the previous example, but with one minor difference: the split is set to be 'test' rather than 'val'. The difference between the two partitions of the dataset comes from the fact that the test set should be run as little as possible. Each time you run a trained model on the test set, make a new model decision (such as changing the size of the layers), and remeasure the new retrained model on the test set, you are biasing your modeling decisions toward the test data. In other words, if you repeat that process often enough, the test set will become meaningless as an accurate measure of truly held-out data. Example 3-22 examines this more closely.

Example 3-22. Test set evaluation

```
Input[0]    dataset.set_split('test')
            batch_generator = generate_batches(dataset,
                                                batch_size=args.batch_size,
                                                device=args.device)
            running_loss = 0.
            running_acc = 0.
            classifier.eval()

            for batch_index, batch_dict in enumerate(batch_generator):
                # compute the output
                y_pred = classifier(x_in=batch_dict['x_data'].float())

                # compute the loss
                loss = loss_func(y_pred, batch_dict['y_target'].float())
                loss_batch = loss.item()
                running_loss += (loss_batch - running_loss) / (batch_index + 1)

                # compute the accuracy
                acc_batch = compute_accuracy(y_pred, batch_dict['y_target'])
                running_acc += (acc_batch - running_acc) / (batch_index + 1)

            train_state['test_loss'] = running_loss
            train_state['test_acc'] = running_acc
```

```
Input[1]    print("Test loss: {:.3f}".format(train_state['test_loss']))
            print("Test Accuracy: {:.2f}".format(train_state['test_acc']))
```

```
Output[1]   Test loss: 0.297
            Test Accuracy: 90.55
```

Inference and classifying new data points

Another method for evaluating the model is to do inference on new data and make qualitative judgments about whether the model is working. We can see this in Example 3-23.

Example 3-23. Printing the prediction for a sample review

```
Input[0]  def predict_rating(review, classifier, vectorizer,
                             decision_threshold=0.5):
              """Predict the rating of a review

              Args:
                  review (str): the text of the review
                  classifier (ReviewClassifier): the trained model
                  vectorizer (ReviewVectorizer): the corresponding vectorizer
                  decision_threshold (float): The numerical boundary which
                      separates the rating classes
              """

              review = preprocess_text(review)
              vectorized_review = torch.tensor(vectorizer.vectorize(review))
              result = classifier(vectorized_review.view(1, -1))

              probability_value = F.sigmoid(result).item()

              index = 1
              if probability_value < decision_threshold:
                  index = 0

              return vectorizer.rating_vocab.lookup_index(index)

          test_review = "this is a pretty awesome book"
          prediction = predict_rating(test_review, classifier, vectorizer)
          print("{} -> {}".format(test_review, prediction))
```

```
Output[0]  this is a pretty awesome book -> positive
```

Inspecting model weights

Finally, the last way to understand whether a model is doing well after it has finished training is to inspect the weights and make qualitative judgments about whether they seem correct. As Example 3-24 demonstrates, with the perceptron and a collapsed one-hot encoding this is fairly straightforward because each model weight corresponds exactly to a word in our vocabulary.

Example 3-24. Inspecting what the classifier learned

Input[0]

```
# Sort weights
fc1_weights = classifier.fc1.weight.detach()[0]
_, indices = torch.sort(fc1_weights, dim=0, descending=True)
indices = indices.numpy().tolist()

# Top 20 words
print("Influential words in Positive Reviews:")
print("--------------------------------------")
for i in range(20):
    print(vectorizer.review_vocab.lookup_index(indices[i]))
```

Output[0]

```
Influential words in Positive Reviews:
--------------------------------------
great
awesome
amazing
love
friendly
delicious
best
excellent
definitely
perfect
fantastic
wonderful
vegas
favorite
loved
yummy
fresh
reasonable
always
recommend
```

Input[1]

```
# Top 20 negative words
print("Influential words in Negative Reviews:")
print("--------------------------------------")
indices.reverse()
for i in range(20):
    print(vectorizer.review_vocab.lookup_index(indices[i]))
```

```
Output[1]    Influential words in Negative Reviews:
             ------------------------------------
             worst
             horrible
             mediocre
             terrible
             not
             rude
             bland
             disgusting
             dirty
             awful
             poor
             disappointing
             ok
             no
             overpriced
             sorry
             nothing
             meh
             manager
             gross
```

Summary

In this chapter, you learned some foundational concepts of supervised neural network training. We covered:

- The simplest of neural network models, the perceptron

- Foundational concepts like activation functions, loss functions, and their different kinds

- In the context of a toy example, the training loop, batch sizes, and epochs

- What generalization means, and good practices to measure generalization performance using training/test/validation splits

- Early stopping and other criteria to determine the termination or convergence of the training algorithm

- What hyperparameters are and a few examples of them, such as the batch size, the learning rate, and so on

- How to classify Yelp restaurant reviews in English using the perceptron model implemented in PyTorch, and how to interpret the model by examining its weights

In Chapter 4, we introduce *feed-forward networks*. We first build on the humble perceptron model by stacking them vertically and horizontally, leading to the *multilayer perceptron* model. We then study a new kind of feed-forward network based on con-volution operations to capture language substructure.

References

1. Zhang, Xiang, et al. (2015). "Character-Level Convolutional Networks for Text Classification." *Proceedings of NIPS*.

Feed-Forward Networks for Natural Language Processing

In Chapter 3, we covered the foundations of neural networks by looking at the perceptron, the simplest neural network that can exist. One of the historic downfalls of the perceptron was that it cannot learn modestly nontrivial patterns present in data. For example, take a look at the plotted data points in Figure 4-1. This is equivalent to an either-or (XOR) situation in which the decision boundary cannot be a single straight line (otherwise known as being *linearly separable*). In this case, the perceptron fails.

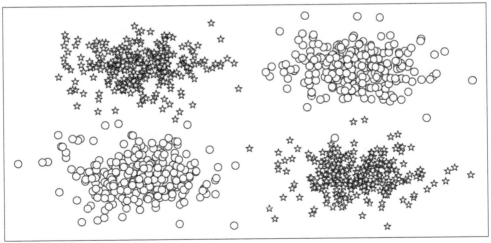

Figure 4-1. Two classes in the XOR dataset plotted as circles and stars. Notice how no single line can separate the two classes.

In this chapter, we explore a family of neural network models traditionally called *feed-forward networks*. We focus on two kinds of feed-forward neural networks: the multilayer perceptron (MLP) and the convolutional neural network (CNN).[1] The multilayer perceptron structurally extends the simpler perceptron we studied in Chapter 3 by grouping many perceptrons in a single layer and stacking multiple layers together. We cover multilayer perceptrons in just a moment and show their use in multiclass classification in "Example: Surname Classification with an MLP" on page 89.

The second kind of feed-forward neural networks studied in this chapter, the convolutional neural network, is deeply inspired by windowed filters in the processing of digital signals. Through this windowing property, CNNs are able to learn localized patterns in their inputs, which has not only made them the workhorse of computer vision but also an ideal candidate for detecting substructures in sequential data, such as words and sentences. We explore CNNs in "Convolutional Neural Networks" on page 100 and demonstrate their use in "Example: Classifying Surnames by Using a CNN" on page 110.

In this chapter, MLPs and CNNs are grouped together because they are both feed-forward neural networks and stand in contrast to a different family of neural networks, recurrent neural networks (RNNs), which allow for feedback (or cycles) such that each computation is informed by the previous computation. In Figures 6 and 7, we cover RNNs and why it can be beneficial to allow cycles in the network structure.

As we walk through these different models, one useful way to make sure you understand how things work is to pay attention to the size and shape of the data tensors as they are being computed. Each type of neural network layer has a specific effect on the size and shape of the data tensor it is computing on, and understanding that effect can be extremely conducive to a deeper understanding of these models.

The Multilayer Perceptron

The multilayer perceptron is considered one of the most basic neural network building blocks. The simplest MLP is an extension to the perceptron of Chapter 3. The perceptron takes the data vector[2] as input and computes a single output value. In an MLP, many perceptrons are grouped so that the output of a single layer is a new vector instead of a single output value. In PyTorch, as you will see later, this is done sim-

---

1 A "feed-forward" network is any neural network in which the data flows in one direction (i.e., from input to output). By this definition, the perceptron is also a "feed-forward" model, but usually the term is reserved for more complicated models with multiple units.

2 In PyTorch terminology, this is a tensor. Remember that a vector is a special case of a tensor. In this chapter, and rest of this book, we use "vector" and tensor interchangeably when it makes sense.

---

ply by setting the number of output features in the `Linear` layer. An additional aspect of an MLP is that it combines multiple layers with a nonlinearity in between each layer.

The simplest MLP, displayed in Figure 4-2, is composed of three stages of representation and two `Linear` layers. The first stage is the *input vector*. This is the vector that is given to the model. In "Example: Classifying Sentiment of Restaurant Reviews" on page 56, the input vector was a collapsed one-hot representation of a Yelp review. Given the input vector, the first `Linear` layer computes a *hidden vector*—the second stage of representation. The hidden vector is called such because it is the output of a layer that's between the input and the output. What do we mean by "output of a layer"? One way to understand this is that the values in the hidden vector are the output of different perceptrons that make up that layer. Using this hidden vector, the second `Linear` layer computes an *output vector*. In a binary task like classifying the sentiment of Yelp reviews, the output vector could still be of size 1. In a multiclass setting, as you'll see in "Example: Surname Classification with an MLP" on page 89, the size of the output vector is equal to the number of classes. Although in this illustration we show only one hidden vector, it is possible to have multiple intermediate stages, each producing its own hidden vector. Always, the final hidden vector is mapped to the output vector using a combination of `Linear` layer and a nonlinearity.

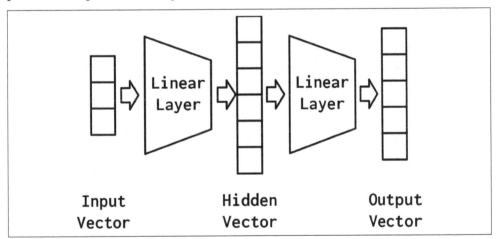

Figure 4-2. A visual representation of an MLP with two linear layers and three stages of representation—the input vector, the hidden vector, and the output vector.

The power of MLPs comes from adding the second `Linear` layer and allowing the model to learn an intermediate representation that is *linearly separable*—a property of representations in which a single straight line (or more generally, a hyperplane) can be used to distinguish the data points by which side of the line (or hyperplane) they fall on. *Learning intermediate representations that have specific properties, like*

*being linearly separable for a classification task, is one of the most profound conse-
quences of using neural networks and is quintessential to their modeling capabilities.* In
the next section, we take a much closer, in-depth look at what that means.

A Simple Example: XOR

Let's take a look at the XOR example described earlier and see what would happen
with a perceptron versus an MLP. In this example, we train both the perceptron and
an MLP in a binary classification task: identifying stars and circles. Each data point is
a 2D coordinate. Without diving into the implementation details yet, the final model
predictions are shown in Figure 4-3. In this plot, incorrectly classified data points are
filled in with black, whereas correctly classified data points are not filled in. In the left
panel, you can see that the perceptron has difficulty in learning a decision boundary
that can separate the stars and circles, as evidenced by the filled in shapes. However,
the MLP (right panel) learns a decision boundary that classifies the stars and circles
much more accurately.

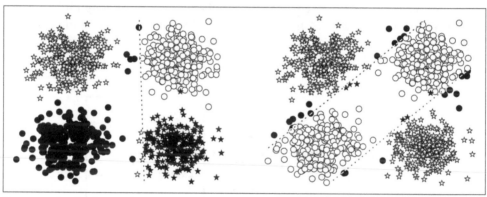

*Figure 4-3. The learned solutions from the perceptron (left) and MLP (right) for the
XOR problem. The true class of each data point is the point's shape: star or circle.
Incorrect classifications are filled in with black and correct classifications are not filled
in. The lines are the decision boundaries of each model. In the left panel, a perceptron
learns a decision boundary that cannot correctly separate the circles from the stars. In
fact, no single line can. In the right panel, an MLP has learned to separate the stars
from the circles.*

Although it appears in the plot that the MLP has two decision boundaries, and that is
its advantage, it is actually just one decision boundary! The decision boundary just
appears that way because the intermediate representation has morphed the space to
allow one hyperplane to appear in both of those positions. In Figure 4-4, we can see
the intermediate values being computed by the MLP. The shapes of the points indicate the class (star or circle). What we see is that the neural network (an MLP in this

case) has learned to "warp" the space in which the data lives so that it can divide the dataset with a single line by the time it passes through the final layer.

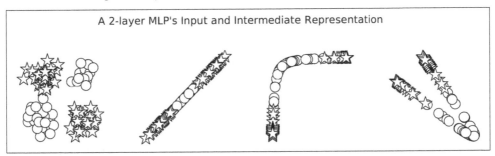

Figure 4-4. The input and intermediate representations for an MLP. From left to right: (1) the input to the network, (2) the output of the first linear module, (3) the output of the first nonlinearity, and (4) the output of the second linear module. As you can see, the output of the first linear module groups the circles and stars, whereas the output of the second linear module reorganizes the data points to be linearly separable.

In contrast, as Figure 4-5 demonstrates, the perceptron does not have an extra layer that lets it massage the shape of the data until it becomes linearly separable.

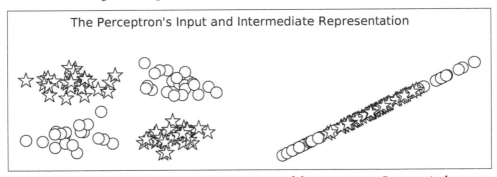

Figure 4-5. The input and output representations of the perceptron. Because it does not have an intermediate representation to group and reorganize as the MLP can, it cannot separate the circles and stars.

Implementing MLPs in PyTorch

In the previous section, we outlined the core ideas of the MLP. In this section, we walk through an implementation in PyTorch. As described, the MLP has an additional layer of computation beyond the simpler perceptron we saw in Chapter 3. In the implementation that we present in Example 4-1, we instantiate this idea with two of PyTorch's `Linear` modules. The `Linear` objects are named `fc1` and `fc2`, following a common convention that refers to a `Linear` module as a "fully connected layer," or "fc layer" for short.[3] In addition to these two Linear layers, there is a Rectified Linear Unit (ReLU) nonlinearity (introduced in Chapter 3, in "Activation Functions" on page 41) which is applied to the output of the first Linear layer before it is provided as input to the second Linear layer. Because of the sequential nature of the layers, you must take care to ensure that the number of outputs in a layer is equal to the number of inputs to the next layer. Using a nonlinearity between two Linear layers is essential because without it, two Linear layers in sequence are mathematically equivalent to a single Linear layer[4] and thus unable to model complex patterns. Our implementation of the MLP implements only the forward pass of the backpropagation. This is because PyTorch automatically figures out how to do the backward pass and gradient updates based on the definition of the model and the implementation of the forward pass.

Example 4-1. Multilayer perceptron using PyTorch

```
import torch.nn as nn
import torch.nn.functional as F

class MultilayerPerceptron(nn.Module):
    def __init__(self, input_dim, hidden_dim, output_dim):
        """
        Args:
            input_dim (int): the size of the input vectors
            hidden_dim (int): the output size of the first Linear layer
            output_dim (int): the output size of the second Linear layer
        """
        super(MultilayerPerceptron, self).__init__()
        self.fc1 = nn.Linear(input_dim, hidden_dim)
        self.fc2 = nn.Linear(hidden_dim, output_dim)

    def forward(self, x_in, apply_softmax=False):
        """The forward pass of the MLP

        Args:
            x_in (torch.Tensor): an input data tensor
                x_in.shape should be (batch, input_dim)
            apply_softmax (bool): a flag for the softmax activation
                should be false if used with the cross-entropy losses
        Returns:
            the resulting tensor. tensor.shape should be (batch, output_dim)
        """
        intermediate = F.relu(self.fc1(x_in))
```

---

3 This is common practice in deep learning literature. If there is more than one fully connected layer, they are numbered from left to right as fc-1, fc-2, and so on.

4 This is easy to prove if you write down the equations of a Linear layer. We invite you to do this as an exercise.

```
        output = self.fc2(intermediate)

        if apply_softmax:
            output = F.softmax(output, dim=1).
        return output
```

In Example 4-2, we instantiate the MLP. Due to the generality of the MLP implementation, we can model inputs of any size. To demonstrate, we use an input dimension of size 3, an output dimension of size 4, and a hidden dimension of size 100. Notice how in the output of the print statement, the number of units in each layer nicely line up to produce an output of dimension 4 for an input of dimension 3.

Example 4-2. An example instantiation of an MLP

Input[0]
```
batch_size = 2 # number of samples input at once
input_dim = 3
hidden_dim = 100
output_dim = 4

# Initialize model
mlp = MultilayerPerceptron(input_dim, hidden_dim, output_dim)
print(mlp)
```

Output[0]
```
MultilayerPerceptron(
    (fc1): Linear(in_features=3, out_features=100, bias=True)
    (fc2): Linear(in_features=100, out_features=4, bias=True)
    (relu): ReLU()
)
```

We can quickly test the "wiring" of the model by passing some random inputs, as shown in Example 4-3. Because the model is not yet trained, the outputs are random. Doing this is a useful sanity check before spending time training a model. Notice how PyTorch's interactivity allows us to do all this in real time during development, in a way not much different from using NumPy or Pandas.

Example 4-3. Testing the MLP with random inputs

Input[0]
```
def describe(x):
    print("Type: {}".format(x.type()))
    print("Shape/size: {}".format(x.shape))
    print("Values: \n{}".format(x))

x_input = torch.rand(batch_size, input_dim)
describe(x_input)
```

```
Output[0]    Type: torch.FloatTensor
             Shape/size: torch.Size([2, 3])
             Values:
             tensor([[ 0.8329,  0.4277,  0.4363],
                     [ 0.9686,  0.6316,  0.8494]])
```

```
Input[1]     y_output = mlp(x_input, apply_softmax=False)
             describe(y_output)
```

```
Output[1]    Type: torch.FloatTensor
             Shape/size: torch.Size([2, 4])
             Values:
             tensor([[-0.2456,  0.0723,  0.1589, -0.3294],
                     [-0.3497,  0.0828,  0.3391, -0.4271]])
```

It is important to learn how to read inputs and outputs of PyTorch models. In the preceding example, the output of the MLP model is a tensor that has two rows and four columns. The rows in this tensor correspond to the batch dimension, which is the number of data points in the minibatch. The columns are the final feature vectors for each data point.[5] In some cases, such as in a classification setting, the feature vector is a *prediction vector*. The name "prediction vector" means that it corresponds to a probability distribution. What happens with the prediction vector depends on whether we are currently conducting training or performing inference. During training, the outputs are used as is with a loss function and a representation of the target class labels.[6] We cover this in depth in "Example: Surname Classification with an MLP" on page 89.

However, if you want to turn the prediction vector into probabilities, an extra step is required. Specifically, you require the softmax activation function, which is used to transform a vector of values into probabilities. The softmax function has many roots. In physics, it is known as the Boltzmann or Gibbs distribution; in statistics, it's multinomial logistic regression; and in the natural language processing (NLP) community it's known as the maximum entropy (MaxEnt) classifier.[7] Whatever the name, the intuition underlying the function is that large positive values will result in higher probabilities, and lower negative values will result in smaller probabilities. In

---

5 Sometimes also called a "representation vector."

6 There is a coordination between model outputs and loss functions in PyTorch. The documentation (*http://bit.ly/2RFOIjM*) goes into more detail on this; for example, it states which loss functions expect a pre-softmax prediction vector and which don't. The exact reasons are based upon mathematical simplifications and numerical stability.

7 This is actually a very significant point. A deeper investigation of these concepts is beyond the scope of this book, but we invite you to work through Frank Ferraro and Jason Eisner's tutorial on the topic (*http://bit.ly/2rPeW8G*).

Example 4-3, the `apply_softmax` argument applies this extra step. In Example 4-4, you can see the same output, but this time with the `apply_softmax` flag set to `True`.

Example 4-4. Producing probabilistic outputs with a multilayer perceptron classifier (notice the apply_softmax = True option)

```
Input[0]    y_output = mlp(x_input, apply_softmax=True)
            describe(y_output)
```

```
Output[0]   Type: torch.FloatTensor
            Shape/size: torch.Size([2, 4])
            Values:
            tensor([[ 0.2087,  0.2868,  0.3127,  0.1919],
                    [ 0.1832,  0.2824,  0.3649,  0.1696]])
```

To conclude, MLPs are stacked `Linear` layers that map tensors to other tensors. Non-linearities are used between each pair of `Linear` layers to break the linear relationship and allow for the model to twist the vector space around. In a classification setting, this twisting should result in linear separability between classes. Additionally, you can use the softmax function to interpret MLP outputs as probabilities, but you should not use softmax with specific loss functions,[8] because the underlying implementations can leverage superior mathematical/computational shortcuts.

Example: Surname Classification with an MLP

In this section, we apply the MLP to the task of classifying surnames to their country of origin. Inferring demographic information (like nationality) from publicly observable data has applications from product recommendations to ensuring fair outcomes for users across different demographics. However, demographic and other self-identifying attributes are collectively called "protected attributes." You must exercise care in the use of such attributes in modeling and in products.[9] We begin by splitting the characters of each surname and treating them the same way we treated words in "Example: Classifying Sentiment of Restaurant Reviews" on page 56. Aside from the

---

8 While we acknowledge this point, we do not go into all of the interactions between output nonlinearity and loss functions. The PyTorch documentation (*http://bit.ly/2RFOIjM*) makes it clear and should be the place you consult for details on such matters.

9 For ethical discussions in NLP, we refer you to *ethicsinnlp.org*.

data difference, character-level models are mostly similar to word-based models in structure and implementation.[10]

An important lesson that you should take away from this example is that implementation and training of an MLP is a straightforward progression from the implementation and training we saw for a perceptron in Chapter 3. In fact, we point back to the example in Chapter 3 throughout the book as the place to go to get a more thorough overview of these components. Further, we will not include code that you can see in "Example: Classifying Sentiment of Restaurant Reviews" on page 56 If you want to see the example code in one place, we highly encourage you to follow along with the supplementary material.[11]

This section begins with a description of the surnames dataset and its preprocessing steps. Then, we step through the pipeline from a surname string to a vectorized mini-batch using the Vocabulary, Vectorizer, and DataLoader classes. If you read through Chapter 3, you should recognize these auxiliary classes as old friends, with some small modifications.

We continue the section by describing the surnameclassifier model and the thought process underlying its design. The MLP is similar to the perceptron example we saw in Chapter 3, but in addition to the model change, we introduce multiclass outputs and their corresponding loss functions in this example. After describing the model, we walk through the training routine. This is quite similar to what you saw in "The Training Routine" on page 68 so for brevity we do not go into as much depth here as we did in that section. We strongly recommend that you refer back that section for additional clarification.

We conclude the example by evaluating the model on the test portion of the dataset and describing the inference procedure on a new surname. A nice property of multiclass predictions is that we can look at more than just the top prediction, and we additionally walk through how to infer the top k predictions for a new surname.

The Surnames Dataset

In this example, we introduce the *surnames dataset*, a collection of 10,000 surnames from 18 different nationalities collected by the authors from different name sources on the internet. This dataset will be reused in several examples in the book and has several properties that make it interesting. The first property is that it is fairly imbalanced. The top three classes account for more than 60% of the data: 27% are English,

---

10 Interestingly, recent research has shown incorporating character-level models can improve word-level models. See Peters et al. (2018).

11 See */chapters/chapter_4/4_2_mlp_surnames/4_2_Classifying_Surnames_with_an_MLP.ipynb* in this book's GitHub repo (*https://nlproc.info/PyTorchNLPBook/repo/*).

21% are Russian, and 14% are Arabic. The remaining 15 nationalities have decreasing frequency—a property that is endemic to language, as well. The second property is that there is a valid and intuitive relationship between nationality of origin and surname orthography (spelling). There are spelling variations that are strongly tied to nation of origin (such in "O'Neill," "Antonopoulos," "Nagasawa," or "Zhu").

To create the final dataset, we began with a less-processed version than what is included in this book's supplementary material and performed several dataset modification operations. The first was to reduce the imbalance—the original dataset was more than 70% Russian, perhaps due to a sampling bias or a proliferation in unique Russian surnames. For this, we subsampled this overrepresented class by selecting a randomized subset of surnames labeled as Russian. Next, we grouped the dataset based on nationality and split the dataset into three sections: 70% to a training dataset, 15% to a validation dataset, and the last 15% to the testing dataset, such that the class label distributions are comparable across the splits.

The implementation of the `SurnameDataset` is nearly identical to the `ReviewDataset` as seen in "Example: Classifying Sentiment of Restaurant Reviews" on page 56, with only minor differences in how the `__getitem__()` method is implemented.[12] Recall that the dataset classes presented in this book inherit from PyTorch's `Dataset` class, and as such, we need to implement two functions: the `__getitem__()` method, which returns a data point when given an index; and the `__len__()` method, which returns the length of the dataset. The difference between the example in Chapter 3 and this example is in the `__getitem__` method as shown in Example 4-5. Rather than returning a vectorized review as in "Example: Classifying Sentiment of Restaurant Reviews" on page 56, it returns a vectorized surname and the index corresponding to its nationality.

Example 4-5. Implementing SurnameDataset.__getitem__()

```
class SurnameDataset(Dataset):
    # Implementation is nearly identical to Example 3-14

    def __getitem__(self, index):
        row = self._target_df.iloc[index]
        surname_vector = \
            self._vectorizer.vectorize(row.surname)
        nationality_index = \
            self._vectorizer.nationality_vocab.lookup_token(row.nationality)

        return {'x_surname': surname_vector,
                'y_nationality': nationality_index}
```

---

12 Some variable names are also changed to reflect their role/content.

Vocabulary, Vectorizer, and DataLoader

To classify surnames using their characters, we use the Vocabulary, Vectorizer, and DataLoader to transform surname strings into vectorized minibatches. These are the same data structures used in "Example: Classifying Sentiment of Restaurant Reviews" on page 56, exemplifying a polymorphism that treats the character tokens of surnames in the same way as the word tokens of Yelp reviews. Instead of vectorizing by mapping word tokens to integers, the data is vectorized by mapping characters to integers.

The Vocabulary class

The Vocabulary class used in this example is exactly the same as the one used in Example 3-16 to map the words in Yelp reviews to their corresponding integers. As a brief overview, the Vocabulary is a coordination of two Python dictionaries that form a bijection between tokens (characters, in this example) and integers; that is, the first dictionary maps characters to integer indices, and the second maps the integer indices to characters. The add_token() method is used to add new tokens into the Vocabulary, the lookup_token() method is used to retrieve an index, and the lookup_index() method is used to retrieve a token given an index (which is useful in the inference stage). In contrast with the Vocabulary for Yelp reviews, we use a one-hot representation[13] and do not count the frequency of characters and restrict only to frequent items. This is mainly because the dataset is small and most characters are frequent enough.

The SurnameVectorizer

Whereas the Vocabulary converts individual tokens (characters) to integers, the SurnameVectorizer is responsible for applying the Vocabulary and converting a surname into a vector. The instantiation and use are very similar to the ReviewVectorizer in "Vectorizer" on page 64, but with one key difference: the string is not split on whitespace. Surnames are sequences of characters, and each character is an individual token in our Vocabulary. However, until "Convolutional Neural Networks" on page 100, we will ignore the sequence information and create a collapsed one-hot vector representation of the input by iterating over each character in the string input. We designate a special token, UNK, for characters not encountered before. The UNK symbol is still used in the character Vocabulary because we instanti-

---

13 See "One-Hot Representation" on page 6 for a description of one-hot representations.

ate the Vocabulary from the training data only and there could be unique characters in the validation or testing data.[14]

You should note that although we used the collapsed one-hot representation in this example, you will learn about other methods of vectorization in later chapters that are alternatives to, and sometimes better than, the one-hot encoding. Specifically, in "Example: Classifying Surnames by Using a CNN" on page 110, you will see a one-hot matrix in which each character is a position in the matrix and has its own one-hot vector. Then, in Chapter 5, you will learn about the embedding layer, the vectorization that returns a vector of integers, and how those are used to create a matrix of dense vectors. But for now, let's take a look at the code for the SurnameVectorizer in Example 4-6.

Example 4-6. Implementing SurnameVectorizer

```
class SurnameVectorizer(object):
    """ The Vectorizer which coordinates the Vocabularies and puts them to use"""
    def __init__(self, surname_vocab, nationality_vocab):
        self.surname_vocab = surname_vocab
        self.nationality_vocab = nationality_vocab

    def vectorize(self, surname):
        """Vectorize the provided surname

        Args:
            surname (str): the surname
        Returns:
            one_hot (np.ndarray): a collapsed one-hot encoding
        """
        vocab = self.surname_vocab
        one_hot = np.zeros(len(vocab), dtype=np.float32)
        for token in surname:
            one_hot[vocab.lookup_token(token)] = 1
        return one_hot

    @classmethod
    def from_dataframe(cls, surname_df):
        """Instantiate the vectorizer from the dataset dataframe

        Args:
            surname_df (pandas.DataFrame): the surnames dataset
        Returns:
            an instance of the SurnameVectorizer
        """
        surname_vocab = Vocabulary(unk_token="@")
```

---

14 And in the data splits provided, there *are* unique characters in the validation data set that will break the training if UNKs are not used.

```
nationality_vocab = Vocabulary(add_unk=False)

for index, row in surname_df.iterrows():
    for letter in row.surname:
        surname_vocab.add_token(letter)
    nationality_vocab.add_token(row.nationality)

return cls(surname_vocab, nationality_vocab)
```

The SurnameClassifier Model

The SurnameClassifier (Example 4-7) is an implementation of the MLP introduced earlier in this chapter. The first Linear layer maps the input vectors to an intermediate vector, and a nonlinearity is applied to that vector. A second Linear layer maps the intermediate vector to the prediction vector.

In the last step, the softmax function is optionally applied to make sure the outputs sum to 1; that is, are interpreted as "probabilities."[15] The reason it is optional has to do with the mathematical formulation of the loss function we use—the cross-entropy loss, introduced in "Loss Functions" on page 45. Recall that cross-entropy loss is most desirable for multiclass classification, but computation of the softmax during training is not only wasteful but also not numerically stable in many situations.

Example 4-7. The SurnameClassifier using an MLP

```python
import torch.nn as nn
import torch.nn.functional as F

class SurnameClassifier(nn.Module):
    """ A 2-layer multilayer perceptron for classifying surnames """
    def __init__(self, input_dim, hidden_dim, output_dim):
        """
        Args:
            input_dim (int): the size of the input vectors
            hidden_dim (int): the output size of the first Linear layer
            output_dim (int): the output size of the second Linear layer
        """
        super(SurnameClassifier, self).__init__()
        self.fc1 = nn.Linear(input_dim, hidden_dim)
        self.fc2 = nn.Linear(hidden_dim, output_dim)

    def forward(self, x_in, apply_softmax=False):
        """The forward pass of the classifier
```

---

15 We intentionally put probabilities in quotation marks just to emphasize that these are not true posterior probabilities in a Bayesian sense, but since the output sums to 1 it is a valid distribution and hence can be interpreted as probabilities. This is also one of the most pedantic footnotes in this book, so feel free to ignore this, close your eyes, hold your nose, and call them probabilities.

```
Args:
    x_in (torch.Tensor): an input data tensor
        x_in.shape should be (batch, input_dim)
    apply_softmax (bool): a flag for the softmax activation
        should be false if used with the cross-entropy losses
Returns:
    the resulting tensor. tensor.shape should be (batch, output_dim).
"""
intermediate_vector = F.relu(self.fc1(x_in))
prediction_vector = self.fc2(intermediate_vector)

if apply_softmax:
    prediction_vector = F.softmax(prediction_vector, dim=1)

return prediction_vector
```

The Training Routine

Although we use a different model, dataset, and loss function in this example, the training routine remains the same as that described in the previous chapter. Thus, in Example 4-8, we show only the args and the major differences between the training routine in this example and the one in "Example: Classifying Sentiment of Restaurant Reviews" on page 56.

Example 4-8. Hyperparameters and program options for the MLP-based Yelp review classifier

```
args = Namespace(
    # Data and path information
    surname_csv="data/surnames/surnames_with_splits.csv",
    vectorizer_file="vectorizer.json",
    model_state_file="model.pth",
    save_dir="model_storage/ch4/surname_mlp",
    # Model hyper parameters
    hidden_dim=300
    # Training  hyper parameters
    seed=1337,
    num_epochs=100,
    early_stopping_criteria=5,
    learning_rate=0.001,
    batch_size=64,
    # Runtime options omitted for space
)
```

The most notable difference in training has to do with the kinds of outputs in the model and the loss function being used. In this example, the output is a multiclass prediction vector that can be turned into probabilities. The loss functions that can be used for this output are limited to `CrossEntropyLoss()` and `NLLLoss()`. Due to its simplifications, we use `CrossEntropyLoss()`.

In Example 4-9, we show the instantiations for the dataset, the model, the loss function, and the optimizer. These instantiations should look nearly identical to those from the example in Chapter 3. In fact, this pattern will repeat for every example in later chapters in this book.

Example 4-9. Instantiating the dataset, model, loss, and optimizer

```
dataset = SurnameDataset.load_dataset_and_make_vectorizer(args.surname_csv)
vectorizer = dataset.get_vectorizer()

classifier = SurnameClassifier(input_dim=len(vectorizer.surname_vocab),
                               hidden_dim=args.hidden_dim,
                               output_dim=len(vectorizer.nationality_vocab))

classifier = classifier.to(args.device)

loss_func = nn.CrossEntropyLoss(dataset.class_weights)
optimizer = optim.Adam(classifier.parameters(), lr=args.learning_rate)
```

The training loop

The training loop for this example is nearly identical to that described in compared to the training loop in "The training loop" on page 71, except for the variable names. Specifically, Example 4-10 shows that different keys are used to get the data out of the batch_dict. Aside from this cosmetic difference, the functionality of the training loop remains the same. Using the training data, compute the model output, the loss, and the gradients. Then, we use the gradients to update the model.

Example 4-10. A snippet of the training loop

```
# the training routine is these 5 steps:

# -------------------------------------
# step 1. zero the gradients
optimizer.zero_grad()

# step 2. compute the output
y_pred = classifier(batch_dict['x_surname'])

# step 3. compute the loss
loss = loss_func(y_pred, batch_dict['y_nationality'])
loss_batch = loss.to("cpu").item()
running_loss += (loss_batch - running_loss) / (batch_index + 1)

# step 4. use loss to produce gradients
loss.backward()
```

```
# step 5. use optimizer to take gradient step
optimizer.step()
```

Model Evaluation and Prediction

To understand a model's performance, you should analyze the model with quantitative and qualitative methods. Quantitatively, measuring the error on the held-out test data determines whether the classifier can generalize to unseen examples. Qualitatively, you can develop an intuition for what the model has learned by looking at the classifier's top *k* predictions for a new example.

Evaluating on the test dataset

To evaluate the `SurnameClassifier` on the test data, we perform the same routine as for the restaurant review text classification example in "Evaluation, Inference, and Inspection" on page 74: we set the split to iterate `'test'` data, invoke the `classifier.eval()` method, and iterate over the test data in the same way we did with the other data. In this example, invoking `classifier.eval()` prevents PyTorch from updating the model parameters when the test/evaluation data is used.

The model achieves around 50% accuracy on the test data. If you run the training routine in the accompanying notebook, you will notice that the performance on the training data is higher. This is because the model will always fit better to the data on which it is training, so the performance on the training data is not indicative of performance on new data. If you are following along with the code, we encourage you to try different sizes of the hidden dimension. You should notice an increase in performance.[16] However, the increase will not be substantial (especially when compared with the model from "Example: Classifying Surnames by Using a CNN" on page 110). The primary reason is that the collapsed one-hot vectorization method is a weak representation. Although it does compactly represent each surname as a single vector, it throws away order information between the characters, which can be vital for identifying the origin.

Classifying a new surname

Example 4-11 shows the code for classifying a new surname. Given a surname as a string, the function will first apply the vectorization process and then get the model prediction. Notice that we include the `apply_softmax` flag so that `result` contains probabilities. The model prediction, in the multinomial case, is the list of class proba-

---

16 Reminder from Chapter 3: when experimenting with hyperparameters, such as the size of the hidden dimension, and number of layers, the choices should be evaluated on the validation set and not the test set. When you're happy with the set of hyperparameters, you can run the evaluation on the test data.

bilities. We use the PyTorch tensor max() function to get the best class, represented by the highest predicted probability.

Example 4-11. Inference using an existing model (classifier): Predicting the nationality given a name

```python
def predict_nationality(name, classifier, vectorizer):
    vectorized_name = vectorizer.vectorize(name)
    vectorized_name = torch.tensor(vectorized_name).view(1, -1)
    result = classifier(vectorized_name, apply_softmax=True)

    probability_values, indices = result.max(dim=1)
    index = indices.item()

    predicted_nationality = vectorizer.nationality_vocab.lookup_index(index)
    probability_value = probability_values.item()

    return {'nationality': predicted_nationality,
            'probability': probability_value}
```

Retrieving the top k predictions for a new surname

It is often useful to look at more than just the best prediction. For example, it is standard practice in NLP to take the top *k* best predictions and rerank them using another model. PyTorch provides a torch.topk() function that offers provides a convenient way to get these predictions, as demonstrated in Example 4-12.

Example 4-12. Predicting the top-k nationalities

```python
def predict_topk_nationality(name, classifier, vectorizer, k=5):
    vectorized_name = vectorizer.vectorize(name)
    vectorized_name = torch.tensor(vectorized_name).view(1, -1)
    prediction_vector = classifier(vectorized_name, apply_softmax=True)
    probability_values, indices = torch.topk(prediction_vector, k=k)

    # returned size is 1,k
    probability_values = probability_values.detach().numpy()[0]
    indices = indices.detach().numpy()[0]

    results = []
    for prob_value, index in zip(probability_values, indices):
        nationality = vectorizer.nationality_vocab.lookup_index(index)
        results.append({'nationality': nationality,
                        'probability': prob_value})

    return results
```

Regularizing MLPs: Weight Regularization and Structural Regularization (or Dropout)

In Chapter 3, we explained how regularization was a solution for the overfitting problem and studied two important types of weight regularization—L1 and L2. These weight regularization methods also apply to MLPs as well as convolutional neural networks, which we'll look at in the next section. In addition to weight regularization, for deep models (i.e., models with multiple layers) such as the feed-forward networks discussed in this chapter, a structural regularization approach called *dropout* becomes very important.

In simple terms, dropout probabilistically drops connections between units belonging to two adjacent layers during training. Why should that help? We begin with an intuitive (and humorous) explanation by Stephen Merity:[17]

> Dropout, simply described, is the concept that if you can learn how to do a task repeatedly whilst drunk, you should be able to do the task even better when sober. This insight has resulted in numerous state-of-the-art results and a nascent field dedicated to preventing dropout from being used on neural networks.

Neural networks—especially deep networks with a large number of layers—can create interesting coadaptation between the units. "Coadaptation" is a term from neuroscience, but here it simply refers to a situation in which the connection between two units becomes excessively strong at the expense of connections between other units. This usually results in the model overfitting to the data. By probabilistically dropping connections between units, we can ensure no single unit will always depend on another single unit, leading to robust models. Dropout does not add additional parameters to the model, but requires a single hyperparameter—the "drop probability."[18] This, as you might have guessed, is the probability with which the connections between units are dropped. It is typical to set the drop probability to 0.5. Example 4-13 presents a reimplementation of the MLP with dropout.

Example 4-13. MLP with dropout

```
import torch.nn as nn
import torch.nn.functional as F

class MultilayerPerceptron(nn.Module):
    def __init__(self, input_dim, hidden_dim, output_dim):
        """
```

---

17 This definition comes from Stephen's April Fool's "paper," (*http://bit.ly/2Cq1FJR*) which is a highly entertaining read.

18 Some deep learning libraries confusingly refer to (and interpret) this probability as "keep probability," with the opposite meaning of a drop probability.

```
        Args:
            input_dim (int): the size of the input vectors
            hidden_dim (int): the output size of the first Linear layer
            output_dim (int): the output size of the second Linear layer
        """
        super(MultilayerPerceptron, self).__init__()
        self.fc1 = nn.Linear(input_dim, hidden_dim)
        self.fc2 = nn.Linear(hidden_dim, output_dim)

    def forward(self, x_in, apply_softmax=False):
        """The forward pass of the MLP

        Args:
            x_in (torch.Tensor): an input data tensor
                x_in.shape should be (batch, input_dim)
            apply_softmax (bool): a flag for the softmax activation
                should be false if used with the cross-entropy losses
        Returns:
            the resulting tensor. tensor.shape should be (batch, output_dim).
        """
        intermediate = F.relu(self.fc1(x_in))
        output = self.fc2(F.dropout(intermediate, p=0.5))

        if apply_softmax:
            output = F.softmax(output, dim=1)
        return output
```

It is important to note that *dropout is applied only during training and not during evaluation*. As an exercise, we encourage you to experiment with the `SurnameClassi fier` model with dropout and see how it changes the results.

Convolutional Neural Networks

In the first part of this chapter, we took an in-depth look at MLPs, neural networks built from a series of linear layers and nonlinear functions. MLPs are not the best tool for taking advantage of sequential patterns.[19] For example, in the surnames dataset, surnames can have segments that reveal quite a bit about their nation of origin (such as the "O'" in "O'Neill," "opoulos" in "Antonopoulos," "sawa" in "Nagasawa," or "Zh" in "Zhu"). These segments can be of variable lengths, and the challenge is to capture them without encoding them explicitly.

---

19 It is possible to design an MLP that takes as input character bigrams to capture some of these dependencies. For the 26 characters in English, the number of character bigrams is 325. So, if we have a hidden layer of 100 nodes, the number of parameters for the input-hidden layer will be 325 * 100. If we also consider all possible character trigrams, that will be an additional 2,600 * 100 parameters. CNNs efficiently capture the same information with far fewer parameters, as we will see, using parameter sharing.

In this section we cover the convolutional neural network, a type of neural network that is well suited to detecting spatial substructure (and creating meaningful spatial substructure as a consequence). CNNs accomplish this by having a small number of weights they use to scan the input data tensors. From this scanning, they produce output tensors that represent the detection (or not) of substructures.

In this section, we begin by describing the ways in which a CNN can function and the concerns you should have when designing CNNs. We dive deep into the CNN hyperparameters, with the goal of providing intuitions on the behavior and effects of these hyperparameters on the outputs. Finally, we step through a few simple examples that illustrate the mechanics of CNNs. In "Example: Classifying Surnames by Using a CNN" on page 110, we delve into a more extensive example.

Historical Context

The name and basic functionality of CNNs stem from a classic mathematical operation called *convolution*. Convolutions have been used in various engineering disciplines, including digital signal processing and computer graphics, for decades now. Classically, convolutions have used parameters specified by the programmer. The parameters are specified to match some functional design, such as highlighting edges or dampening high-frequency sounds. In fact, many Photoshop filters are fixed-convolution operations applied to an image. However, in deep learning and in this chapter, we learn the parameters of the convolution filter from data so it is optimal for solving the task at hand.

CNN Hyperparameters

To get an understanding of what the different design decisions mean to a CNN, we show an example in Figure 4-6. In this example, a single "kernel" is applied to an input matrix. The exact mathematical expression for a convolution operation (a linear operator) is not important for understanding this section; the intuition you should develop from this figure is that a kernel is a small square matrix that is applied at different positions in the input matrix in a systematic way.

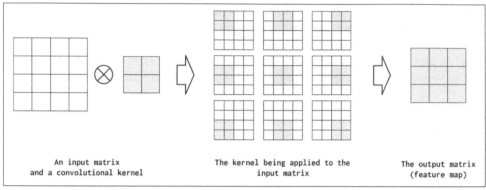

An input matrix
and a convolutional kernel

The kernel being applied to the
input matrix

The output matrix
(feature map)

Figure 4-6. A two-dimensional convolution operation. An input matrix is convolved with a single convolutional kernel to produce an output matrix (also called a feature map). The convolving is the application of the kernel to each position in the input matrix. In each application, the kernel multiplies the values of the input matrix with its own values and then sums up these multiplications. In this example, the kernel has the following hyperparameter configuration: kernel_size=2, stride=1, padding=0, and dilation=1. These hyperparameters are explained in the following text.

Although classic convolutions[20] are designed by specifying the values of the kernel,[21] CNNs are designed by specifying hyperparameters that control the behavior of the CNN and then using gradient descent to find the best parameters for a given dataset. The two primary hyperparameters control the shape of the convolution (called the `kernel_size`) and the positions the convolution will multiply in the input data tensor (called the `stride`). There are additional hyperparameters that control how much the input data tensor is padded with 0s (called `padding`) and how far apart the multiplications should be when applied to the input data tensor (called `dilation`). In the following subsections, we develop intuitions for these hyperparameters in more detail.

Dimension of the convolution operation

The first concept to understand is the *dimensionality* of the convolution operation. In Figure 4-6 and rest of the figures in this section, we illustrate using a two-dimensional convolution, but there are convolutions of other dimensions that may be more suitable depending on the nature of the data. In PyTorch, convolutions can be one-dimensional, two-dimensional, or three-dimensional and are implemented by the `Conv1d`, `Conv2d`, and `Conv3d` modules, respectively. The one-dimensional convolutions are useful for time series in which each time step has a feature vector. In this

---

20 See the box "Historical Context" on page 101 for more information about classic convolutions.

21 Many filters in image-editing programs such as Photoshop operate by doing this. For example, you can highlight edges using a convolutional filter specifically designed for that purpose.

situation, we can learn patterns on the sequence dimension. Most convolution operations in NLP are one-dimensional convolutions. A two-dimensional convolution, on the other hand, tries to capture spatio-temporal patterns along two directions in the data—for example, in images along the height and width dimensions, which is why two-dimensional convolutions are popular for image processing. Similarly, in three-dimensional convolutions the patterns are captured along three dimensions in the data. For example, in video data, information lies in three dimensions (the two dimensions representing the frame of the image, and the time dimension representing the sequence of frames). As far as this book is concerned, we use `Conv1d` primarily.

Channels

Informally, *channels* refers to the feature dimension along each point in the input. For example, in images there are three channels for each pixel in the image, corresponding to the RGB components. A similar concept can be carried over to text data when using convolutions. Conceptually, if "pixels" in a text document are words, the number of channels is the size of the vocabulary. If we go finer-grained and consider convolution over characters, the number of channels is the size of the character set (which happens to be the vocabulary in this case). In PyTorch's convolution implementation, the number of channels in the input is the `in_channels` argument. The convolution operation can produce more than one channel in the output (`out_chan nels`). You can consider this as the convolution operator "mapping" the input feature dimension to an output feature dimension. Figures 4-7 and 4-8 illustrate this concept.

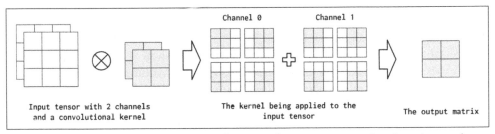

Figure 4-7. A convolution operation is shown with two input matrices (two input channels). The corresponding kernel also has two layers; it multiplies each layer separately and then sums the results. Configuration: input_channels=2, output_channels=1, kernel_size=2, stride=1, padding=0, and dilation=1.

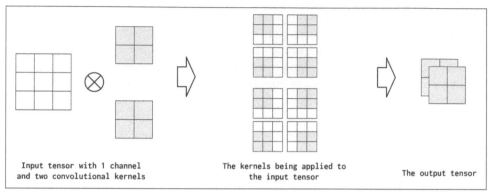

Input tensor with 1 channel
and two convolutional kernels

The kernels being applied to
the input tensor

The output tensor

Figure 4-8. A convolution operation with one input matrix (one input channel) and two convolutional kernels (two output channels). The kernels apply individually to the input matrix and are stacked in the output tensor. Configuration: input_channels=1, output_channels=2, kernel_size=2, stride=1, padding=0, and dilation=1.

It's difficult to immediately know how many output channels are appropriate for the problem at hand. To simplify this difficulty, let's say that the bounds are 1 and 1,024 —we can have a convolutional layer with a single channel, up to a maximum of 1,024 channels. Now that we have bounds, the next thing to consider is how many input channels there are. A common design pattern is not to shrink the number of channels by more than a factor of two from one convolutional layer to the next. This is not a hard-and-fast rule, but it should give you some sense of what an appropriate number of out_channels would look like.

Kernel size

The width of the kernel matrix is called the *kernel size* (kernel_size in PyTorch). In Figure 4-6 the kernel size was 2, and for contrast, we show a kernel with size 3 in Figure 4-9. The intuition you should develop is that convolutions combine spatially (or temporally) local information in the input and the amount of local information per convolution is controlled by the kernel size. However, by increasing the size of the kernel, you also decrease the size of the output (Dumoulin and Visin, 2016). This is why the output matrix is 2×2 in Figure 4-9 when the kernel size is 3, but 3×3 in Figure 4-6 when the kernel size is 2.

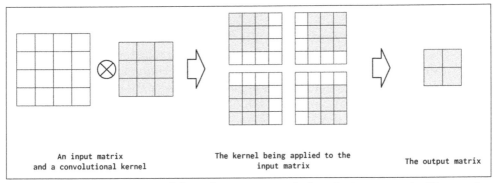

An input matrix and a convolutional kernel

The kernel being applied to the input matrix

The output matrix

Figure 4-9. A convolution with kernel_size=3 is applied to the input matrix. The result is a trade-off: more local information is used for each application of the kernel to the matrix, but the output size is smaller.

Additionally, you can think of the behavior of kernel size in NLP applications as being similar to the behavior of *n-grams*, which capture patterns in language by looking at groups of words. With smaller kernel sizes, smaller, more frequent patterns are captured, whereas larger kernel sizes lead to larger patterns, which might be more meaningful but occur less frequently. Small kernel sizes lead to fine-grained features in the output, whereas large kernel sizes lead to coarse-grained features.

Stride

Stride controls the step size between convolutions. If the stride is the same size as the kernel, the kernel computations do not overlap. On the other hand, if the stride is 1, the kernels are maximally overlapping. The output tensor can be deliberately shrunk to summarize information by increasing the stride, as demonstrated in Figure 4-10.

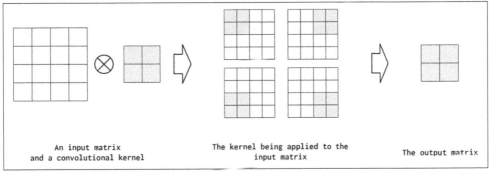

An input matrix and a convolutional kernel

The kernel being applied to the input matrix

The output matrix

Figure 4-10. A convolutional kernel with kernel_size=2 applied to an input with the hyperparameter stride equal to 2. This has the effect that the kernel takes larger steps, resulting in a smaller output matrix. This is useful for subsampling the input matrix more sparsely.

Padding

Even though `stride` and `kernel_size` allow for controlling how much scope each computed feature value has, they have a detrimental, and sometimes unintended, side effect of shrinking the total size of the feature map (the output of a convolution). To counteract this, the input data tensor is artificially made larger in length (if 1D, 2D, or 3D), height (if 2D or 3D, and depth (if 3D) by appending and prepending 0s to each respective dimension. This consequently means that the CNN will perform *more* convolutions, but the output shape can be controlled without compromising the desired kernel size, stride, or dilation. Figure 4-11 illustrates padding in action.

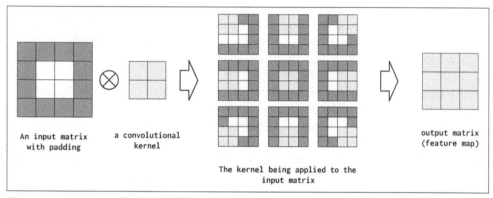

An input matrix with padding

a convolutional kernel

The kernel being applied to the input matrix

output matrix (feature map)

Figure 4-11. A convolution with kernel_size=2 applied to an input matrix that has height and width equal to 2. However, because of padding (indicated as dark-gray squares), the input matrix's height and width can be made larger. This is most commonly used with a kernel of size 3 so that the output matrix will exactly equal the size of the input matrix.

Dilation

Dilation controls how the convolutional kernel is applied to the input matrix. In Figure 4-12 we show that increasing the dilation from 1 (the default) to 2 means that the elements of the kernel are two spaces away from each other when applied to the input matrix. Another way to think about this is striding in the kernel itself—there is a step size between the elements in the kernel or application of kernel with "holes." This can be useful for summarizing larger regions of the input space without an increase in the number of parameters. Dilated convolutions have proven very useful when convolution layers are stacked. Successive dilated convolutions exponentially increase the size of the "receptive field"; that is, the size of the input space seen by the network before a prediction is made.

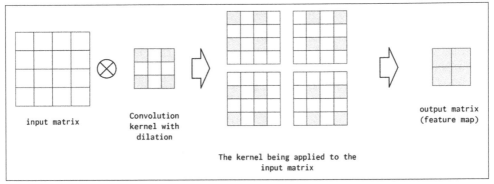

| input matrix | Convolution kernel with dilation | | output matrix (feature map) |

The kernel being applied to the input matrix

Figure 4-12. A convolution with kernel_size=2 applied to an input matrix with the hyperparameter dilation=2. The increase in dilation from its default value means the elements of the kernel matrix are spread further apart as they multiply the input matrix. Increasing dilation further would accentuate this spread.

Implementing CNNs in PyTorch

In this section, we work through an end-to-end example that will utilize the concepts introduced in the previous section. Generally, the goal of neural network design is to find a configuration of hyperparameters that will accomplish a task. We again consider the now-familiar surname classification task introduced in "Example: Surname Classification with an MLP" on page 89, but we will use CNNs instead of an MLP. We still need to apply a final Linear layer that will learn to create a prediction vector from a feature vector created by a series of convolution layers. This implies that the goal is to determine a configuration of convolution layers that results in the desired feature vector. All CNN applications are like this: there is an initial set of convolutional layers that extract a feature map that becomes input in some upstream processing. In classification, the upstream processing is almost always the application of a Linear (or fc) layer.

The implementation walk through in this section iterates over the design decisions to construct a feature vector.[22] We begin by constructing an artificial data tensor mirroring the actual data in shape. The size of the data tensor is going to be three-dimensional—this is the size of the minibatch of vectorized text data. If you use a one-hot vector for each character in a sequence of characters, a sequence of one-hot vectors is a matrix, and a minibatch of one-hot matrices is a three-dimensional tensor. Using the terminology of convolutions, the size of each one-hot vector (usually

---

22 Most deep learning books skip this detail and just present the end network as if it came from divine providence. We think this section should walk an unfamiliar reader through the process of how a certain convolutional network is arrived at, starting from the input. In most situations, especially when you are implementing an existing paper, you don't need to do this. You can simply use the values supplied by the authors.

the size of the vocabulary) is the number of "input channels" and the length of the character sequence is the "width."

As illustrated in Example 4-14, the first step to constructing a feature vector is applying an instance of PyTorch's Conv1d class to the three-dimensional data tensor. By checking the size of the output, you can get a sense of how much the tensor has been reduced. We refer you to Figure 4-9 for a visual explanation of why the output tensor is shrinking.

Example 4-14. Artificial data and using a Conv1d class

```
Input[0]
batch_size = 2
one_hot_size = 10
sequence_width = 7
data = torch.randn(batch_size, one_hot_size, sequence_width)
conv1 = Conv1d(in_channels=one_hot_size, out_channels=16,
                  kernel_size=3)
intermediate1 = conv1(data)
print(data.size())
print(intermediate1.size())
```

```
Output[0]
torch.Size([2, 10, 7])
torch.Size([2, 16, 5])
```

There are three primary methods for reducing the output tensor further. The first method is to create additional convolutions and apply them in sequence. Eventually, the dimension that had been corresponding sequence_width (dim=2) will have size=1. We show the result of applying two additional convolutions in Example 4-15. In general, the process of applying convolutions to reduce the size of the output tensor is iterative and requires some guesswork. Our example is constructed so that after three convolutions, the resulting output has size=1 on the final dimension.[23]

---

23 For larger tensors, you will need more convolutions. You'll also need to modify the convolutions to reduce the tensor at a faster rate. The hyperparameters to try out are increasing stride, increasing dilation, and increasing the kernel_size.

Example 4-15. The iterative application of convolutions to data

| Input[0] | ```
conv2 = nn.Conv1d(in_channels=16, out_channels=32, kernel_size=3)
conv3 = nn.Conv1d(in_channels=32, out_channels=64, kernel_size=3)

intermediate2 = conv2(intermediate1)
intermediate3 = conv3(intermediate2)

print(intermediate2.size())
print(intermediate3.size())
``` |
|---|---|
| Output[0] | ```
torch.Size([2, 32, 3])
torch.Size([2, 64, 1])
``` |
| Input[1] | ```
y_output = intermediate3.squeeze()
print(y_output.size())
``` |
| Output[1] | ```
torch.Size([2, 64])
``` |

With each convolution, the size of the channel dimension is increased because the channel dimension is intended to be the feature vector for each data point. The final step to the tensor actually being a feature vector is to remove the pesky `size=1` dimension. You can do this by using the `squeeze()` method. This method will drop any dimensions that have `size=1` and return the result. The resulting feature vectors can then be used in conjunction with other neural network components, such as a `Linear` layer, to compute prediction vectors.

There are two other methods for reducing a tensor to one feature vector per data point: flattening the remaining values into a feature vector, and averaging[24] over the extra dimensions. The two methods are shown in Example 4-16. Using the first method, you just flatten all vectors into a single vector using PyTorch's `view()` method.[25] The second method uses some mathematical operation to summarize the information in the vectors. The most common operation is the arithmetic mean, but summing and using the max value along the feature map dimensions are also common. Each approach has its advantages and disadvantages. Flattening retains all of the information but can result in larger feature vectors than is desirable (or computa-

---

24 In actuality, you can also compute the sum or use an attention-based mechanism, as described in Chapter 8. For simplicity, we discuss only these two methods.

25 For more details on the `view()` method, refer to Chapter 1.

tionally feasible). Averaging becomes agnostic to the size of the extra dimensions but can lose information.[26]

Example 4-16. Two additional methods for reducing to feature vectors

```
Input[0]      # Method 2 of reducing to feature vectors
              print(intermediate1.view(batch_size, -1).size())

              # Method 3 of reducing to feature vectors
              print(torch.mean(intermediate1, dim=2).size())
              # print(torch.max(intermediate1, dim=2).size())
              # print(torch.sum(intermediate1, dim=2).size())

Output[0]     torch.Size([2, 80])
              torch.Size([2, 16])
```

This method for designing a series of convolutions is empirically based: you start with the expected size of your data, play around with the series of convolutions, and eventually get a feature vector that suits you. Although this works well in practice, there is another method of computing the output size of a tensor given the convolution's hyperparameters and an input tensor, by using a mathematical formula derived from the convolution operation itself.

Example: Classifying Surnames by Using a CNN

To demonstrate the effectiveness of CNNs, let's apply a simple CNN model to the task of classifying surnames.[27] Many of the details remain the same as in the earlier MLP example for this task, but what does change is the construction of the model and the vectorization process. The input to the model, rather than the collapsed one-hots we saw in the last example, will be a matrix of one-hots. This design will allow the CNN to get a better "view" of the arrangement of characters and encode the sequence information that was lost in the collapsed one-hot encoding used in "Example: Surname Classification with an MLP" on page 89.

---

[26] Additionally, careful bookkeeping is needed for variable-length sequences, which are introduced in Chapter 6. In short, some positions may be all 0s to allow for sequences of different length. In this situation, while averaging, you would sum over the extra dimensions and divide by the number of nonzero entries.

[27] You can find the notebook for this example at */chapters/chapter_4/4_4_cnn_surnames/4_4_Classifying_Surnames_with_a_CNN.ipynb* in this book's GitHub repo (*https://nlproc.info/PyTorchNLPBook/repo/*).

The SurnameDataset Class

The Surnames dataset was previously described in "The Surnames Dataset" on page 90. We're using the same dataset in this example, but there is one difference in the implementation: the dataset is composed of a matrix of one-hot vectors rather than a collapsed one-hot vector. To accomplish this, we implement a dataset class that tracks the longest surname and provides it to the vectorizer as the number of rows to include in the matrix. The number of columns is the size of the one-hot vectors (the size of the `Vocabulary`). Example 4-17 shows the change to the `SurnameDataset.__getitem__()` method we show the change to `SurnameVectorizer.vectorize()` in the next subsection.

Example 4-17. SurnameDataset modified for passing the maximum surname length

```python
class SurnameDataset(Dataset):
    # ... existing implementation from
    "Example: Surname Classification with an MLP" on page 89

    def __getitem__(self, index):
        row = self._target_df.iloc[index]

        surname_matrix = \
            self._vectorizer.vectorize(row.surname, self._max_seq_length)

        nationality_index = \
            self._vectorizer.nationality_vocab.lookup_token(row.nationality)

        return {'x_surname': surname_matrix,
                'y_nationality': nationality_index}
```

There are two reasons why we use the longest surname in the dataset to control the size of the one-hot matrix. First, each minibatch of surname matrices is combined into a three-dimensional tensor, and there is a requirement that they all be the same size. Second, using the longest surname in the dataset means that each minibatch can be treated in the same way.[28]

Vocabulary, Vectorizer, and DataLoader

In this example, even though the `Vocabulary` and `DataLoader` are implemented in the same way as the example in "Vocabulary, Vectorizer, and DataLoader" on page 92, the `Vectorizer`'s `vectorize()` method has been changed to fit the needs of a CNN model. Specifically, as we show in the code in Example 4-18, the function maps

---

[28] We could have alternatively used the max surname length in each minibatch, but having a dataset-wide max length is a simpler option.

each character in the string to an integer and then uses that integer to construct a matrix of one-hot vectors. Importantly, each column in the matrix is a different one-hot vector. The primary reason for this is because the Conv1d layers we will use require the data tensors to have the batch on the 0th dimension, channels on the 1st dimension, and features on the 2nd.

In addition to the change to using a one-hot matrix, we also modify the Vectorizer to compute and save the maximum length of a surname as max_surname_length.

Example 4-18. Implementing the SurnameVectorizer for CNNs

```python
class SurnameVectorizer(object):
    """ The Vectorizer which coordinates the Vocabularies and puts them to use"""
    def vectorize(self, surname):
        """
        Args:
            surname (str): the surname
        Returns:
            one_hot_matrix (np.ndarray): a matrix of one-hot vectors
        """

        one_hot_matrix_size = (len(self.character_vocab), self.max_surname_length)
        one_hot_matrix = np.zeros(one_hot_matrix_size, dtype=np.float32)

        for position_index, character in enumerate(surname):
            character_index = self.character_vocab.lookup_token(character)
            one_hot_matrix[character_index][position_index] = 1

        return one_hot_matrix

    @classmethod
    def from_dataframe(cls, surname_df):
        """Instantiate the vectorizer from the dataset dataframe

        Args:
            surname_df (pandas.DataFrame): the surnames dataset
        Returns:
            an instance of the SurnameVectorizer
        """
        character_vocab = Vocabulary(unk_token="@")
        nationality_vocab = Vocabulary(add_unk=False)
        max_surname_length = 0

        for index, row in surname_df.iterrows():
            max_surname_length = max(max_surname_length, len(row.surname))
            for letter in row.surname:
                character_vocab.add_token(letter)
            nationality_vocab.add_token(row.nationality)

        return cls(character_vocab, nationality_vocab, max_surname_length)
```

Reimplementing the SurnameClassifier with Convolutional Networks

The model we use in this example is built using the methods we walked through in "Convolutional Neural Networks" on page 100. In fact, the "artificial" data that we created to test the convolutional layers in that section exactly matched the size of the data tensors in the surnames dataset using the Vectorizer from this example. As you can see in Example 4-19, there are both similarities to the sequence of Conv1d that we introduced in that section and new additions that require explaining. Specifically, the model is similar to the previous one in that it uses a series of one-dimensional convolutions to compute incrementally more features that result in a single-feature vector.

New in this example, however, are the use of the Sequential and ELU PyTorch modules. The Sequential module is a convenience wrapper that encapsulates a linear sequence of operations. In this case, we use it to encapsulate the application of the Conv1d sequence. ELU is a nonlinearity similar to the ReLU introduced in Chapter 3, but rather than clipping values below 0, it exponentiates them. ELU has been shown to be a promising nonlinearity to use between convolutional layers (Clevert et al., 2015).

In this example, we tie the number of channels for each of the convolutions with the num_channels hyperparameter. We could have alternatively chosen a different number of channels for each convolution operation separately. Doing so would entail optimizing more hyperparameters. We found that 256 was large enough for the model to achieve a reasonable performance.

Example 4-19. The CNN-based SurnameClassifier

```python
import torch.nn as nn
import torch.nn.functional as F

class SurnameClassifier(nn.Module):
    def __init__(self, initial_num_channels, num_classes, num_channels):
        """
        Args:
            initial_num_channels (int): size of the incoming feature vector
            num_classes (int): size of the output prediction vector
            num_channels (int): constant channel size to use throughout network
        """
        super(SurnameClassifier, self).__init__()

        self.convnet = nn.Sequential(
            nn.Conv1d(in_channels=initial_num_channels,
                    out_channels=num_channels, kernel_size=3),
            nn.ELU(),
            nn.Conv1d(in_channels=num_channels, out_channels=num_channels,
                    kernel_size=3, stride=2),
            nn.ELU(),
```

```
            nn.Conv1d(in_channels=num_channels, out_channels=num_channels,
                    kernel_size=3, stride=2),
            nn.ELU(),
            nn.Conv1d(in_channels=num_channels, out_channels=num_channels,
                    kernel_size=3),
            nn.ELU()
        )
        self.fc = nn.Linear(num_channels, num_classes)

    def forward(self, x_surname, apply_softmax=False):
        """The forward pass of the classifier

        Args:
            x_surname (torch.Tensor): an input data tensor
                x_surname.shape should be (batch, initial_num_channels,
                                            max_surname_length)
            apply_softmax (bool): a flag for the softmax activation
                should be false if used with the cross-entropy losses
        Returns:
            the resulting tensor. tensor.shape should be (batch, num_classes).
        """

        features = self.convnet(x_surname).squeeze(dim=2)
        prediction_vector = self.fc(features)

        if apply_softmax:
            prediction_vector = F.softmax(prediction_vector, dim=1)

        return prediction_vector
```

The Training Routine

Training routines consist of the following now-familiar sequence of operations: instantiate the dataset, instantiate the model, instantiate the loss function, instantiate the optimizer, iterate over the dataset's training partition and update the model parameters, iterate over the dataset's validation partition and measure the performance, and then repeat the dataset iterations a certain number of times. This is the third training routine implementation in the book so far, and this sequence of operations should be internalized. We will not describe the specific training routine in any more detail for this example because it is the exact same routine from "Example: Surname Classification with an MLP" on page 89. The input arguments, however, are different, which you can see in Example 4-20.

Example 4-20. Input arguments to the CNN surname classifier

```
args = Namespace(
    # Data and path information
    surname_csv="data/surnames/surnames_with_splits.csv",
    vectorizer_file="vectorizer.json",
    model_state_file="model.pth",
```

```
    save_dir="model_storage/ch4/cnn",
    # Model hyperparameters
    hidden_dim=100,
    num_channels=256,
    # Training hyperparameters
    seed=1337,
    learning_rate=0.001,
    batch_size=128,
    num_epochs=100,
    early_stopping_criteria=5,
    dropout_p=0.1,
    # Runtime options omitted for space
)
```

Model Evaluation and Prediction

To understand the model's performance, you need quantitative and qualitative measures of performance. The basic components for these two measures are described
next. We encourage you to expand upon them to explore the model and what it has
learned.

Evaluating on the test dataset

Just as the training routine did not change between the previous example and this
one, the code performing the evaluation has not changed either. To summarize, the
classifier's eval() method is invoked to prevent backpropagation, and the test dataset
is iterated over. The test set performance of this model is around 56% accurate as
compared to the approximate 50% accuracy of the MLP. Although these performance
numbers are not by any means upper bounds for these specific architectures, the
improvement obtained by a relatively simple CNN model should be convincing
enough to encourage you to try out CNNs on textual data.

Classifying or retrieving top predictions for a new surname

In this example, one part of the predict_nationality() function changes, as shown
in Example 4-21: rather than using the view() method to reshape the newly created
data tensor to add a batch dimension, we use PyTorch's unsqueeze() function to add
a dimension with size=1 where the batch should be. The same change is reflected in
the predict_topk_nationality() function.

Example 4-21. Using the trained model to make predictions

```
def predict_nationality(surname, classifier, vectorizer):
    """Predict the nationality from a new surname

    Args:
        surname (str): the surname to classifier
```

```
    classifier (SurnameClassifer): an instance of the classifier
    vectorizer (SurnameVectorizer): the corresponding vectorizer
Returns:
    a dictionary with the most likely nationality and its probability
"""
vectorized_surname = vectorizer.vectorize(surname)
vectorized_surname = torch.tensor(vectorized_surname).unsqueeze(0)
result = classifier(vectorized_surname, apply_softmax=True)

probability_values, indices = result.max(dim=1)
index = indices.item()

predicted_nationality = vectorizer.nationality_vocab.lookup_index(index)
probability_value = probability_values.item()

return {'nationality': predicted_nationality, 'probability': probability_value}
```

Miscellaneous Topics in CNNs

To conclude our discussion, in this section we outline a few additional topics that are central to CNNs but have a primary role in their common use. In particular, you will see descriptions of pooling operations, batch normalization, network-in-network connections, and residual connections.

Pooling

Pooling is an operation to summarize a higher-dimensional feature map to a lower-dimensional feature map. The output of a convolution is a feature map. The values in the feature map summarize some region of the input. Due to the overlapping nature of convolution computation, many of the computed features can be redundant. Pooling is a way to summarize a high-dimensional, and possibly redundant, feature map into a lower-dimensional one. Formally, pooling is an arithmetic operator like sum, mean, or max applied over a local region in a feature map in a systematic way, and the resulting pooling operations are known as *sum pooling*, *average pooling*, and *max pooling*, respectively. Pooling can also function as a way to improve the statistical strength of a larger but weaker feature map into a smaller but stronger feature map. Figure 4-13 illustrates pooling.

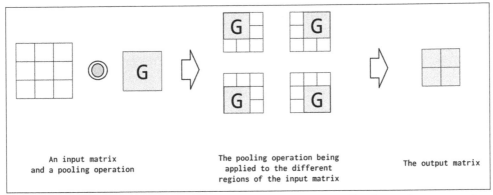

| An input matrix and a pooling operation | The pooling operation being applied to the different regions of the input matrix | The output matrix |

Figure 4-13. The pooling operation as shown here is functionally identical to a convolution: it is applied to different positions in the input matrix. However, rather than multiply and sum the values of the input matrix, the pooling operation applies some function G that pools the values. G can be any operation, but summing, finding the max, and computing the average are the most common.

Batch Normalization (BatchNorm)

Batch normalization, or BatchNorm, is an often-used tool in designing CNNs. Batch-Norm applies a transformation to the output of a CNN by scaling the activations to have zero mean and unit variance. The mean and variance values it uses for the Z-transform[29] are updated per batch such that fluctuations in any single batch won't shift or affect it too much. BatchNorm allows models to be less sensitive to initialization of the parameters and simplifies the tuning of learning rates (Ioffe and Szegedy, 2015). In PyTorch, BatchNorm is defined in the nn module. Example 4-22 shows how to instantiate and use BatchNorm with convolution and Linear layers.

Example 4-22. Using a Conv1D layer with batch normalization

```
        # ...
        self.conv1 = nn.Conv1d(in_channels=1, out_channels=10,
                               kernel_size=5,
                               stride=1)
        self.conv1_bn = nn.BatchNorm1d(num_features=10)
        # ...

    def forward(self, x):
        # ...
        x = F.relu(self.conv1(x))
        x = self.conv1_bn(x)
        # ...
```

---

29 For motivation, see Standard score on Wikipedia (*http://bit.ly/2V0x64z*).

Network-in-Network Connections (1x1 Convolutions)

Network-in-network (NiN) connections are convolutional kernels with `kernel_size=1` and have a few interesting properties. In particular, a 1×1 convolution acts like a fully connected linear layer across the channels.[30] This is useful in mapping from feature maps with many channels to shallower feature maps. In Figure 4-14, we show a single NiN connection being applied to an input matrix. As you can see, it reduces the two channels down to a single channel. Thus, NiN or 1×1 convolutions provide an inexpensive way to incorporate additional nonlinearity with few parameters (Lin et al., 2013).

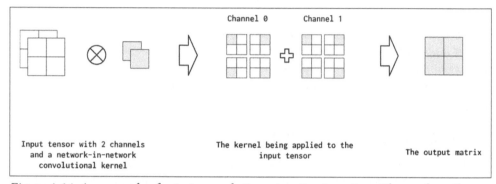

Figure 4-14. An example of a 1×1 convolution operation in action. Observe how the 1×1 convolution operation reduces the number of channels from two to one.

Residual Connections/Residual Block

One of the most significant trends in CNNs that has enabled really deep networks (more than 100 layers) is the residual connection. It is also called a *skip connection*. If we let the convolution function be represented as *conv*, the output of a residual block is as follows:[31]

$$output = conv (input) + input$$

There is an implicit trick to this operation, however, which we show in Figure 4-15. For the input to be added to the output of the convolution, they must have the same shape. To accomplish this, the standard practice is to apply a padding before convolution. In Figure 4-15, the padding is of size 1 for a convolution of size 3. To learn more about the details of residual connections, the original paper by He et al. (2016)

---

30 If you recall from earlier diagrams, there is a parameter for each incoming channel so a convolutional kernel with `kernel_size=1` is a vector as large as the number of incoming channels.

31 Here, "input" refers to input to the residual block, not necessarily input to the neural network.

---

is still a great reference. For an example of residual networks used in NLP, see Huang and Wang (2017).

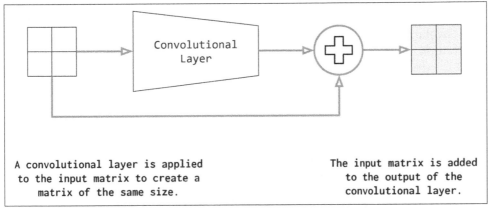

Figure 4-15. A residual connection is a method for adding the original matrix to the output of a convolution. This is described visually above as the convolutional layer is applied to the input matrix and the resultant added to the input matrix. A common hyper parameter setting to create outputs that are the size as the inputs is let `kernel_size=3 and padding=1`. In general, any odd `kernel_size` with `padding=(floor(kernel_size)/2 - 1)` will result in an output that is the same size as its input. See Figure 4-11 for a visual explanation of padding and convolutions. The matrix resulting from the convolutional layer is added to the input and the final resultant is the output of the residual connection computation. (The figure inspired by Figure 2 in He et al. [2016])

Summary

In this chapter, you learned two basic feed-forward architectures: the multilayer perceptron (MLP; also called "fully-connected" network) and the convolutional neural network (CNN). We saw the power of MLPs in approximating any nonlinear function and showed applications of MLPs in NLP with the application of classifying nationalities from surnames. We studied one of the major disadvantages/limitations of MLPs—lack of parameter sharing—and introduced the convolutional network architecture as a possible solution. CNNs, originally developed for computer vision, have become a mainstay in NLP; primarily because of their highly efficient implementation and low memory requirements. We studied different variants of convolutions—padded, dilated, and strided—and how they transform the input space. This chapter also dedicated a nontrivial length of discussion on the practical matter of choosing input and output sizes for the convolutional filters. We showed how the convolution operation helps capture substructure information in language by extending the surname classification example to use convnets. Finally, we discussed some miscellaneous, but important, topics related to convolutional network design: 1) Pooling, 2) BatchNorm, 3) 1x1 convolutions, and 4) residual connections. In modern CNN design, it is common to see many of these tricks employed at once as seen in the Inception architecture (Szegedy et al., 2015) in which a mindful use of these tricks led convolutional networks hundreds of layers deep that were not only accurate but fast to train. In the Chapter 5, we explore the topic of learning and using representations for discrete units, like words, sentences, documents, and other feature types using *Embeddings*.

References

1. Min Lin, Qiang Chen, and Shuicheng Yan. (2013). "Network in network." arXiv preprint arXiv:1312.4400.

2. Christian Szegedy, Wei Liu, Yangqing Jia, Pierre Sermanet, Scott Reed, Dragomir Anguelov, Dumitru Erhan, Vincent Vanhoucke, and Andrew Rabinovich. "Going deeper with convolutions." In *CVPR* 2015.

3. Djork-Arné Clevert, Thomas Unterthiner, and Sepp Hochreiter. (2015). "Fast and accurate deep network learning by exponential linear units (elus)." arXiv preprint arXiv:1511.07289.

4. Sergey Ioffe and Christian Szegedy. (2015). "Batch normalization: Accelerating deep network training by reducing internal covariate shift." arXiv preprint arXiv: 1502.03167.

5. Vincent Dumoulin and Francesco Visin. (2016). "A guide to convolution arithmetic for deep learning." arXiv preprint arXiv:1603.07285.

6. Kaiming He, Xiangyu Zhang, Shaoqing Ren, and Jian Sun. 2016 "Identity mappings in deep residual networks." In *ECCV*.

7. Yi Yao Huang and William Yang Wang. (2017). "Deep Residual Learning for Weakly-Supervised Relation Extraction." arXiv preprint arXiv:1707.08866.

Embedding Words and Types

When implementing natural language processing tasks, we need to deal with different kinds of discrete types. The most obvious example is words. Words come from a finite set (aka vocabulary). Other examples of discrete types include characters, part-of-speech tags, named entities, named entity types, parse features, items in a product catalog, and so on. Essentially, when any input feature comes from a finite (or a countably infinite) set, it is a *discrete type*.

Representing discrete types (e.g., words) as dense vectors is at the core of deep learning's successes in NLP. The terms "representation learning" and "embedding" refer to learning this mapping from one discrete type to a point in the vector space. When the discrete types are words, the dense vector representation is called a *word embedding*. We saw examples of *count-based* embedding methods, like Term-Frequency-Inverse-Document-Frequency (TF-IDF), in Chapter 2. In this chapter, we focus on *learning-based* or *prediction-based* (Baroni et al., 2014) embedding methods, in which the representations are learned by maximizing an objective for a specific learning task; for example, predicting a word based on context. Learning-based embedding methods are now *de jure* because of their broad applicability and performance. In fact, the ubiquity of word embeddings in NLP tasks has earned them the title of the "Sriracha of NLP," because you can utilize word embeddings in any NLP task and expect the performance of the task to improve.[1] But we contend that this sobriquet is misleading, as, unlike Sriracha, embeddings are not usually added as an afterthought to a model, but are a fundamental ingredient of the model itself.

In this chapter, we discuss vector representations as they pertain to word embeddings: methods to embed words, methods to optimize word embeddings for both

---

[1] For folks who are not aware of the brand, Sriracha is a hot chili pepper–based condiment popular in the United States.

supervised and unsupervised language tasks, methods to visualize word embeddings, and methods to combine word embeddings for sentences and documents. However, you must keep in mind that the methods we describe here apply to any discrete type.

Why Learn Embeddings?

In the previous chapters, you saw traditional methods for creating vector representations of words. Specifically, you learned that you can use one-hot representations—vectors that are the same length as the size of the vocabulary and that have 0s everywhere except a single position that has the value 1 to represent a specific word. Additionally, you saw count representations—vectors that are also the same length as the number of unique words in your model but instead have counts at positions in the vector corresponding to the frequency of words in a sentence. The count-based representations are also called *distributional representations* because their significant content or meaning is represented by multiple dimensions in the vector. Distributional representations have a long history (Firth, 1935) and work well with many machine learning and neural network models. These representations are not *learned* from the data but heuristically constructed.[2]

Distributed representations earn their name from the fact that the words are now represented by a much lower-dimension dense vector (say $d=100$, as opposed to the size of the entire vocabulary, which can be around 10^5 to 10^6 or higher), and the meaning and other properties of a word are distributed across different dimensions of this dense vector.

Low-dimensional learned dense representations have several benefits over the one-hot and count-based vectors we saw in previous chapters. First, reducing the dimensionality is computationally efficient. Second, the count-based representations result in high-dimensional vectors that redundantly encode similar information along many dimensions, and do not share statistical strength. Third, very high dimensions in the input can result in real problems in machine learning and optimization—a phenomenon that's often called the *curse of dimensionality* (*http://bit.ly/2CrhQXm*). Traditionally, to deal with this dimensionality problem, dimensionality reduction approaches like singular value decomposition (SVD) and principal component analysis (PCA) are employed, but somewhat ironically, these approaches do not scale well when dimensionality is on the order of millions (the typical case in NLP). Fourth, representations learned (or fine-tuned) from task-specific data are optimal for the task at hand. With heuristics like TF-IDF or low-dimensional approaches like SVD it

---

2 For an excellent review of traditional (non-neural-network-based) embedding methods, see *"Distributional approaches to word meanings"* by Chris Potts at Stanford (*https://stanford.io/2LuklLp*).

is not clear if the optimization objective of the embedding approach is relevant to the task.

Efficiency of Embeddings

To understand how embeddings work, let's take a look at an example of a one-hot vector multiplying the weight matrix in a Linear layer, as demonstrated in Figure 5-1. In Chapters 3 and 4, the one-hot vectors were the same size as the vocabularies. The vector is called "one-hot" because it has a 1 in an index that indicates the presence of specific word.

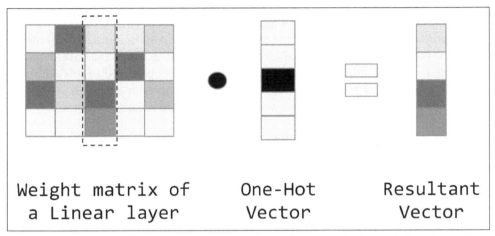

Figure 5-1. An example of matrix multiplication using a one-hot encoded vector and the weight matrix of a Linear layer. Because a one-hot vector is all 0s and a single 1, the placement of the single 1 will act as a selector in the matrix multiplication. This is visually shown using the shading patterns in the weight matrix and resultant vector. Although functional, this method of lookup is computationally expensive and inefficient because the one-hot vector is multiplying every number in the weight matrix and computing the sum for each row.

By definition, the weight matrix of a Linear layer that accepts as input this one-hot vector must have the same number of rows as the size of the one-hot vector. When you perform the matrix multiplication, as shown in Figure 5-1, the resulting vector is actually just selecting the row indicated by the non zero entry. Based on this observation, we can just skip the multiplication step and instead directly use an integer as an index to retrieve the selected row.

One final note about the efficiency of embeddings: despite the example in Figure 5-1 showing a weight matrix that has the same dimensionality as the incoming one-hot vector, this is not always the case. In fact, embeddings are often used to represent words in a lower-dimensional space than would be needed if a one-hot vector or a count-based representation was used. Typical sizes for embeddings in the research literature range from 25 dimensions to 500 dimensions, and the exact choice can boil down to the amount of GPU memory you have to spare.

Approaches to Learning Word Embeddings

The goal of this chapter is not to teach specific word embedding techniques, but to help you understand what embeddings are, how and where they are applicable, how to use them reliably in models, and their limitations. Our choice in doing so is because practitioners rarely find themselves in situations in which they need to write new word embedding training algorithms. However, in this section, we provide a brief overview of the current approaches to train word embeddings. All word embedding methods train with just words (i.e., unlabeled data), but in a *supervised fashion*. This is possible by constructing auxiliary supervised tasks in which the data is implicitly labeled, with the intuition that a representation that is optimized to solve the auxiliary task will capture many statistical and linguistic properties of the text corpus in order to be generally useful. Here are some examples of such auxiliary tasks:

- Given a sequence of words, predict the next word. This is also called the *language modeling task*.
- Given a sequence of words before and after, predict the missing word.
- Given a word, predict words that occur within a window, independent of the position.

Of course, this list is not complete, and the choice of the auxiliary task depends on the intuition of the algorithm designer and the computational expense. Examples include *GloVe*, *Continuous Bag-of-Words (CBOW)*, *Skipgrams*, and so on. We refer you to Goldberg, 2017, Chapter 10, for details, but we will briefly study the CBOW model. However, for most purposes, using pretrained word embeddings and finetuning them for the task at hand appears sufficient.

The Practical Use of Pretrained Word Embeddings

The bulk of this chapter, and later ones in the book, concerns itself with using *pretrained word embeddings*. Pretrained word embeddings trained on a large corpus—like all Google News, Wikipedia, or Common Crawl[3]—using one of the many methods described earlier are available freely to download and use. The rest of this chapter shows how to load and look up these embeddings efficiently, examines some proper-

---

3 Common Crawl is a Creative Commons–licensed webcrawl corpus, available via *commoncrawl.org* (*https://www.commoncrawl.org*).

ties of word embeddings, and gives some examples of using pretrained embeddings in NLP tasks.

Loading embeddings

Word embeddings have become popular and pervasive enough that you can download many different varieties, from the original Word2Vec[4] to Stanford's GLoVe (*https://stanford.io/2PSIvPZ*), Facebook's FastText (*https://fasttext.cc/*),[5] and many others. Typically, the embeddings will come in the following format: each line starts with the word/type that is being embedded and is followed by a sequence of numbers (i.e., the vector representation). The length of this sequence is the dimension of the representation (aka the *embedding dimension*). The embedding dimension is usually on the order of hundreds. The number of token types is usually the size of the vocabulary and on the order of a million. For example, here are the first seven dimensions for the dog and cat vectors from GloVe:

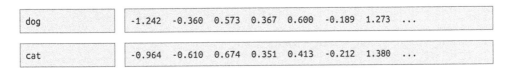

```
dog    -1.242  -0.360  0.573  0.367  0.600  -0.189  1.273  ...

cat    -0.964  -0.610  0.674  0.351  0.413  -0.212  1.380  ...
```

To efficiently load and process embeddings, we describe a utility class called Pre TrainedEmbeddings (Example 5-1). The class builds an in-memory index of all the word vectors to facilitate quick lookups and nearest-neighbor queries using an approximate nearest-neighbor package, annoy.

Example 5-1. Using pretrained word embeddings

```
Input[0]    import numpy as np
            from annoy import AnnoyIndex

            class PreTrainedEmbeddings(object):
                def __init__(self, word_to_index, word_vectors):
                    """
                    Args:
                        word_to_index (dict): mapping from word to integers
                        word_vectors (list of numpy arrays)
                    """
```

---

4 Word2Vec is a collection of embedding methods. In this chapter, we look at the Continuous Bag-of-Words embedding from the Word2Vec paper. To download the Word2Vec embeddings, visit *https://goo.gl/ZER2d5*.

5 As of this writing, FastText is the only package we know of that offers embeddings in multiple languages. FastText also offers more than embeddings.

```
Input[0]        self.word_to_index = word_to_index
                self.word_vectors = word_vectors
                self.index_to_word = \
                    {v: k for k, v in self.word_to_index.items()}
                self.index = AnnoyIndex(len(word_vectors[0]),
                                        metric='euclidean')
                for _, i in self.word_to_index.items():
                    self.index.add_item(i, self.word_vectors[i])
                self.index.build(50)

            @classmethod
            def from_embeddings_file(cls, embedding_file):
                """Instantiate from pretrained vector file.

                Vector file should be of the format:
                    word0 x0_0 x0_1 x0_2 x0_3 ... x0_N
                    word1 x1_0 x1_1 x1_2 x1_3 ... x1_N

                Args:
                    embedding_file (str): location of the file
                Returns:
                    instance of PretrainedEmbeddings
                """
                word_to_index = {}
                word_vectors = []
                with open(embedding_file) as fp:
                    for line in fp.readlines():
                        line = line.split(" ")
                        word = line[0]
                        vec = np.array([float(x) for x in line[1:]])

                        word_to_index[word] = len(word_to_index)
                        word_vectors.append(vec)
                return cls(word_to_index, word_vectors)
```

```
Input[1]    embeddings = \
                PreTrainedEmbeddings.from_embeddings_file('glove.6B.100d.txt')
```

In these examples, we use the GloVe word embeddings. After you download them, you can instantiate with the `PretrainedEmbeddings` class, as shown in the second input in Example 5-1.

Relationships between word embeddings

The core feature of word embeddings is that the encode syntactic and semantic relationships that manifest as regularities in word use. For example, cats and dogs are talked about in very similar ways (discussions of pets, feeding, etc.). As a consequence, their embeddings are far closer to each other than they are to those of other animals, like ducks and elephants.

We can explore the semantic relationships encoded in word embeddings in several ways. One of the most popular methods is an analogy task (a popular category of reasoning tasks at exams like SAT):

```
Word1 : Word2 :: Word3 : _____
```

In this task, you are provided with the first three words and need to determine the fourth word that's congruent to the relationship between the first two words. Using word embeddings, we can encode this spatially. First, we subtract Word2> from Word1. This difference vector encodes the relationship between Word1 and Word2. This difference can then be added to Word3 to produce a vector that's close to the fourth word, where the blank symbol is. Doing a nearest-neighbor query on the index with this result vector solves the analogy problem. A function for computing this, shown in Example 5-2, does exactly what was just described: using vector arithmetic and the approximate nearest-neighbor index, it completes the analogy.

Example 5-2. The analogy task using word embeddings

```
Input[0]    import numpy as np
            from annoy import AnnoyIndex

            class PreTrainedEmbeddings(object):
                """ implementation continued from previous code example"""
                def get_embedding(self, word):
                    """
                    Args:
                        word (str)
                    Returns
                        an embedding (numpy.ndarray)
                    """
                    return self.word_vectors[self.word_to_index[word]]
                def get_closest_to_vector(self, vector, n=1):
                    """Given a vector, return its n nearest neighbors
                    Args:
                        vector (np.ndarray): should match the size of the vectors
                            in the Annoy index
                        n (int): the number of neighbors to return
                    Returns:
                        [str, str, ...]: words nearest to the given vector
                            The words are not ordered by distance
                    """
```

```
            nn_indices = self.index.get_nns_by_vector(vector, n)
            return [self.index_to_word[neighbor]
                        for neighbor in nn_indices]

    def compute_and_print_analogy(self, word1, word2, word3):
        """Prints the solutions to analogies using word embeddings

        Analogies are word1 is to word2 as word3 is to __
        This method will print: word1 : word2 :: word3 : word4

        Args:
            word1 (str)
            word2 (str)
            word3 (str)
        """
        vec1 = self.get_embedding(word1)
        vec2 = self.get_embedding(word2)
        vec3 = self.get_embedding(word3)

        # Simple hypothesis: Analogy is a spatial relationship
        spatial_relationship = vec2 - vec1
        vec4 = vec3 + spatial_relationship

        closest_words = self.get_closest_to_vector(vec4, n=4)
        existing_words = set([word1, word2, word3])
        closest_words = [word for word in closest_words
                            if word not in existing_words]

        if len(closest_words) == 0:
            print("Could not find nearest neighbors for the vector!")
            return

        for word4 in closest_words:
            print("{} : {} :: {} : {}".format(word1, word2, word3,
                                                word4))
```

Interestingly, the simple word analogy task can demonstrate that word embeddings capture a variety of semantic and syntactic relationships, as demonstrated in Example 5-3.

Example 5-3. Word embeddings encode many linguistics relationships, as illustrated using the SAT analogy task

Input[0]
```
# Relationship 1: the relationship between gendered nouns and pronouns
embeddings.compute_and_print_analogy('man', 'he', 'woman')
```

Output[0]
```
man : he :: woman : she
```

```
Input[1]    # Relationship 2: Verb-noun relationships
            embeddings.compute_and_print_analogy('fly', 'plane', 'sail')
```

```
Output[1]   fly : plane :: sail : ship
```

```
Input[2]    # Relationship 3: Noun-noun relationships
            embeddings.compute_and_print_analogy('cat', 'kitten', 'dog')
```

```
Output[2]   cat : kitten :: dog : puppy
```

```
Input[3]    # Relationship 4: Hypernymy (broader category)
            embeddings.compute_and_print_analogy('blue', 'color', 'dog')
```

```
Output[3]   blue : color :: dog : animal
```

```
Input[4]    # Relationship 5: Meronymy (part-to-whole)
            embeddings.compute_and_print_analogy('toe', 'foot', 'finger')
```

```
Output[4]   toe : foot :: finger : hand
```

```
Input[5]    # Relationship 6: Troponymy (difference in manner)
            embeddings.compute_and_print_analogy('talk', 'communicate', 'read')
```

```
Output[5]   talk : communicate :: read : interpret
```

```
Input[6]    # Relationship 7: Metonymy (convention / figures of speech)
            embeddings.compute_and_print_analogy('blue', 'democrat', 'red')
```

```
Output[6]   blue : democrat :: red : republican
```

```
Input[7]    # Relationship 8: Adjectival scales
            embeddings.compute_and_print_analogy('fast', 'fastest', 'young')
```

```
Output[7]   fast : fastest :: young : youngest
```

Although it seems like the relationships are systematic to how language functions, things can get tricky. As Example 5-4 shows, because word vectors are just based on cooccurrences, relationships can be wrong.

Example 5-4. An example illustrating the danger of using cooccurrences to encode meaning—sometimes they do not!

Input[0]	`embeddings.compute_and_print_analogy('fast', 'fastest', 'small')`
Output[0]	`fast : fastest :: small : largest`

Example 5-5 illustrates how one of the most common analogy pairings is encoding gendered roles.

Example 5-5. Watch out for protected attributes such as gender encoded in word embeddings. This can introduce unwanted biases in downstream models.

Input[0]	`embeddings.compute_and_print_analogy('man', 'king', 'woman')`
Output[0]	`man : king :: woman : queen`

It turns out that differentiating between language regularities and codified cultural biases is difficult. For example, doctors are not de facto men and nurses are not de facto women, but these long-standing biases in culture are observed as the regularities in language and are codified in the word vectors, as shown in Example 5-6.

Example 5-6. Cultural gender bias encoded in vector analogy

Input[0]	`embeddings.compute_and_print_analogy('man', 'doctor', 'woman')`
Output[0]	`man : doctor :: woman : nurse`

You need to be aware of the biases in embeddings, given that their popularity and use in NLP applications are on the rise. Debiasing existing word embeddings is a new and exciting research area (see Bolukbasi et al., 2016). Further, we recommend that you visit *ethicsinnlp.org* for latest results at the intersectionality of ethics and NLP.

Example: Learning the Continuous Bag of Words Embeddings

In this example, we walk through one of the most famous models intended to construct and learn general-purpose word embeddings, the Word2Vec Continuous Bag-of-Words (CBOW) model.[6] In this section, when we refer to "the CBOW task" or "the CBOW classification task," it is implicit that we are constructing a classification task for the purpose of learning CBOW embeddings. The CBOW model is a multi-class classification task represented by scanning over texts of words, creating a context window of words, removing the center word from the context window, and classifying the context window to the missing word. Intuitively, you can think of it like a fill-in-the-blank task. There is a sentence with a missing word, and the model's job is to figure out what that word should be.

The goal of this example is to introduce the `nn.Embedding` layer, a PyTorch module that encapsulates an embedding matrix. Using the `Embedding` layer, we can map a token's integer ID to a vector that is used in the neural network computation. When the optimizer updates the model weights to minimize the loss, it also updates the values of the vector. Through this process, the model will learn to embed words in the most useful way it can for that task.

In the remainder of this example, we follow our standard example format. In the first section, we introduce the dataset, Mary Shelley's *Frankenstein*. Then, we discuss the vectorization pipeline from token to vectorized minibatch. After that, we outline the CBOW classification model and how the `Embedding` layer is used. Next, we cover the training routine (although if you have been reading the book sequentially, the training should be fairly familiar at this point). Finally, we discuss the model evaluation, model inference, and how you can inspect the model.

The Frankenstein Dataset

For this example, we will build a text dataset from a digitized version of Mary Shelley's novel *Frankenstein*, available via Project Gutenberg (*http://bit.ly/2T5iU8J*). This section walks through the preprocessing; building a PyTorch `Dataset` class for this text dataset; and finally splitting the dataset into training, validation, and test sets.

Starting with the raw text file that Project Gutenberg distributes, the preprocessing is minimal: we use NLTK's `Punkt` tokenizer (*http://bit.ly/2GvRO9j*) to split the text into separate sentences, then each sentence is converted to lowercase and the punctuation is completely removed. This preprocessing allows for us to later split the strings on whitespace in order to retrieve a list of tokens. This preprocessing function is reused from "Example: Classifying Sentiment of Restaurant Reviews" on page 56.

The next step is to enumerate the dataset as a sequence of windows so that the CBOW model can be optimized. To do this, we iterate over the list of tokens in each

---

6 See */chapters/chapter_5/5_2_CBOW/5_2_Continuous_Bag_of_Words_CBOW.ipynb* in this book's *GitHub repo* (*https://nlproc.info/PyTorchNLPBook/repo/*).

sentence and group them into windows of a specified window size,[7] as visually demonstrated in Figure 5-2.

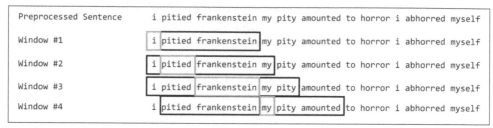

Figure 5-2. The CBOW task: predict a word using the left and the right context. The context windows are of length 2 on either side. A sliding window over the text produces many "supervised" examples, each with its target word (in the middle). The windows that are not of length 2 are padded appropriately. For example, for window #3, given the contexts "i pitied" and "my pity," the CBOW classifier is set up to predict "frankenstein".

The final step in constructing the dataset is to split the data into three sets: the training, validation, and test sets. Recall that the training and validation sets are used during model training: the training set is used to update the parameters, and the validation set is used to measure the model's performance.[8] The test set is used at most once to provide a less biased measurement. In this example (and in most examples in this book), we use a split of 70% for the training set, 15% for the validation set, and 15% for the test set.

The resulting dataset of windows and targets is loaded with a Pandas DataFrame and indexed in the CBOWDataset class. Example 5-7 shows the __getitem__() code snippet, which utilizes the Vectorizer to convert the context—the left and right windows —into a vector. The target—the word at the center of the window—is converted to an integer using the Vocabulary.

---

7 The exact window size used is a hyperparameter, and one that is fairly critical to CBOW. Too large of a window, and the model might fail to capture regularities; too small of a window, and the window might miss out on interesting dependencies.

8 It is worth repeating that you should never interpret performance measurements on the data upon which a model is trained as measurements of eventual model performance. The model is not trained on the validation data, and thus the model's performance on this set better represents eventual performance. However, decisions made by you, the computational experimentalist, can be biased by observing validation set performance and the model could be falsely reporting higher performance than it will achieve on new data.

Example 5-7. Constructing a dataset class for the CBOW task

```python
class CBOWDataset(Dataset):
    # ... existing implementation from Example 3-15
    @classmethod
    def load_dataset_and_make_vectorizer(cls, cbow_csv):
        """Load dataset and make a new vectorizer from scratch

        Args:
            cbow_csv (str): location of the dataset
        Returns:
            an instance of CBOWDataset
        """
        cbow_df = pd.read_csv(cbow_csv)
        train_cbow_df = cbow_df[cbow_df.split=='train']
        return cls(cbow_df, CBOWVectorizer.from_dataframe(train_cbow_df))

    def __getitem__(self, index):
        """the primary entry point method for PyTorch datasets

        Args:
            index (int): the index to the data point
        Returns:
            a dict with features (x_data) and label (y_target)
        """
        row = self._target_df.iloc[index]

        context_vector = \
            self._vectorizer.vectorize(row.context, self._max_seq_length)
        target_index = self._vectorizer.cbow_vocab.lookup_token(row.target)

        return {'x_data': context_vector,
                'y_target': target_index}
```

Vocabulary, Vectorizer, and DataLoader

In the CBOW classification task, the pipeline from text to vectorized minibatch is mostly standard: both the Vocabulary and the DataLoader function exactly as they did in "Example: Classifying Sentiment of Restaurant Reviews" on page 56. However, unlike the Vectorizers we saw in Chapters 3 and 4, the Vectorizer in this case does not construct one-hot vectors. Instead, a vector of integers representing the indices of the context is constructed and returned. Example 5-8 presents the code for the vec torize() function.

Example 5-8. A Vectorizer for the CBOW data

```python
class CBOWVectorizer(object):
    """ The Vectorizer which coordinates the Vocabularies and puts them to use"""
```

```
def vectorize(self, context, vector_length=-1):
    """
    Args:
        context (str): the string of words separated by a space
        vector_length (int): an argument for forcing the length of index vector
    """

    indices = \
        [self.cbow_vocab.lookup_token(token) for token in context.split(' ')]
    if vector_length < 0:
        vector_length = len(indices)

    out_vector = np.zeros(vector_length, dtype=np.int64)
    out_vector[:len(indices)] = indices
    out_vector[len(indices):] = self.cbow_vocab.mask_index

    return out_vector
```

Note that if the number of tokens in the context is less than the max length, the remaining entries are filled with zeros. This can be referred to as *padding* with zeros, but in practice.

The CBOWClassifier Model

The CBOWClassifier shown in Example 5-9 has three essential steps. First, indices representing the words of the context are used with an Embedding layer to create vectors for each word in the context. Second, the goal is to combine the vectors in some way such that it captures the overall context. In this example, we sum over the vectors. However, other options include taking the max, the average, or even using a Multilayer Perceptron on top. Third, the context vector is used with a Linear layer to compute a prediction vector. This prediction vector is a probability distribution over the entire vocabulary. The largest (most probable) value in the prediction vector indicates the likely prediction for the target word—the center word missing from the context.

The Embedding layer that is used here is parameterized primarily by two numbers: the number of embeddings (size of the vocabulary) and the size of the embeddings (embedding dimension). A third argument is used in the code snippet in Example 5-9: padding_idx. This argument is used as a sentinel value to the Embedding layer for situations like ours where the data points might not all be the same length.[9] The layer forces both the vector corresponding to that index and its gradients to be all 0s.

---

9 This pattern of indicating the padding index so that variable-length data points can be used will be repeated for many examples because it occurs so often in language data.

Example 5-9. The CBOWClassifier model

```python
class CBOWClassifier(nn.Module):
    def __init__(self, vocabulary_size, embedding_size, padding_idx=0):
        """
        Args:
            vocabulary_size (int): number of vocabulary items, controls the
                number of embeddings and prediction vector size
            embedding_size (int): size of the embeddings
            padding_idx (int): default 0; Embedding will not use this index
        """
        super(CBOWClassifier, self).__init__()

        self.embedding =  nn.Embedding(num_embeddings=vocabulary_size,
                                       embedding_dim=embedding_size,
                                       padding_idx=padding_idx)
        self.fc1 = nn.Linear(in_features=embedding_size,
                             out_features=vocabulary_size)

    def forward(self, x_in, apply_softmax=False):
        """The forward pass of the classifier

        Args:
            x_in (torch.Tensor): an input data tensor
                x_in.shape should be (batch, input_dim)
            apply_softmax (bool): a flag for the softmax activation
                should be false if used with the cross-entropy losses
        Returns:
            the resulting tensor. tensor.shape should be (batch, output_dim).
        """
        x_embedded_sum = self.embedding(x_in).sum(dim=1)
        y_out = self.fc1(x_embedded_sum)

        if apply_softmax:
            y_out = F.softmax(y_out, dim=1)

        return y_out
```

The Training Routine

In this example, the training routine follows the standard we've used throughout the book. First, initialize the dataset, vectorizer, model, loss function, and optimizer. Then iterate through the training and validation portions of the dataset for a certain number of epochs, optimizing for loss minimization on the training portion and measuring progress on the validation portion. For more details on the training routine, we refer you to "Example: Classifying Sentiment of Restaurant Reviews" on page 56, where we cover it in great detail. Example 5-10 presents the arguments we used for training.

Example 5-10. Arguments to the CBOW training script

```
Input[0]    args = Namespace(
                # Data and path information
                cbow_csv="data/books/frankenstein_with_splits.csv",
                vectorizer_file="vectorizer.json",
                model_state_file="model.pth",
                save_dir="model_storage/ch5/cbow",
                # Model hyperparameters
                embedding_size=300,
                # Training hyperparameters
                seed=1337,
                num_epochs=100,
                learning_rate=0.001,
                batch_size=128,
                early_stopping_criteria=5,
                # Runtime options omitted for space
            )
```

Model Evaluation and Prediction

The evaluation in this example is based on predicting a target word from a provided word context for each target and context pair in the test set.[10] A correctly classified word means that the model is learning to predict words from contexts. In this example, the model achieves 15% target word classification accuracy on the test set. There are a few reasons why the result is not super high. First, the construction of the CBOW in this example was meant to be illustrative of how one might construct general-purpose embeddings. As such, there are many properties of the original implementation that have been left out because they add complexity unnecessary for learning (but necessary for optimal performance). The second is that the dataset we are using is minuscule—a single book with roughly 70,000 words is not enough data to identify many regularities when training from scratch. In contrast, state-of-the-art embeddings are typically trained on datasets with terabytes of text.[11]

In this example, we showed how you can use the PyTorch nn.Embedding layer to train embeddings from scratch by setting up an artificial supervised task called CBOW classification. In the next example we examine how, given an embedding pretrained on one corpus, we can use it and fine-tune it for another task. In machine learning, using a model trained on one task as an initializer for another task is called *transfer learning*.

---

10 "The Frankenstein Dataset" on page 131 describes the test set construction.

11 The Common Crawl dataset has more than 100 TB of data.

Example: Transfer Learning Using Pretrained Embeddings for Document Classification

The previous example used an Embedding layer to do simple classification. This example builds on that in three ways: first by loading pretrained word embeddings, then by fine-tuning these pretrained embeddings by classifying entire news articles, and finally by using a convolutional neural network to capture the spatial relationships between words.

In this example, we use the AG News dataset. To model the sequences of words in AG News, we introduce a variant of the Vocabulary class SequenceVocabulary, to bundle several tokens vital for modeling sequences. The Vectorizer demonstrates how to use this class.

After describing the dataset and how the vectorized minibatches are constructed, we step through the loading of pretrained word vectors into an Embedding layer and demonstrate how they are customized to our setting. Then, the model combines the pretrained Embedding layer with the CNN used in "Example: Classifying Surnames by Using a CNN" on page 110. In an effort to scale up the complexity of the model to a more realistic construction, we also identify the places where we utilize dropout as a regularization technique. We then discuss the training routine. It might not surprise you that this has once again barely changed from the previous examples in Chapter 4 and this chapter. Finally, we conclude the example by evaluating the model on a test set and discussing the results.

The AG News Dataset

The AG News dataset (*http://bit.ly/2SbWzpL*) is a collection of more than one million news articles collected in 2005 by academics for experimenting with data mining and information extraction methods. The goal of this example is to illustrate the effectiveness of pretrained word embeddings in classifying texts. For this example, we use a slimmed-down version consisting of 120,000 news articles that are split evenly between four categories: Sports, Science/Technology, World, and Business. In addition to slimming down the dataset, we focus on the article headlines as our observations and create the multiclass classification task of predicting the category given the headline.

As before, we preprocess the text by removing punctuation symbols, adding spaces around punctuation (such as around commas, apostrophes, and periods), and converting the text to lowercase. Additionally, we split the dataset into training, validation, and testing sets by first aggregating the data points by class label and then assigning each data point to one of the three splits. In this way, the class distribution is guaranteed to be identical across the splits.

The NewsDataset.__getitem__() method, shown in Example 5-11, follows a fairly basic formula you should now be familiar with: the string representing the input to the model is retrieved from a specific row in the dataset, vectorized by the Vector izer, and paired with the integer representing the news category (class label).

Example 5-11. The NewsDataset.__getitem__() method

```
class NewsDataset(Dataset):
    @classmethod
    def load_dataset_and_make_vectorizer(cls, news_csv):
        """Load dataset and make a new vectorizer from scratch

        Args:
            news_csv (str): location of the dataset
        Returns:
            an instance of NewsDataset
        """
        news_df = pd.read_csv(news_csv)
        train_news_df = news_df[news_df.split=='train']
        return cls(news_df, NewsVectorizer.from_dataframe(train_news_df))

    def __getitem__(self, index):
        """the primary entry point method for PyTorch datasets

        Args:
            index (int): the index to the data point
        Returns:
            a dict holding the data point's features (x_data) and label (y_target)
        """
        row = self._target_df.iloc[index]

        title_vector = \
            self._vectorizer.vectorize(row.title, self._max_seq_length)

        category_index = \
            self._vectorizer.category_vocab.lookup_token(row.category)

        return {'x_data': title_vector,
                'y_target': category_index}
```

Vocabulary, Vectorizer, and DataLoader

In this example we introduce SequenceVocabulary, a subclass of the standard Vocabu lary class that bundles four special tokens used for sequence data: the UNK token, the MASK token, the BEGIN-OF-SEQUENCE token, and the END-OF-SEQUENCE token. We describe these tokens in more detail in Chapter 6, but in brief, they serve three different purposes. The UNK token (short for unknown), which we saw in Chapter 4, allows the model to learn a representation for rare words so that it can accommodate words that it has never seen at test time. The MASK token serves as a sentinel for Embedding layers and loss calculations when we have sequences of variable length. Finally, the BEGIN-OF-SEQUENCE and END-OF-SEQUENCE tokens give the neural network hints about the sequence boundaries. Figure 5-3 shows the result of using these special tokens in the broader vectorization pipeline.

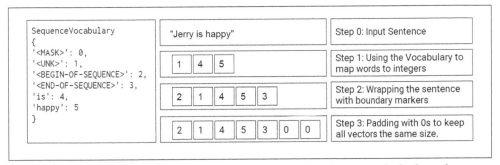

Figure 5-3. A simple example of the vectorization pipeline begins with the bare-bones SequenceVocabulary, which has the four special tokens described in the text. First, it is used to map the words to a sequence of integers. Because the word "Jerry" is not in the SequenceVocabulary, it is mapped to the <UNK> integer. Next, the special tokens that mark sentence boundaries are prepended and appended to the integers. Finally, the integers are right-padded with 0s to a specific length, which allows every vector in the dataset to be the same length.

The second part of the text-to-vectorized-minibatch pipeline is the Vectorizer, which both instantiates and encapsulates the use of the SequenceVocabulary. In this example, the Vectorizer follows the pattern we demonstrated in "Vectorizer" on page 64 of restricting the total set of words allowed in the Vocabulary by counting and thresholding on a certain frequency. The core purpose of this action is to improve the signal quality for the model and limit the memory model's memory usage by removing noisy, low-frequency words.

After instantiation, the Vectorizer's vectorize() method takes as input a news title and returns a vector that is as long as the longest title in the dataset. It has two key behaviors. The first is that it stores the maximum sequence length locally. Normally, the dataset tracks the maximum sequence length, and at inference time, the length of the test sequence is taken as the length of the vector. However, because we have a CNN model, it's important to maintain a static size even at inference time. The second key behavior, shown in the code snippet in Example 5-11, is that it outputs a zero-padded vector of integers, which represent the words in the sequence. Additionally, this vector of integers has the integer for the BEGIN-OF-SEQUENCE token prepended to the beginning and the integer for the END-OF-SEQUENCE token appended to the end. From the classifier's perspective, these special tokens provide evidence of the sequence boundaries, allowing it to react to words near the boundary differently than to words near the center.[12]

Example 5-12. Implementing a Vectorizer for the AG News dataset

```
class NewsVectorizer(object):
    def vectorize(self, title, vector_length=-1):
        """
        Args:
            title (str): the string of words separated by spaces
            vector_length (int): forces the length of the index vector
        Returns:
            the vectorized title (numpy.array)
        """
        indices = [self.title_vocab.begin_seq_index]
        indices.extend(self.title_vocab.lookup_token(token)
                        for token in title.split(" "))
        indices.append(self.title_vocab.end_seq_index)

        if vector_length < 0:
            vector_length = len(indices)

        out_vector = np.zeros(vector_length, dtype=np.int64)
        out_vector[:len(indices)] = indices
        out_vector[len(indices):] = self.title_vocab.mask_index

        return out_vector

    @classmethod
    def from_dataframe(cls, news_df, cutoff=25):
        """Instantiate the vectorizer from the dataset dataframe

        Args:
            news_df (pandas.DataFrame): the target dataset
            cutoff (int): frequency threshold for including in Vocabulary
        Returns:
            an instance of the NewsVectorizer
        """
        category_vocab = Vocabulary()
        for category in sorted(set(news_df.category)):
            category_vocab.add_token(category)

        word_counts = Counter()
        for title in news_df.title:
            for token in title.split(" "):
                if token  not in string.punctuation:
                    word_counts[token] += 1
```

---

12 It's important to note that it only *allows* for this behavior. The dataset must provide evidence that it's useful and that it makes a difference in the final loss.

```
    title_vocab = SequenceVocabulary()
    for word, word_count in word_counts.items():
        if word_count >= cutoff:
            title_vocab.add_token(word)

    return cls(title_vocab, category_vocab)
```

The NewsClassifier Model

Earlier in this chapter, we showed how you can load pretrained embeddings from disk and use them efficiently using an approximate nearest-neighbors data structure from Spotify's annoy library. In that example, we compared the vectors against one another to discover interesting linguistics insights. However, pretrained word vectors have a much more impactful use: we can use them to initialize the embedding matrix of an Embedding layer.

The process for using word embeddings as the initial embedding matrix involves first loading the embeddings from the disk, then selecting the correct subset of embeddings for the words that are actually present in the data, and finally setting the Embedding layer's weight matrix as the loaded subset. The first and second steps are demonstrated in Example 5-13. One issue that commonly arises is the existence of words that are in the dataset but are not among the pretrained GloVe embeddings. One common method for handling this is to use an initialization method from the PyTorch library, such as the Xavier Uniform method, as shown in Example 5-13 (Glorot and Bengio, 2010).

Example 5-13. Selecting a subset of the word embeddings based on the vocabulary

```
def load_glove_from_file(glove_filepath):
    """Load the GloVe embeddings

    Args:
        glove_filepath (str): path to the glove embeddings file
    Returns:
        word_to_index (dict), embeddings (numpy.ndarray)
    """
    word_to_index = {}
    embeddings = []
    with open(glove_filepath, "r") as fp:
        for index, line in enumerate(fp):
            line = line.split(" ") # each line: word num1 num2 ...
            word_to_index[line[0]] = index # word = line[0]
            embedding_i = np.array([float(val) for val in line[1:]])
            embeddings.append(embedding_i)
    return word_to_index, np.stack(embeddings)

def make_embedding_matrix(glove_filepath, words):
```

```
"""Create embedding matrix for a specific set of words.

Args:
    glove_filepath (str): file path to the glove embeddings
    words (list): list of words in the dataset
Returns:
    final_embeddings (numpy.ndarray): embedding matrix
"""
word_to_idx, glove_embeddings = load_glove_from_file(glove_filepath)
embedding_size = glove_embeddings.shape[1]
final_embeddings = np.zeros((len(words), embedding_size))

for i, word in enumerate(words):
    if word in word_to_idx:
        final_embeddings[i, :] = glove_embeddings[word_to_idx[word]]
    else:
        embedding_i = torch.ones(1, embedding_size)
        torch.nn.init.xavier_uniform_(embedding_i)
        final_embeddings[i, :] = embedding_i

return final_embeddings
```

The NewsClassifier in this example builds on the ConvNet classifier from section 4-4, in which we classified surnames using a CNN on the one-hot embeddings of characters. Specifically, we use the Embedding layer, which maps the input token indices to a vector representation. We use the pretrained embedding subset by replacing the Embedding layer's weight matrix, as shown in Example 5-14.[13] The embedding is then used in the forward() method to map from the indices to the vectors. Aside from the embedding layer, everything is exactly the same as the example in "Example: Classifying Surnames by Using a CNN" on page 110.

Example 5-14. Implementing the NewsClassifier

```
class NewsClassifier(nn.Module):
    def __init__(self, embedding_size, num_embeddings, num_channels,
                 hidden_dim, num_classes, dropout_p,
                 pretrained_embeddings=None, padding_idx=0):
        """
        Args:
            embedding_size (int): size of the embedding vectors
            num_embeddings (int): number of embedding vectors
            filter_width (int): width of the convolutional kernels
            num_channels (int): number of convolutional kernels per layer
            hidden_dim (int): size of the hidden dimension
```

---

13 In newer versions of PyTorch, replacing the Embedding's weight matrix is abstracted away and you only have to pass in the embedding subset to the Embedding's constructor. Check the PyTorch documentation (*http://bit.ly/2T0cdVp*) for the latest information on accomplishing this.

```
            num_classes (int): number of classes in the classification
            dropout_p (float): a dropout parameter
            pretrained_embeddings (numpy.array): previously trained word embeddings
                default is None. If provided,
            padding_idx (int): an index representing a null position
        """
        super(NewsClassifier, self).__init__()

        if pretrained_embeddings is None:
            self.emb = nn.Embedding(embedding_dim=embedding_size,
                                    num_embeddings=num_embeddings,
                                    padding_idx=padding_idx)
        else:
            pretrained_embeddings = torch.from_numpy(pretrained_embeddings).float()
            self.emb = nn.Embedding(embedding_dim=embedding_size,
                                    num_embeddings=num_embeddings,
                                    padding_idx=padding_idx,
                                    _weight=pretrained_embeddings)


        self.convnet = nn.Sequential(
            nn.Conv1d(in_channels=embedding_size,
                    out_channels=num_channels, kernel_size=3),
            nn.ELU(),
            nn.Conv1d(in_channels=num_channels, out_channels=num_channels,
                    kernel_size=3, stride=2),
            nn.ELU(),
            nn.Conv1d(in_channels=num_channels, out_channels=num_channels,
                    kernel_size=3, stride=2),
            nn.ELU(),
            nn.Conv1d(in_channels=num_channels, out_channels=num_channels,
                    kernel_size=3),
            nn.ELU()
        )

        self._dropout_p = dropout_p
        self.fc1 = nn.Linear(num_channels, hidden_dim)
        self.fc2 = nn.Linear(hidden_dim, num_classes)

    def forward(self, x_in, apply_softmax=False):
        """The forward pass of the classifier

        Args:
            x_in (torch.Tensor): an input data tensor
                x_in.shape should be (batch, dataset._max_seq_length)
            apply_softmax (bool): a flag for the softmax activation
                should be false if used with the cross-entropy losses
        Returns:
            the resulting tensor. tensor.shape should be (batch, num_classes).
        """
        # embed and permute so features are channels
        x_embedded = self.emb(x_in).permute(0, 2, 1)
```

```
        features = self.convnet(x_embedded)

        # average and remove the extra dimension
        remaining_size = features.size(dim=2)
        features = F.avg_pool1d(features, remaining_size).squeeze(dim=2)
        features = F.dropout(features, p=self._dropout_p)

        # final linear layer to produce classification outputs
        intermediate_vector = F.relu(F.dropout(self.fc1(features),
                                               p=self._dropout_p))
        prediction_vector = self.fc2(intermediate_vector)

        if apply_softmax:
            prediction_vector = F.softmax(prediction_vector, dim=1)

        return prediction_vector
```

The Training Routine

Training routines consist of the following sequence of operations: instantiate the
dataset, instantiate the model, instantiate the loss function, instantiate the optimizer,
iterate over the dataset's training partition and update the model parameters, iterate
over the dataset's validation partition and measure the performance, and then repeat
the dataset iterations a certain number of times. At this point, this sequence should
be very familiar to you. The hyperparameters and other training arguments for this
example are shown in Example 5-15.

Example 5-15. Arguments to the CNN NewsClassifier using pretrained embeddings

```
args = Namespace(
    # Data and path hyperparameters
    news_csv="data/ag_news/news_with_splits.csv",
    vectorizer_file="vectorizer.json",
    model_state_file="model.pth",
    save_dir="model_storage/ch5/document_classification",
    # Model hyperparameters
    glove_filepath='data/glove/glove.6B.100d.txt',
    use_glove=False,
    embedding_size=100,
    hidden_dim=100,
    num_channels=100,
    # Training hyperparameter
    seed=1337,
    learning_rate=0.001,
    dropout_p=0.1,
    batch_size=128,
    num_epochs=100,
    early_stopping_criteria=5,
```

```
    # Runtime options omitted for space
)
```

Model Evaluation and Prediction

In this example, the task was to classify news headlines to their respective categories. As you have seen in previous examples, there are two kinds of methods for understanding how well the model is carrying out the task: a quantitative evaluation using the test dataset, and a qualitative evaluation to personally inspect classification results.

Evaluating on the test dataset

Although this is the first time you are seeing the task of classifying news headlines, the quantitative evaluation routine is the same as all the previous ones: set the model in eval mode to turn off dropout and backpropagation (using `classifier.eval()`) and then iterate over the test set in the same manner as the training and validation sets. In a typical setting, you should experiment with different training options, and when you're satisfied, you should perform model evaluation. We will leave that as an exercise for you to complete. What is the final accuracy you can get on this test set? Remember that you can use the test set only once in the entire experimentation process.

Predicting the category of novel news headlines

The goal of training a classifier is to deploy it in production so that it can perform inference or prediction on unseen data. To predict the category of a news headline that isn't already processed and in the dataset, there are a few steps. The first is to preprocess the text in a manner similar to preprocessing data in the training. For inference, we use the same preprocessing function on the input as the one used in training. This preprocessed string is vectorized using the `Vectorizer` used during training, and converted into a PyTorch tensor. Next, the classifier is applied to it. The maximum of the prediction vector is computed to look up the name of the category. Example 5-16 presents the code.

Example 5-16. Predicting with the trained model

```
def predict_category(title, classifier, vectorizer, max_length):
    """Predict a news category for a new title

    Args:
        title (str): a raw title string
        classifier (NewsClassifier): an instance of the trained classifier
        vectorizer (NewsVectorizer): the corresponding vectorizer
        max_length (int): the max sequence length
            Note: CNNs are sensitive to the input data tensor size.
```

```
                      This ensures it's kept to the same size as the training data.
    """
    title = preprocess_text(title)
    vectorized_title = \
        torch.tensor(vectorizer.vectorize(title, vector_length=max_length))
    result = classifier(vectorized_title.unsqueeze(0), apply_softmax=True)
    probability_values, indices = result.max(dim=1)
    predicted_category = vectorizer.category_vocab.lookup_index(indices.item())

    return {'category': predicted_category,
            'probability': probability_values.item()}
```

Summary

In this chapter we studied word embeddings, which are a way to represent discrete items like words as fixed-dimension vectors in a space such that the distance between the vectors encodes a variety of linguistic properties. It is important to remember that the techniques introduced in this chapter are applicable to any discrete units, like sentences, paragraphs, documents, database records, and so on. This makes embedding techniques indispensable to deep learning, particularly in NLP. We showed how to use pretrained embeddings in a black-box fashion. We briefly discussed a few ways to learn these embeddings directly from data, including the Continuous Bag-of-Words (CBOW) method. We then showed how to train a CBOW model in the context of language modeling. Finally, we worked through an example of using pretrained embeddings and explored fine-tuning embeddings in a task like document classification.

This chapter, unfortunately, leaves out a lot of important topics due to lack of space, such as debiasing word embeddings, modeling context, and polysemy. Language data is a reflection of the world. Societal biases can become encoded into models via biased training corpora. In one study, the words closest to the pronoun "she" were *homemaker, nurse, receptionist, librarian, hairdresser,* and so on, whereas the ones closest to "he" were *surgeon, protege, philosopher, architect, financier,* and so on. Models trained on such biased embeddings can continue making decisions that could produce inequitable outcomes. Debiasing word embeddings is still a nascent area of research; and we recommend that you read Bolukbasi et al. (2016) and recent papers citing that. Also note that the word embeddings we used did not consider context. For example, depending on the context, the word "play" might have different meanings, but all the embedding methods discussed here collapse the meanings. Recent works like that of Peters et al. (2018) explore ways to provide embeddings conditioned on the context.

References

1. Firth, John. (1935). "The Technique of Semantics." Transactions of the Philological Society.

2. Baroni, Marco, Georgiana Dinu, and Germán Kruszewski. (2014). "Don't Count, Predict! A Systematic Comparison of Context-Counting vs. Context-Predicting Semantic Vectors." *Proceedings of the 52nd Annual Meeting of the ACL.*

3. Bolukbasi, Tolga, et al. (2016). "Man Is to Computer Programmer as Woman Is to Homemaker? Debiasing Word Embeddings." NIPS.

4. Goldberg, Yoav. (2017). *Neural Network Methods for Natural Language Processing.* Morgan and Claypool.

5. Peters, Matthew et al. (2018). "Deep Contextualized Word Representations." arXiv preprint arXiv:1802.05365.

6. Glorot, Xavier, and Yoshua Bengio. (2010). "Understanding the Difficulty of Training Deep Feedforward Neural Networks." Proceedings of the *13th International Conference on Artificial Intelligence and Statistics.*

CHAPTER 6
Sequence Modeling for Natural Language Processing

A sequence is an ordered collection of items. Traditional machine learning assumes data points to be independently and identically distributed (IID), but in many situations, like with language, speech, and time-series data, one data item depends on the items that precede or follow it. Such data is also called *sequence data*. Sequential information is everywhere in human language. For example, speech can be considered a sequence of basic units called *phonemes*. In a language like English, words in a sentence are not haphazard. They might be constrained by the words that come before or after them. For example, in the English language, the preposition "of" is likely followed by the article "the"; for example, "The lion is the king of the jungle." As another example, in many languages, including English, the number of a verb must agree with the number of the subject in a sentence. Here's an example:

```
The book is on the table
The books are on the table.
```

Sometimes these dependencies or constraints can be arbitrarily long. For example:

```
The book that I got yesterday is on the table.
The books read by the second-grade children are shelved in the lower rack.
```

In short, understanding sequences is essential to understanding human language. In the previous chapters, you were introduced to feed-forward neural networks, like multilayer perceptrons and convolutional neural networks, and to the power of vector representations. Although a wide range of natural language processing tasks can be approached using these techniques, as we will learn in this and the following two chapters, they do not adequately model sequences.[1]

Traditional approaches to modeling sequences in NLP using hidden Markov models, conditional random fields, and other kinds of probabilistic graphical models, although not discussed in this book, are still relevant.[2]

In deep learning, modeling sequences involves maintaining hidden "state information," or a *hidden state*. As each item in the sequence is encountered—for example, as each word in a sentence is seen by the model—the hidden state is updated. Thus, the hidden state (usually a vector) encapsulates everything seen by the sequence so far.[3] This hidden state vector, also called a *sequence representation*, can then be used in many sequence modeling tasks in myriad ways depending on the task we are solving, ranging from classifying sequences to predicting sequences. In this chapter we study the classification of sequence data, but Chapter 7 covers how you can use sequence models to generate sequences.

We begin by introducing the most basic neural network sequence model: the *recurrent neural network* (RNN). After this, we present an end-to-end example of the RNN in a classification setting. Specifically, you will see how to use a character-based RNN to classify surnames to their respective nationality. The surname example demonstrates that sequence models can capture orthographic (subword) patterns in language. This example is developed in a way to enable the reader to apply the model to other situations, including modeling sequences of text in which the data items are words and not characters.

Introduction to Recurrent Neural Networks

The purpose of recurrent neural networks is to model sequences of tensors.[4] RNNs, like feed-forward networks, are a family of models. There are several different members in the RNN family, but in this chapter, we work with only the most basic form,

---

1 An exception to that is CNNs. As we mention in Chapter 9, CNNs can be effectively utilized to capture sequence information.

2 For details, see Koller and Friedman (2009).

3 In Chapter 7, we'll see variants of sequence models that "forget" irrelevant information from the past.

4 Recall from Chapter 1 that everything can be expressed as a tensor. So here, an RNN is modeling a sequence of items at discrete time steps. Each of the items can be represented as a tensor. In the rest of the chapter, we use "vector" interchangeably for "tensor" sometimes. The dimensionality should be understood from the context.

---

sometimes called the *Elman RNN*.[5] The goal of recurrent networks—both the basic Elman form and the more complicated forms outlined in Chapter 7—is to learn a representation of a sequence. This is done by maintaining a hidden state vector that captures the current state of the sequence. The hidden state vector is computed from both a current input vector and the previous hidden state vector. These relationships are shown in Figure 6-1, which shows both the functional (left) and the "unrolled" (right) view of the computational dependencies. In both illustrations, the output is same as the hidden vector. This is not always the case, but in the case of an Elman RNN, the hidden vector is what's predicted.

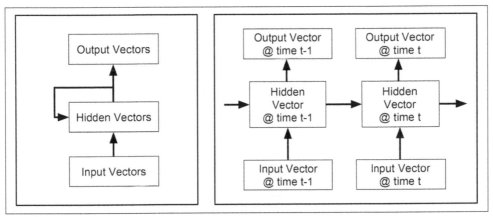

Figure 6-1. The functional view of the Elman RNN (left) displays the recurrent relationship as a feedback loop on the hidden vectors. The "unrolled" view (right) displays the computational relationship clearly; the hidden vector of each time step is dependent on both the input at that time step and the hidden vector from the previous time step.

Let's look at a slightly more specific description to understand what is happening in the Elman RNN. As shown in the unrolled view in Figure 6-1, also known as *backpropagation through time* (BPTT), the input vector from the current time step and the hidden state vector from the previous time step are mapped to the hidden state vector of the current time step. Shown in more detail in Figure 6-2, a new hidden vector is computed using a hidden-to-hidden weight matrix to map the previous hidden state vector and an input-to-hidden weight matrix to map the input vector.

---

5 In this chapter, we use "RNN" to refer to the Elman RNN. In fact, everything we model in this chapter can be modeled using other recurrent neural network types (the subject of Chapter 8), but for simplicity, we stick to the Elman RNN. You should keep this distinction in mind throughout this chapter.

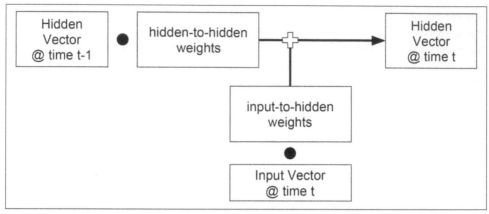

Figure 6-2. The explicit computation inside an Elman RNN is shown as the addition of two quantities: the dot product between the hidden vector of the previous time step and a hidden-to-hidden weight matrix and the dot product of the input vector and an input-to-hidden weight matrix.

Crucially, the hidden-to-hidden and input-to-hidden weights are shared across the different time steps. The intuition you should take away from this fact is that, during training, these weights will be adjusted so that the RNN is learning how to incorporate incoming information and maintain a state representation summarizing the input seen so far. The RNN does not have any way of knowing which time step it is on. Instead, it is simply learning how to transition from one time step to another and maintain a state representation that will minimize its loss function.

Using the same weights to transform inputs into outputs at every time step is another example of parameter sharing. In Chapter 4, we saw how CNNs share parameters across space. CNNs use parameters, called *kernels*, to compute outputs from subregions in the input data. Convolutional kernels are shifted across the input, computing outputs from every possible position in order to learn translation invariance. In contrast, RNNs use the same parameters to compute outputs at every time step by relying on a hidden state vector to capture the state of the sequence. In this way, the goal of RNNs is to learn sequence invariance by being able to compute any output given the hidden state vector and the input vector. You can think of an RNN sharing parameters across time and a CNN sharing parameters across space.

Because words and sentences can be of different lengths, the RNN or any sequence model should be equipped to handle *variable-length sequences*. One possible technique is to restrict sequences to a fixed length artificially. In this book, we use another technique, called *masking*, to handle variable-length sequences by taking advantage of knowledge of the lengths of the sequences. In brief, masking allows for the data to signal when certain inputs should not count toward the gradient or the eventual output. PyTorch provides primitives for handling variable-length sequences called Pack edSequences that create dense tensors from these less-dense ones. "Example: Classifying Surname Nationality Using a Character RNN" on page 155 illustrates an example of this.[6]

Implementing an Elman RNN

To explore the details of RNNs, let us step through a simple implementation of the Elman RNN. PyTorch offers many useful classes and helper functions to build RNNs. The PyTorch RNN class implements the Elman RNN. Instead of using this class directly, in this chapter we use RNNCell, an abstraction for a single time step of the RNN, and construct an RNN from that. Our intention in doing so is to show you the RNN computations explicitly. The class shown in Example 6-1, ElmanRNN, utilizes RNNCell to create the input-to-hidden and hidden-to-hidden weight matrices described earlier. Each call to RNNCell() accepts a matrix of input vectors and a matrix of hidden vectors. It returns the matrix of hidden vectors that results from one step.

Example 6-1. An implementation of the Elman RNN using PyTorch's RNNCell

```python
class ElmanRNN(nn.Module):
    """ an Elman RNN built using RNNCell """
    def __init__(self, input_size, hidden_size, batch_first=False):
        """
        Args:
            input_size (int): size of the input vectors
            hidden_size (int): size of the hidden state vectors
            batch_first (bool): whether the 0th dimension is batch
        """
        super(ElmanRNN, self).__init__()

        self.rnn_cell = nn.RNNCell(input_size, hidden_size)

        self.batch_first = batch_first
        self.hidden_size = hidden_size

    def _initialize_hidden(self, batch_size):
        return torch.zeros((batch_size, self.hidden_size))

    def forward(self, x_in, initial_hidden=None):
        """The forward pass of the ElmanRNN
```

---

6 Masking and PackedSequences are "implementation details" that are often glossed over in papers and books on deep learning. Although not critical to get a conceptual understanding of RNNs, a deep familiarity with these concepts, as we develop in this chapter, is indispensable for the practitioner. Pay special attention to them!

```
Args:
    x_in (torch.Tensor): an input data tensor.
        If self.batch_first: x_in.shape = (batch_size, seq_size, feat_size)
        Else: x_in.shape = (seq_size, batch_size, feat_size)
    initial_hidden (torch.Tensor): the initial hidden state for the RNN
Returns:
    hiddens (torch.Tensor): The outputs of the RNN at each time step.
        If self.batch_first:
            hiddens.shape = (batch_size, seq_size, hidden_size)
        Else: hiddens.shape = (seq_size, batch_size, hidden_size)
"""
if self.batch_first:
    batch_size, seq_size, feat_size = x_in.size()
    x_in = x_in.permute(1, 0, 2)
else:
    seq_size, batch_size, feat_size = x_in.size()

hiddens = []

if initial_hidden is None:
    initial_hidden = self._initialize_hidden(batch_size)
    initial_hidden = initial_hidden.to(x_in.device)

hidden_t = initial_hidden

for t in range(seq_size):
    hidden_t = self.rnn_cell(x_in[t], hidden_t)
    hiddens.append(hidden_t)

hiddens = torch.stack(hiddens)

if self.batch_first:
    hiddens = hiddens.permute(1, 0, 2)

return hiddens
```

In addition to controlling the input and hidden size hyperparameters in the RNN, there is a Boolean argument for specifying whether the dimension will be on the 0th dimension. This flag is present in all PyTorch RNNs implementations, as well. When set to True, the RNN swaps the 0th and 1st dimensions on the input tensor.

In the ElmanRNN class, the forward() method loops over the input tensor to compute the hidden state vector for each time step. Notice that there is an option for specifying the initial hidden state, but if it is not provided, a default hidden state vector of all 0s is used. As the ElmanRNN class loops over the length of the input vector, it computes a new hidden state. These hidden states are aggregated and ultimately stacked.[7]

---

7 For a discussion of the PyTorch stacking operation, see "Tensor Operations" on page 17.

Before they are returned, the `batch_first` flag is checked again. If it is `True`, the output hidden vectors are permuted so that the batch is once again on the `0`th dimension.

The output of the class is a three-dimensional tensor—there is a hidden state vector for each data point on the batch dimension and each time step. You can use these hidden vectors in several different ways, depending on the task at hand. One way that you can use them is to classify each time step to some discrete set of options. This method means that the RNN weights will be adjusted to track information relevant to predictions at each time step. Additionally, you can use the final vector for classifying the entire sequence. This means that the RNN weights will be adjusted to track information important for the eventual classification. In this chapter we see only the classification setting, but in the next two chapters we will examine stepwise predictions more closely.

Example: Classifying Surname Nationality Using a Character RNN

Now that we have outlined the basic properties of RNNs and stepped through an implementation of the `ElmanRNN`, let's apply it to a task. The task we will consider is the surname classification task from Chapter 4 in which character sequences (surnames) are classified to the nationality of origin.

The SurnameDataset Class

The dataset in this example is the surnames dataset, previously covered in Chapter 4. Each data point is represented by a surname and the corresponding nationality. We will avoid repeating the details of the dataset, but you should refer back to "The Surnames Dataset" on page 90 for a refresher.

In this example, like in "Example: Classifying Surnames by Using a CNN" on page 110, we treat each surname as a sequence of characters. As usual, we implement a dataset class, shown in Example 6-2, that returns the vectorized surname as well as the integer representing its nationality. Additionally returned is the length of the sequence, which is used in downstream computations to know where the final vector in the sequence is located. This is a part of the familiar sequence of steps—implementing `Dataset`, a `Vectorizer`, and a `Vocabulary`—before the actual training can take place.

Example 6-2. Implementing the SurnameDataset class

```
class SurnameDataset(Dataset):
    @classmethod
    def load_dataset_and_make_vectorizer(cls, surname_csv):
```

```
"""Load dataset and make a new vectorizer from scratch

Args:
    surname_csv (str): location of the dataset
Returns:
    an instance of SurnameDataset
"""
surname_df = pd.read_csv(surname_csv)
train_surname_df = surname_df[surname_df.split=='train']
return cls(surname_df, SurnameVectorizer.from_dataframe(train_surname_df))

def __getitem__(self, index):
    """the primary entry point method for PyTorch datasets

    Args:
        index (int): the index to the data point
    Returns:
        a dictionary holding the data point's:
            features (x_data)
            label (y_target)
            feature length (x_length)
    """
    row = self._target_df.iloc[index]

    surname_vector, vec_length = \
        self._vectorizer.vectorize(row.surname, self._max_seq_length)

    nationality_index = \
        self._vectorizer.nationality_vocab.lookup_token(row.nationality)

    return {'x_data': surname_vector,
            'y_target': nationality_index,
            'x_length': vec_length}
```

The Vectorization Data Structures

The first stage in the vectorization pipeline is to map each character token in the surname to a unique integer. To accomplish this, we use the SequenceVocabulary data structure, which we first introduced and described in "Example: Transfer Learning Using Pretrained Embeddings for Document Classification" on page 137. Recall that this data structure not only maps characters in the names to integers, but also utilizes four special-purpose tokens: the UNK token, the MASK token, the BEGIN-OF-SEQUENCE token, and the END-OF-SEQUENCE token. The first two tokens are vital for language data: the UNK token is used for unseen out-of-vocabulary tokens in the input and the MASK token enables handling variable-length inputs. The latter two tokens provide the model with sentence boundary features and are prepended and appended to the sequence, respectively. We refer you to "Vocabulary, Vectorizer, and DataLoader" on page 138 for a longer description of the SequenceVocabulary.

The overall vectorization procedure is managed by the `SurnameVectorizer`, which uses a `SequenceVocabulary` to manage the mapping between characters in surnames and integers. Example 6-3 shows its implementation, which should look very familiar; in the previous chapter we looked at classifying the titles of news articles to specific categories, and the vectorization pipeline was almost identical.

Example 6-3. A vectorizer for surnames

```
class SurnameVectorizer(object):
    """ The Vectorizer which coordinates the Vocabularies and puts them to use"""
    def vectorize(self, surname, vector_length=-1):
        """
        Args:
            title (str): the string of characters
            vector_length (int): an argument for forcing the length of index vector
        """
        indices = [self.char_vocab.begin_seq_index]
        indices.extend(self.char_vocab.lookup_token(token)
                        for token in surname)
        indices.append(self.char_vocab.end_seq_index)

        if vector_length < 0:
            vector_length = len(indices)

        out_vector = np.zeros(vector_length, dtype=np.int64)
        out_vector[:len(indices)] = indices
        out_vector[len(indices):] = self.char_vocab.mask_index

        return out_vector, len(indices)

    @classmethod
    def from_dataframe(cls, surname_df):
        """Instantiate the vectorizer from the dataset dataframe

        Args:
            surname_df (pandas.DataFrame): the surnames dataset
        Returns:
            an instance of the SurnameVectorizer
        """
        char_vocab = SequenceVocabulary()
        nationality_vocab = Vocabulary()

        for index, row in surname_df.iterrows():
            for char in row.surname:
                char_vocab.add_token(char)
            nationality_vocab.add_token(row.nationality)

        return cls(char_vocab, nationality_vocab)
```

The SurnameClassifier Model

The `SurnameClassifier` model is composed of an Embedding layer, the `ElmanRNN`, and a `Linear` layer. We assume that the input to the model is tokens represented as a set of integers after they have been mapped to integers by the `SequenceVocabulary`. The model first embeds the integers using the embedding layer. Then, using the RNN, sequence representation vectors are computed. These vectors represent the hidden state for each character in the surname. Because the goal is to classify each surname, the vector corresponding to the final character position in each surname is extracted. One way to think about this vector is that the final vector is a result of passing over the entire sequence input, and hence it's a summary vector for the surname. These summary vectors are passed through the `Linear` layer to compute a prediction vector. The prediction vector is used in the training loss, or we can apply the softmax function to create a probability distribution over surnames.[8]

The arguments to the model are the size of the embeddings, the number of embeddings (i.e., vocabulary size), the number of classes, and the hidden state size of the RNN. Two of these arguments—the number of embeddings and the number of classes—are determined by the data. The remaining hyperparameters are the size of the embeddings and the size of the hidden state. Although these can take on any value, it is usually good to start with something small that will train fast to verify that the model will work.

Example 6-4. Implementing the SurnameClassifier model using an Elman RNN

```
class SurnameClassifier(nn.Module):
    """ An RNN to extract features & an MLP to classify """
    def __init__(self, embedding_size, num_embeddings, num_classes,
                 rnn_hidden_size, batch_first=True, padding_idx=0):
        """
        Args:
            embedding_size (int): The size of the character embeddings
            num_embeddings (int): The number of characters to embed
            num_classes (int): The size of the prediction vector
                Note: the number of nationalities
            rnn_hidden_size (int): The size of the RNN's hidden state
            batch_first (bool): Informs whether the input tensors will
                have batch or the sequence on the 0th dimension
            padding_idx (int): The index for the tensor padding;
                see torch.nn.Embedding
        """
        super(SurnameClassifier, self).__init__()
```

---

8 In this example, the number of classes is small. In many situations in NLP, the number of output classes can be on the order of thousands or hundreds of thousands. In such situations, a hierarchical softmax might be warranted instead of the vanilla softmax.

```python
        self.emb = nn.Embedding(num_embeddings=num_embeddings,
                                embedding_dim=embedding_size,
                                padding_idx=padding_idx)
        self.rnn = ElmanRNN(input_size=embedding_size,
                            hidden_size=rnn_hidden_size,
                            batch_first=batch_first)
        self.fc1 = nn.Linear(in_features=rnn_hidden_size,
                             out_features=rnn_hidden_size)
        self.fc2 = nn.Linear(in_features=rnn_hidden_size,
                             out_features=num_classes)

    def forward(self, x_in, x_lengths=None, apply_softmax=False):
        """The forward pass of the classifier

        Args:
            x_in (torch.Tensor): an input data tensor
                x_in.shape should be (batch, input_dim)
            x_lengths (torch.Tensor): the lengths of each sequence in the batch
                used to find the final vector of each sequence
            apply_softmax (bool): a flag for the softmax activation
                should be false if used with the cross-entropy losses
        Returns:
            out (torch.Tensor); `out.shape = (batch, num_classes)`
        """
        x_embedded = self.emb(x_in)
        y_out = self.rnn(x_embedded)

        if x_lengths is not None:
            y_out = column_gather(y_out, x_lengths)
        else:
            y_out = y_out[:, -1, :]

        y_out = F.dropout(y_out, 0.5)
        y_out = F.relu(self.fc1(y_out))
        y_out = F.dropout(y_out, 0.5)
        y_out = self.fc2(y_out)

        if apply_softmax:
            y_out = F.softmax(y_out, dim=1)

        return y_out
```

You will notice that the forward() function requires the lengths of the sequences. The lengths are used to retrieve the final vector of each sequence in the tensor that is returned from the RNN with a function named column_gather(), shown in Example 6-5. The function iterates over batch row indices and retrieves the vector that's at the position indicated by the corresponding length of sequence.

Example 6-5. Retrieving the final output vector in each sequence using column_gather()

```python
def column_gather(y_out, x_lengths):
    """Get a specific vector from each batch data point in `y_out`.

    Args:
        y_out (torch.FloatTensor, torch.cuda.FloatTensor)
            shape: (batch, sequence, feature)
        x_lengths (torch.LongTensor, torch.cuda.LongTensor)
            shape: (batch,)

    Returns:
        y_out (torch.FloatTensor, torch.cuda.FloatTensor)
            shape: (batch, feature)
    """
    x_lengths = x_lengths.long().detach().cpu().numpy() - 1

    out = []
    for batch_index, column_index in enumerate(x_lengths):
        out.append(y_out[batch_index, column_index])

    return torch.stack(out)
```

The Training Routine and Results

The training routine follows the standard formula. For a single batch of data, apply the model and compute the prediction vectors. Use the CrossEntropyLoss() function and the ground truth to compute a loss value. Using the loss value and an optimizer, compute the gradients and update the weights of the model using those gradients. Repeat this for each batch in the training data. Proceed similarly with the validation data, but set the model in eval mode so as to prevent backpropagating. Instead, the validation data is used only to give a less-biased sense of how the model is performing. Repeat this routine for a specific number of epochs. For the code, please see the supplementary material. We encourage you to play with the hyperparameters to get a sense of what affects performance and by how much, and to tabulate the results. We also leave writing a suitable baseline model for this task as an exercise for you to complete.[9] The model implemented in "The SurnameClassifier Model" on page 158 is general and not restricted to characters. The embedding layer in the

---

9 As a warmup, consider an MLP with a bag of unigram characters as input. Then modify it to consider a bag of character bigrams as input. It is likely, for this problem, that the baseline models might perform better than this simple RNN model. That is instructive: you are doing feature engineering by telling the baseline model that there is signal in character bigrams. Calculate the number of parameters in the unigram and the bigram input cases, and compare these with the RNN model in this chapter. Does it have more or fewer parameters, and why? Finally, can you think of a baseline model much simpler than an MLP for this task that performs well?

model can map any discrete item in a sequence of discrete items; for example, a sentence is a sequence of words. We encourage you to use the code in Example 6-6 in other sequence classification tasks, like sentence classification.

Example 6-6. Arguments to the RNN-based SurnameClassifier

```
args = Namespace(
    # Data and path information
    surname_csv="data/surnames/surnames_with_splits.csv",
    vectorizer_file="vectorizer.json",
    model_state_file="model.pth",
    save_dir="model_storage/ch6/surname_classification",
    # Model hyperparameter
    char_embedding_size=100,
    rnn_hidden_size=64,
    # Training hyperparameter
    num_epochs=100,
    learning_rate=1e-3,
    batch_size=64,
    seed=1337,
    early_stopping_criteria=5,
    # Runtime options omitted for space
)
```

Summary

In this chapter we introduced the use of recurrent neural networks for modeling sequence data and looked at one of the simplest kinds of recurrent networks, called the Elman RNN. We established that the goal of sequence modeling is to learn a representation (i.e., a vector) for the sequence. This learned representation can be used in different ways depending on the task. We considered an example task involving classification of this hidden-state representation to one of many classes. The surname classification task showed an example of using RNNs to capture information at a sub-word level.

References

1. Koller, Daphne, and Nir Friedman. (2009). *Probabilistic Graphical Models: Principles and Techniques*. MIT Press.

Intermediate Sequence Modeling for Natural Language Processing

The goal of this chapter is *sequence prediction*. Sequence prediction tasks require us to label each item of a sequence. Such tasks are common in natural language processing. Some examples include *language modeling* (see Figure 7-1), in which we predict the next word given a sequence of words at each step; *part-of-speech tagging*, in which we predict the grammatical part of speech for each word; *named entity recognition*, in which we predict whether each word is part of a named entity, such as `Person`, `Location`, `Product`, or `Organization`; and so on. Sometimes, in NLP literature, the sequence prediction tasks are also referred to as *sequence labeling*.

Although in theory we can use the Elman recurrent neural networks introduced in Chapter 6 for sequence prediction tasks, they fail to capture long-range dependencies well and perform poorly in practice. In this chapter, we spend some time understanding why that is the case and learn about a new type of RNN architecture called the *gated network*.

We also introduce the task of *natural language generation* as an application of sequence prediction and explore conditioned generation in which the output sequence is constrained in some manner.

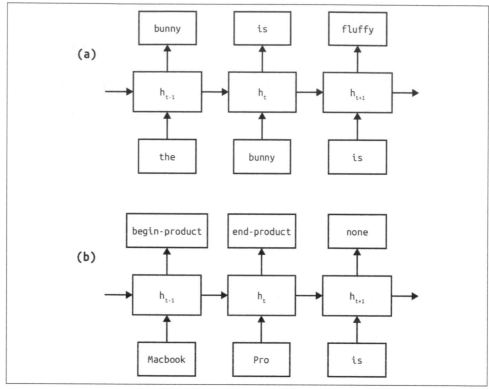

Figure 7-1. Two examples of sequence prediction tasks: (a) language modeling, in which the task is to predict the next word in a sequence; and (b) named entity recognition, which aims to predict boundaries of entity strings in text along with their types.

The Problem with Vanilla RNNs (or Elman RNNs)

Even though the vanilla/Elman RNN, discussed in Chapter 6, is well suited for modeling sequences, it has two issues that make it unsuitable for many tasks: the inability to retain information for long-range predictions, and gradient stability. To understand these two issues, recall that at their core, RNNs are computing a hidden state vector at each time step using the hidden state vector of the previous time step and an input vector at the current time step. It is this core computation that makes the RNN so powerful, but it also creates drastic numerical issues.

The first issue with Elman RNNs is the difficulty in retaining long-range information. With the RNN in Chapter 6, for example, at each time step we simply updated the hidden state vector regardless of whether it made sense. As a consequence, the RNN has no control over which values are retained and which are discarded in the hidden state—that is entirely determined by the input. Intuitively, that doesn't make sense.

What is desired is some way for the RNN to decide if the update is optional, or if the update happens, by how much and what parts of the state vector, and so on.

The second issue with Elman RNNs is their tendency to cause gradients to spiral out of control to zero or to infinity. Unstable gradients that can spiral out of control are called either *vanishing gradients* or *exploding gradients* depending on the direction in which the absolute values of the gradients are shrinking/growing. A really large absolute value of the gradient or a really small (less than 1) value can make the optimization procedure unstable (Hochreiter et al., 2001; Pascanu et al., 2013).

There are solutions to deal with these gradient problems in vanilla RNNs, such as the use of rectified linear units (ReLUs), gradient clipping, and careful initialization. But none of the proposed solutions work as reliably as the technique called *gating*.

Gating as a Solution to a Vanilla RNN's Challenges

To intuitively understand gating, suppose that you were adding two quantities, a and b, but you wanted to control how much of b gets into the sum. Mathematically, you can rewrite the sum $a + b$ as:

$$a + \lambda b$$

where λ is a value between 0 and 1. If $\lambda = 0$, there is no contribution from b and if $\lambda = 1$, b contributes fully. Looking at it this way, you can interpret that λ acts as a "switch" or a "gate" in controlling the amount of b that gets into the sum. This is the intuition behind the gating mechanism. Now let's revisit the Elman RNN and see how gating can be incorporated into vanilla RNNs to make conditional updates. If the previous hidden state was h_{t-1} and the current input is x_t, the recurrent update in the Elman RNN would look something like:

$$h_t = h_{t-1} + F(h_{t-1}, x_t)$$

where F is the recurrent computation of the RNN. Obviously, this is an unconditioned sum and has the evils described in "The Problem with Vanilla RNNs (or Elman RNNs)" on page 164. Now imagine if, instead of a constant, the λ in the previous example was a function of the previous hidden state vector h_{t-1} and the current input x_t, and still produced the desired gating behavior; that is, a value between 0 and 1. With this gating function, our RNN update equation would appear as follows:

$$h_t = h_{t-1} + \lambda(h_{t-1}, x_t)F(h_{t-1}, x_t)$$

Now it becomes clear that the function λ controls how much of the current input gets to update the state h_{t-1}. Further, the function λ is context-dependent. This is the basic intuition behind all gated networks. The function λ is usually a sigmoid function, which we know from Chapter 3 to produce a value between 0 and 1.

In the case of the *long short-term memory* network (LSTM; Hochreiter and Schmidhuber, 1997), this basic intuition is extended carefully to incorporate not only conditional updates, but also intentional forgetting of the values in the previous hidden state h_{t-1}. This "forgetting" happens by multiplying the previous hidden state value h_{t-1} with another function, μ, that also produces values between 0 and 1 and depends on the current input:

$$h_t = \mu(h_{t-1}, x_t)h_{t-1} + \lambda(h_{t-1}, x_t)F(h_{t-1}, x_t)$$

As you might have guessed, μ is another gating function. In an actual LSTM description, this becomes complicated because the gating functions are parameterized, leading to a somewhat complex (to the uninitiated) sequence of operations. Armed with the intuition in this section, you are now ready to dive deep if you want to into the update mechanics of the LSTM. We recommend the classic article by Christopher Olah (*http://colah.github.io/posts/2015-08-Understanding-LSTMs/*). We will refrain from covering any of that in this book because the details are not essential for the application and use of LSTMs in NLP applications.

The LSTM is only one of the many gated variants of the RNN. Another variant that's becoming increasingly popular is the *gated recurrent unit* (GRU; Chung et al., 2015). Fortunately, in PyTorch, you can simply replace the nn.RNN or nn.RNNCell with nn.LSTM or nn.LSTMCell with no other code change to switch to an LSTM (*mutatis mutandis* for GRU)!

The gating mechanism is an effective solution for problems enumerated in "The Problem with Vanilla RNNs (or Elman RNNs)" on page 164. It not only makes the updates controlled, but also keeps the gradient issues under check and makes training relatively easier. Without further ado, we will show these gated architectures in action using two examples.

Example: A Character RNN for Generating Surnames

In this example,[1] we walk through a simple sequence prediction task: generating surnames using an RNN. In practice, this means that for each time step, the RNN is computing a probability distribution over the set of possible characters in the sur-

---

[1] The code is available in */chapters/chapter_7/7_3_surname_generation* in this book's GitHub repo (*https://nlproc.info/PyTorchNLPBook/repo/*).

name. We can use these probability distributions, either to optimize the network to improve its predictions (given that we know what characters should have been predicted), or to generate brand-new surnames.

Although the dataset for this task has been used in earlier examples and will look familiar, there are some differences in the way each data sample is constructed for sequence prediction. After describing the dataset and task, we outline the supporting data structures that enable the sequence prediction through systematic bookkeeping.

We then introduce two models for generating surnames: the unconditioned `Surname GenerationModel` and the conditioned `SurnameGenerationModel`. The unconditioned model predicts sequences of surname characters without knowing anything about the nationality. In contrast, the conditioned model utilizes a specific nationality embedding as the initial hidden state of the RNN to allow the model to bias its predictions of sequences.

The SurnameDataset Class

First introduced in "Example: Surname Classification with an MLP" on page 89, the surnames dataset is a collection of last names and their country of origin. Up until now, the dataset has been used for a classification task—given a new surname, correctly classify from which country the surname originated. However, in this example, we show how you can use the dataset to train a model that can assign probabilities to sequences of characters and generate new sequences.

The `SurnameDataset` class remains mostly the same as in previous chapters: we use a Pandas DataFrame to load the dataset and a vectorizer is constructed which encapsulates the token-to-integer mappings required for the model and task at hand. To accommodate the difference in tasks, the `SurnameDataset.__getitem__()` method is modified to output the sequences of integers for the prediction targets, as illustrated in Example 7-1. The method references the `Vectorizer` for computing the sequence of integers that serve as the input (the `from_vector`) and the sequence of integers that serve as the output (the `to_vector`). The implementation of `vectorize()` is described in the next subsection.

Example 7-1. The SurnameDataset.__getitem__() method for a sequence prediction task

```
class SurnameDataset(Dataset):
    @classmethod
    def load_dataset_and_make_vectorizer(cls, surname_csv):
        """Load dataset and make a new vectorizer from scratch

        Args:
            surname_csv (str): location of the dataset
        Returns:
```

```
        an instance of SurnameDataset
    """

    surname_df = pd.read_csv(surname_csv)
    return cls(surname_df, SurnameVectorizer.from_dataframe(surname_df))

def __getitem__(self, index):
    """the primary entry point method for PyTorch datasets

    Args:
        index (int): the index to the data point
    Returns:
        a dictionary holding the data point: (x_data, y_target, class_index)
    """
    row = self._target_df.iloc[index]

    from_vector, to_vector = \
        self._vectorizer.vectorize(row.surname, self._max_seq_length)

    nationality_index = \
        self._vectorizer.nationality_vocab.lookup_token(row.nationality)

    return {'x_data': from_vector,
            'y_target': to_vector,
            'class_index': nationality_index}
```

The Vectorization Data Structures

As with the previous examples, there are three main data structures that transform each surname's sequence of characters into its vectorized forms: the SequenceVocabulary maps individual tokens to integers, the SurnameVectorizer coordinates the integer mappings, and the DataLoader groups the SurnameVector izer's results into minibatches. Because the DataLoader implementation and its use remain the same in this example, we will skip over its implementation details.[2]

SurnameVectorizer and END-OF-SEQUENCE

For the task of sequence prediction, the training routine is written to expect two sequences of integers which represent the token observations and the token targets at each time step. Commonly, we just want to predict the very sequence we are training on, such as with the surnames in this example. This means that we only have a single sequence of tokens to work with and construct the observations and targets by staggering the single sequence.

---

2 We refer you to "Vocabulary, Vectorizer, and DataLoader" on page 133 for a more in-depth look at Sequence Vocabulary and "The Vocabulary, the Vectorizer, and the DataLoader" on page 62 for an introductory discussion of the Vocabulary and Vectorizer data structures.

To turn it into a sequence prediction problem, each token is mapped to its appropriate index using the SequenceVocabulary. Then, the BEGIN-OF-SEQUENCE token index, begin_seq_index, is prepended to the beginning of the sequence and the END-OF-SEQUENCE token index, end_seq_index, is appended to the end of the sequence. At this point, each data point is a sequence of indices and has the same first and last index. To create the input and output sequences required by the training routine, we simply use two slices of the sequence of indices: the first slice includes all the token indices except the last and the second slice includes all the token indices except the first. When aligned and paired together, the sequences are the correct input-output indices.

To be explicit, we show the code for SurnameVectorizer.vectorize() in Example 7-2. The first step is to map surname, a string of characters, to indices, a list of integers representing those characters. Then, indices is wrapped with the beginning and end-of-sequence indices: specifically, begin_seq_index is prepended to indices and end_seq_index is appended to indices. Next, we test for the vector_length, which is typically provided at runtime (although the code is written to allow for any length of vector). During training, it is important that the vector_length be provided because minibatches are constructed from stacked vector representations. If the vectors are of different lengths, they cannot be stacked in a single matrix. After testing for vector_length, two vectors are created: the from_vector and the to_vector. The slice of the indices that doesn't include the last index is placed inside from_vector and the slice of the indices that doesn't include the first index is placed inside to_vector. The remaining positions of each vector are filled with the mask_index. It is important that the sequences are filled (or padded) to the right, because empty positions will change the output vector and we want those changes to happen after the sequence has been seen.

Example 7-2. The code for SurnameVectorizer.vectorize() in a sequence prediction task

```
class SurnameVectorizer(object):
    """ The Vectorizer which coordinates the Vocabularies and puts them to use"""
    def vectorize(self, surname, vector_length=-1):
        """Vectorize a surname into a vector of observations and targets

        Args:
            surname (str): the surname to be vectorized
            vector_length (int): an argument for forcing the length of index vector
        Returns:
            a tuple: (from_vector, to_vector)
                from_vector (numpy.ndarray): the observation vector
                to_vector (numpy.ndarray): the target prediction vector
        """
        indices = [self.char_vocab.begin_seq_index]
        indices.extend(self.char_vocab.lookup_token(token) for token in surname)
```

```
        indices.append(self.char_vocab.end_seq_index)

        if vector_length < 0:
            vector_length = len(indices) - 1

        from_vector = np.zeros(vector_length, dtype=np.int64)
        from_indices = indices[:-1]
        from_vector[:len(from_indices)] = from_indices
        from_vector[len(from_indices):] = self.char_vocab.mask_index

        to_vector = np.empty(vector_length, dtype=np.int64)
        to_indices = indices[1:]
        to_vector[:len(to_indices)] = to_indices
        to_vector[len(to_indices):] = self.char_vocab.mask_index

        return from_vector, to_vector

    @classmethod
    def from_dataframe(cls, surname_df):
        """Instantiate the vectorizer from the dataset dataframe

        Args:
            surname_df (pandas.DataFrame): the surnames dataset
        Returns:
            an instance of the SurnameVectorizer
        """
        char_vocab = SequenceVocabulary()
        nationality_vocab = Vocabulary()

        for index, row in surname_df.iterrows():
            for char in row.surname:
                char_vocab.add_token(char)
            nationality_vocab.add_token(row.nationality)

        return cls(char_vocab, nationality_vocab)
```

From the ElmanRNN to the GRU

In practice, switching from the vanilla RNN to a gated variant is extremely easy. In
the following models, although we use the GRU in place of the vanilla RNN, using
the LSTM is just as easy. To use the GRU, we instantiate the torch.nn.GRU module
using the same parameters as the ElmanRNN from Chapter 6.

Model 1: The Unconditioned SurnameGenerationModel

The first of the two models is unconditioned: it does not observe the nationality
before generating a surname. In practice, being unconditioned means the GRU does
not bias its computations toward any nationality. In the next example (Example 7-4),
the computational bias is introduced through the initial hidden vector. In this exam-

ple, we use a vector of all 0s so that the initial hidden state vector does not contribute to the computations.[3]

In general, the `SurnameGenerationModel` (Example 7-3) embeds character indices, computes their sequential state using a GRU, and computes the probability of token predictions using a `Linear` layer. More explicitly, the unconditioned `SurnameGenerationModel` starts with initializing an `Embedding` layer, a GRU, and a `Linear` layer. Similar to the sequence models of Chapter 6, a matrix of integers is input to the model. We use a PyTorch `Embedding` instance, the `char_embedding`, to convert the integers to a three-dimensional tensor (a sequence of vectors for each batch item). This tensor is passed to the GRU, which computes a state vector for each position in each sequence.

Example 7-3. The unconditioned surname generation model

```python
class SurnameGenerationModel(nn.Module):
    def __init__(self, char_embedding_size, char_vocab_size, rnn_hidden_size,
                 batch_first=True, padding_idx=0, dropout_p=0.5):
        """
        Args:
            char_embedding_size (int): The size of the character embeddings
            char_vocab_size (int): The number of characters to embed
            rnn_hidden_size (int): The size of the RNN's hidden state
            batch_first (bool): Informs whether the input tensors will
                have batch or the sequence on the 0th dimension
            padding_idx (int): The index for the tensor padding;
                see torch.nn.Embedding
            dropout_p (float): The probability of zeroing activations using
                the dropout method
        """
        super(SurnameGenerationModel, self).__init__()

        self.char_emb = nn.Embedding(num_embeddings=char_vocab_size,
                                     embedding_dim=char_embedding_size,
                                     padding_idx=padding_idx)
        self.rnn = nn.GRU(input_size=char_embedding_size,
                          hidden_size=rnn_hidden_size,
                          batch_first=batch_first)
        self.fc = nn.Linear(in_features=rnn_hidden_size,
                            out_features=char_vocab_size)
        self._dropout_p = dropout_p

    def forward(self, x_in, apply_softmax=False):
        """The forward pass of the model

        Args:
```

---

3 If the initial hidden vector is all 0's, matrix multiplication with it will result in only 0's.

```
    x_in (torch.Tensor): an input data tensor
        x_in.shape should be (batch, input_dim)
    apply_softmax (bool): a flag for the softmax activation
        should be False during training
Returns:
    the resulting tensor. tensor.shape should be (batch, output_dim).
    """
x_embedded = self.char_emb(x_in)

y_out, _ = self.rnn(x_embedded)

batch_size, seq_size, feat_size = y_out.shape
y_out = y_out.contiguous().view(batch_size * seq_size, feat_size)

y_out = self.fc(F.dropout(y_out, p=self._dropout_p))

if apply_softmax:
    y_out = F.softmax(y_out, dim=1)

new_feat_size = y_out.shape[-1]
y_out = y_out.view(batch_size, seq_size, new_feat_size)

return y_out
```

The primary difference between the sequence classification tasks of Chapter 6 and sequence prediction tasks of this chapter is how the state vectors computed by the RNN are handled. In Chapter 6, we retrieved a single vector per batch index and performed predictions using those single vectors. In this example, we reshape our three-dimensional tensor into a two-dimensional tensor (a matrix) so that the row dimension represents every sample (batch and sequence index). Using this matrix and the Linear layer, we compute prediction vectors for every sample. We finish the computation by reshaping the matrix back into a three-dimensional tensor. Because the ordering information is preserved with reshaping operations, each batch and sequence index is still in the same position. The reason why we needed to reshape is because the Linear layer requires a matrix as input.

Model 2: The Conditioned SurnameGenerationModel

The second model takes into account the nationality of the surname to be generated. In practice, this means that there is some mechanism that allows for the model to bias its behavior relative to a specific surname. In this example, we parameterize the initial hidden state of the RNN by embedding each nationality as a vector the size of the hidden state. This means that as the model adjusts its parameters, it also adjusts the values in the embedding matrix so that it biases the predictions to be more sensitive to the specific nationality and the regularities of its surnames. For example, the Irish nationality vector biases toward the starting sequences "Mc" and "O'".

Example 7-4 shows the differences in the conditioned model. Specifically, an extra Embedding is introduced to map the nationality indices to vectors the same size as the RNN's hidden layer. Then, in the forward function, nationality indices are embedded and simply passed in as the initial hidden layer of the RNN. Although this is a very simple modification to the first model, it has a profound effect in letting the RNN change its behavior based on the nationality of the surname being generated.

Example 7-4. The conditioned surname generation model

```
class SurnameGenerationModel(nn.Module):
    def __init__(self, char_embedding_size, char_vocab_size, num_nationalities,
                 rnn_hidden_size, batch_first=True, padding_idx=0, dropout_p=0.5):
        # ...
        self.nation_embedding = nn.Embedding(embedding_dim=rnn_hidden_size,
                                             num_embeddings=num_nationalities)

    def forward(self, x_in, nationality_index, apply_softmax=False):
        # ...
        x_embedded = self.char_embedding(x_in)
        # hidden_size: (num_layers * num_directions, batch_size, rnn_hidden_size)
        nationality_embedded = self.nation_emb(nationality_index).unsqueeze(0)
        y_out, _ = self.rnn(x_embedded, nationality_embedded)
        # ...
```

The Training Routine and Results

In this example, we introduced the task of predicting sequences of characters for generating surnames. Although in many respects the implementation details and training routine are similar to the sequence classification examples in Chapter 6, there are a few major differences. In this section, we focus on the differences, the hyperparameters used, and the results.

Computing the loss in this example requires two changes when compared with previous examples because we are making predictions at every time step in the sequence. First, we reshape three-dimensional tensors[4] to two-dimensional tensors (matrices) to satisfy computational constraints. Second, we coordinate the masking index, which allows for variable-length sequences, with the loss function so that the loss does not use the masked positions in its computations.

We handle both issues—three-dimensional tensors and variable-length sequences—by utilizing the code snippet shown in Example 7-5. First, the predictions and the targets are normalized to sizes that the loss function expects (two dimensions for the predictions and one dimension for the targets). Now, each row represents a single

---

[4] The three-dimensional tensors are batch on the first dimension, sequence on the second, and prediction vector on the third.

sample: one time step in one sequence. Then, cross-entropy loss is used with the ignore_index set to the mask_index. This has the effect of the loss function ignoring any position in the targets that matches the ignore_index.

Example 7-5. Handling three-dimensional tensors and sequence-wide loss computations

```
def normalize_sizes(y_pred, y_true):
    """Normalize tensor sizes

    Args:
        y_pred (torch.Tensor): the output of the model
            If a 3-dimensional tensor, reshapes to a matrix
        y_true (torch.Tensor): the target predictions
            If a matrix, reshapes to be a vector
    """
    if len(y_pred.size()) == 3:
        y_pred = y_pred.contiguous().view(-1, y_pred.size(2))
    if len(y_true.size()) == 2:
        y_true = y_true.contiguous().view(-1)
    return y_pred, y_true


def sequence_loss(y_pred, y_true, mask_index):
    y_pred, y_true = normalize_sizes(y_pred, y_true)
    return F.cross_entropy(y_pred, y_true, ignore_index=mask_index)
```

Using this modified loss computation, we construct a training routine that looks similar to that in every other example in this book. It begins by iterating over the training dataset one minibatch at a time. For each minibatch, the output of the model is computed from the inputs. Because we are performing predictions at each time step, the output of the model is a three-dimensional tensor. Using the previously described sequence_loss() and an optimizer, the error signal for the model's predictions is computed and used to update the model parameters.

Most of the model hyperparameters are determined by the size of the character vocabulary. This size is the number of discrete tokens that can be observed as input to the model and the number of classes in the output classification at each time step. The remaining model hyperparameters are the size of the character embeddings and the size of the internal RNN hidden state. Example 7-6 presents these hyperparameters and training options.

Example 7-6. Hyperparameters for surname generation

```
args = Namespace(
    # Data and path information
    surname_csv="data/surnames/surnames_with_splits.csv",
```

```
    vectorizer_file="vectorizer.json",
    model_state_file="model.pth",
    save_dir="model_storage/ch7/model1_unconditioned_surname_generation",
    # or: save_dir="model_storage/ch7/model2_conditioned_surname_generation",
    # Model hyperparameters
    char_embedding_size=32,
    rnn_hidden_size=32,
    # Training hyperparameters
    seed=1337,
    learning_rate=0.001,
    batch_size=128,
    num_epochs=100,
    early_stopping_criteria=5,
    # Runtime options omitted for space
)
```

Even though the per-character accuracy of the predictions is a measure of model performance, it is better in this example to do qualitative evaluation by inspecting what
kinds of surnames the model will generate. To do this, we write a new loop over a
modified version of the steps in the forward() method to compute predictions at
each time step and use those predictions as the input to the following time step. We
show the code in Example 7-7. The output of the model at each time step is a prediction vector which is turned into a probability distribution using the softmax function.
Using the probability distribution, we take advantage of the torch.multinomial()
sampling function, which selects an index at a rate proportional to the probability of
the index. Sampling is a stochastic procedure that produces different outputs each
time.

Example 7-7. Sampling from the unconditioned generation model

```
def sample_from_model(model, vectorizer, num_samples=1, sample_size=20,
                      temperature=1.0):
    """Sample a sequence of indices from the model

    Args:
        model (SurnameGenerationModel): the trained model
        vectorizer (SurnameVectorizer): the corresponding vectorizer
        num_samples (int): the number of samples
        sample_size (int): the max length of the samples
        temperature (float): accentuates or flattens the distribution
            0.0 < temperature < 1.0 will make it peakier
            temperature > 1.0 will make it more uniform
    Returns:
        indices (torch.Tensor): the matrix of indices
        shape = (num_samples, sample_size)
    """
    begin_seq_index = [vectorizer.char_vocab.begin_seq_index
                       for _ in range(num_samples)]
    begin_seq_index = torch.tensor(begin_seq_index,
```

```
                                    dtype=torch.int64).unsqueeze(dim=1)
    indices = [begin_seq_index]
    h_t = None

    for time_step in range(sample_size):
        x_t = indices[time_step]
        x_emb_t = model.char_emb(x_t)
        rnn_out_t, h_t = model.rnn(x_emb_t, h_t)
        prediction_vector = model.fc(rnn_out_t.squeeze(dim=1))
        probability_vector = F.softmax(prediction_vector / temperature, dim=1)
        indices.append(torch.multinomial(probability_vector, num_samples=1))
    indices = torch.stack(indices).squeeze().permute(1, 0)
    return indices
```

We need to transform the sampled indices from the `sample_from_model()` function into a string for human-readable output. As Example 7-8 demonstrates, to do this, we use the `SequenceVocabulary` that was used to vectorize the surnames. In creating the string, we use only the indices up to the `END-OF-SEQUENCE` index. This assumes that the model learns some sense of when surnames should end.

Example 7-8. Mapping sampled indices to surname strings

```
def decode_samples(sampled_indices, vectorizer):
    """Transform indices into the string form of a surname

    Args:
        sampled_indices (torch.Tensor): the indices from `sample_from_model`
        vectorizer (SurnameVectorizer): the corresponding vectorizer
    """
    decoded_surnames = []
    vocab = vectorizer.char_vocab

    for sample_index in range(sampled_indices.shape[0]):
        surname = ""
        for time_step in range(sampled_indices.shape[1]):
            sample_item = sampled_indices[sample_index, time_step].item()
            if sample_item == vocab.begin_seq_index:
                continue
            elif sample_item == vocab.end_seq_index:
                break
            else:
                surname += vocab.lookup_index(sample_item)
        decoded_surnames.append(surname)
    return decoded_surnames
```

Using these functions, you can inspect the output of the model, shown in Example 7-9, to get a sense of whether the model is learning to generate sensible surnames. What can we learn from inspecting the output? We can see that although the surnames appear to follow several morphological patterns, the names don't appear distinctly to be of one nationality or another. One possibility is that learning a general model of surnames confuses the character distributions between different nationalities. The conditioned SurnameGenerationModel is meant to handle this kind of situation.

Example 7-9. Sampling from the unconditioned model

| Input[0] | `samples = sample_from_model(unconditioned_model, vectorizer,`
`                      num_samples=10)`
`decode_samples(samples, vectorizer)` |

| Output[0] | `['Aqtaliby',`
` 'Yomaghev',`
` 'Mauasheev',`
` 'Unander',`
` 'Virrovo',`
` 'NInev',`
` 'Bukhumohe',`
` 'Burken',`
` 'Rati',`
` 'Jzirmar']` |

For the conditioned SurnameGenerationModel, we modify the sample_from_model() function to accept a list of nationality indices rather than a specified number of samples. In Example 7-10, the modified function uses the nationality indices with the nationality embedding to construct the initial hidden state of the GRU. After that, the sampling procedure is exactly the same as with the unconditioned model.

Example 7-10. Sampling from a sequence model

```python
def sample_from_model(model, vectorizer, nationalities, sample_size=20,
                      temperature=1.0):
    """Sample a sequence of indices from the model

    Args:
        model (SurnameGenerationModel): the trained model
        vectorizer (SurnameVectorizer): the corresponding vectorizer
        nationalities (list): a list of integers representing nationalities
        sample_size (int): the max length of the samples
        temperature (float): accentuates or flattens the distribution
            0.0 < temperature < 1.0 will make it peakier
            temperature > 1.0 will make it more uniform
    Returns:
        indices (torch.Tensor): the matrix of indices
        shape = (num_samples, sample_size)
    """
    num_samples = len(nationalities)
```

```
begin_seq_index = [vectorizer.char_vocab.begin_seq_index
                    for _ in range(num_samples)]
begin_seq_index = torch.tensor(begin_seq_index,
                               dtype=torch.int64).unsqueeze(dim=1)
indices = [begin_seq_index]
nationality_indices = torch.tensor(nationalities,
                                   dtype=torch.int64).unsqueeze(dim=0)
h_t = model.nation_emb(nationality_indices)

for time_step in range(sample_size):
    x_t = indices[time_step]
    x_emb_t = model.char_emb(x_t)
    rnn_out_t, h_t = model.rnn(x_emb_t, h_t)
    prediction_vector = model.fc(rnn_out_t.squeeze(dim=1))
    probability_vector = F.softmax(prediction_vector / temperature, dim=1)
    indices.append(torch.multinomial(probability_vector, num_samples=1))
indices = torch.stack(indices).squeeze().permute(1, 0)
return indices
```

The usefulness of sampling with a conditioning vector means that we have influence over the generated output. In Example 7-11, we iterate over the nationality indices and sample from each of them. To save space, we show only a few of the outputs. From these outputs, we can see that the model is indeed picking up on some patterns of orthography for surnames.

Example 7-11. Sampling from the conditioned SurnameGenerationModel (not all outputs are shown)

```
Input[0]    for index in range(len(vectorizer.nationality_vocab)):
                nationality = vectorizer.nationality_vocab.lookup_index(index)

                print("Sampled for {}: ".format(nationality))

                sampled_indices = sample_from_model(model=conditioned_model,
                                                    vectorizer=vectorizer,
                                                    nationalities=[index] * 3,
                                                    temperature=0.7)

                for sampled_surname in decode_samples(sampled_indices,
                                                      vectorizer):
                    print("-  " + sampled_surname)
```

```
Output[0]    Sampled for Arabic:
             -  Khatso
             -  Salbwa
             -  Gadi
             Sampled for Chinese:
             -  Lie
             -  Puh
             -  Pian
             Sampled for German:
             -  Lenger
             -  Schanger
             -  Schumper
             Sampled for Irish:
             -  Mcochin
             -  Corran
             -  O'Baintin
             Sampled for Russian:
             -  Mahghatsunkov
             -  Juhin
             -  Karkovin
             Sampled for Vietnamese:
             -  Lo
             -  Tham
             -  Tou
```

Tips and Tricks for Training Sequence Models

Sequence models can be challenging to train, and many issues crop up in the process. Here, we summarize a few tips and tricks that we have found useful in our work, and that others have reported in the literature.

When possible, use the gated variants
  Gated architectures simplify training by addressing many of the numerical stability issues of nongated variants.

When possible, prefer GRUs over LSTMs
  GRUs provide almost comparable performance to LSTMs and use far fewer parameters and compute resources. Fortunately, from the point of view of PyTorch, using a GRU rather than an LSTM simply requires using a different Module class.

Use Adam as your optimizer
  Throughout Chapters 6, 7, and 8, we use only Adam as the optimizer, for good reason: it is reliable and typically converges faster than the alternatives. This is especially true for sequence models. If for some reason your models are not converging with Adam, switching to stochastic gradient descent might help.

Gradient clipping

If you notice numerical errors in applying concepts learned in these chapters, instrument your code to plot the values of the gradients during training. After you know the range, clip any outliers. This will ensure smoother training. In PyTorch there is a helpful utility, `clip_grad_norm()`, to do this for you, as demonstrated in Example 7-12. In general, you should develop a habit of clipping gradients.

Example 7-12. Applying gradient clipping in PyTorch

```
# define your sequence model
model = ..
# define loss function
loss_function = ..

# training loop
for _ in ...:
    ...
    model.zero_grad()
    output, hidden = model(data, hidden)
    loss = loss_function(output, targets)
    loss.backward()
    torch.nn.utils.clip_grad_norm(model.parameters(), 0.25)
    ...
```

Early stopping

With sequence models, it is easy to overfit. We recommend that you stop the training procedure early, when the evaluation error, as measured on a development set, starts going up.

In Chapter 8 we continue the discussion of sequence models, exploring how to predict and generate sequences of lengths different from the input using sequence-to-sequence models and considering other variants.

References

1. Hochreiter, Sepp, and Jürgen Schmidhuber. (1997). "Long Short-Term Memory." *Neural Computation 15.*

2. Hochreiter, Sepp et al. (2001). "Gradient Flow in Recurrent Nets: The Difficulty of Learning Long-Term Dependencies." In *A Field Guide to Dynamical Recurrent Neural Networks.* IEEE Press.

3. Pascanu, Razvan, Tomas Mikolov, and Yoshua Bengio. (2013). "On the Difficulty of Training Recurrent Neural Networks." *Proceedings of the 30th International Conference on Machine Learning.*

4. Chung, Junyoung et al. (2015). "Gated Feedback Recurrent Neural Networks." *Proceedings of the 32nd International Concference on Machine Learning.*

Advanced Sequence Modeling for Natural Language Processing

In this chapter, we build on the sequence modeling concepts discussed in Chapters 6 and 7 and extend them to the realm of *sequence-to-sequence modeling*, where the model takes a sequence as input and produces another sequence, of possibly different length, as output. Examples of sequence-to-sequence problems occur everywhere. For example, we might want to, given an email, predict a response, given a French sentence, predict its English translation, or given an article, write an abstract summarizing the article. We also discuss structural variants of sequence models here: particularly, the bidirectional models. To get the most out of the sequence representation, we introduce the attention mechanism and discuss that in depth. Finally, this chapter ends with a detailed walkthrough of neural machine translation (NMT) that implements the concepts described herein.

Sequence-to-Sequence Models, Encoder–Decoder Models, and Conditioned Generation

Sequence-to-sequence (S2S) models are a special case of a general family of models called *encoder–decoder models*. An encoder–decoder model is a composition of two models (Figure 8-1), an "encoder" and a "decoder," that are typically jointly trained. The encoder model takes an input and produces an encoding or a representation (ϕ) of the input, which is usually a vector.[1] The goal of the encoder is to capture important properties of the input with respect to the task at hand. The goal of the decoder is to take the encoded input and produce a desired output. From this understanding

---

1 In this chapter, we reserve the symbol ϕ for encodings.

of encoders and decoders, we define S2S models as encoder–decoder models in which the encoder and decoder are sequence models and the inputs and outputs are both sequences, possibly of different lengths.

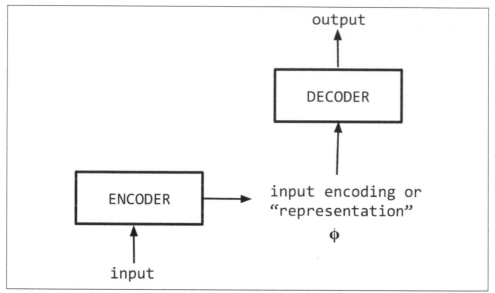

Figure 8-1. An encoder–decoder model is a composition of two models that are jointly trained. The encoder produces a representation or encoding of the input, φ, that's used by the decoder to produce an output.

One way to view encoder–decoder models is as a special case of models called *conditioned generation models*. In conditioned generation, instead of the input representation φ, a general conditioning context *c* influences a decoder to produce an output. When the conditioning context *c* comes from an encoder model, conditioned generation is same as an encoder–decoder model. Not all conditioned generation models are encoder–decoder models, because it is possible for the conditioning context to be derived from a structured source. Consider the example of a weather report generator. The values of the temperature, humidity, and wind speed and direction could "condition" a decoder to generate the textual weather report. In "Model 2: The Conditioned SurnameGenerationModel" on page 172, we saw an example of generation of surnames that were conditioned based on nationality. Figure 8-2 illustrates some real-world examples of conditioned generation models.

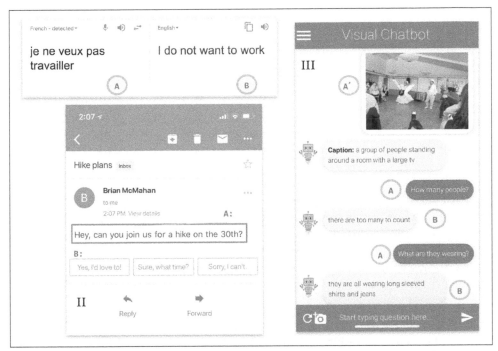

Figure 8-2. Examples of tasks solved by encoder–decoder models include machine translation (top left: the input A is a French sentence and the output B is an English sentence) and email reply suggestions (bottom left: the input A is the text of the email; the output B is one of the many possible replies). The example on the right is a little more complex: here a chatbot is answering questions, marked by A, about an input image (A') by conditioning the generation of the response (B) on encodings of both A and A'. All of these tasks can also be viewed as conditioned generation tasks.

In this chapter, we study S2S models in depth and illustrate their use in the context of a machine translation task. Consider a "smart" iOS/Android keyboard that automatically turns your texts into emojis as you type. A single token in the input can produce zero or more tokens in the output. For example, if you type "omg the house is on fire," you want the keyboard to output something like 🌋 🏠 ↔️ 🔥. Notice the output has a different length (four tokens) than the input (six tokens). The mapping between the output and the input is called an *alignment*, which you can see illustrated in Figure 8-3.

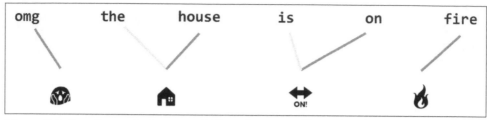

Figure 8-3. Emoji translation as an S2S prediction problem: the alignments between the tokens in the two sequences are indicative of translational equivalences.

Traditionally, many solutions to S2S problems were attempted with engineering and heuristic-heavy statistical approaches. Although reviewing those approaches is beyond the scope of this chapter, we recommend that you read Koehn (2009) and consult the resources listed at *statmt.org*. In Chapter 6, we learned how a sequence model can encode a sequence of arbitrary length into a vector. In Chapter 7, we saw how a single vector can bias a recurrent neural network to conditionally generate different surnames. The S2S models are a natural extension of these concepts.

Figure 8-4 shows the encoder "encoding" the entire input into a representation, ϕ, that conditions the decoder to generate the right output. You can use any RNN as an encoder, be it an Elman RNN, LSTM, or GRU. In the next two sections, we introduce two vital components of modern-day S2S models. First, we look at the bidirectional recurrent model that combines forward and backward passes over a sequence to create richer representations. Then, in "Capturing More from a Sequence: Attention" on page 189, we introduce and survey the attention mechanism, which is useful in focusing on different parts of the input that are relevant to the task. Both sections are vital for building nontrivial S2S model–based solutions.

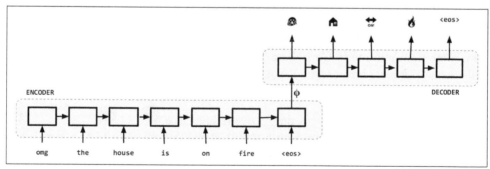

Figure 8-4. An S2S model for translating English to emoji.

Capturing More from a Sequence: Bidirectional Recurrent Models

One way to understand a recurrent model is to look at it as a black box that encodes a sequence into a vector. When modeling a sequence, it is useful to observe not just the words in the past but also the words that appear in the future.[2] Consider the following sentence:[3]

```
The man who hunts ducks out on the weekends.
```

If the model were to observe only from left to right, its representation for "ducks"[4] would be different from that of a model that had also observed the words from right to left. Humans do this sort of retroactive meaning updating all the time.

Taken together, information from the past and the future will be able to robustly represent the meaning of a word in a sequence. This is the goal of bidirectional recurrent models. Any of the models in the recurrent family, such as Elmann RNNs, LSTMs, or GRUs, could be used in such a bidirectional formulation. Bidirectional models, like their unidirectional counterparts seen in Chapters 6 and 7, can be used in both classification and sequence labeling settings, for which we need to predict one label per word in the input.

Figure 8-5 and Figure 8-6 illustrate this in detail.

In Figure 8-5, notice how the model "reads" the sentence in both directions, and produces a sentential representation ϕ that's a composition of the forward and backward representations. What's not shown here is the final classification layer consisting of a Linear layer and a softmax.

The ϕ_{love} in Figure 8-6 is the representation or encoding of the "hidden state" of the network at that time step when the input is the word "love." This state information becomes important in "Capturing More from a Sequence: Attention" on page 189 when we discuss attention.

Notice how there is a "forward" representation and a "backward" representation for each word in the input, which are concatenated to produce the final representation for the word in question. What's not shown here is the final classification layer, consisting of a Linear layer and a softmax, at each time step.

---

2 This is not possible for streaming applications, but a large number of practical applications of NLP happen in a batch (nonstreaming) context anyway.

3 Sentences like the one in this example are called *garden-path sentences* (*https://en.wikipedia.org/wiki/Garden_path_sentence*). Such sentences are more common than one would imagine; for example, newspaper headlines use such constructs regularly.

4 Consider the two meanings of "duck": (i) □ (noun, quack quack) and (ii) evade (verb).

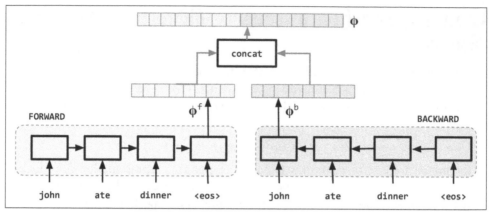

Figure 8-5. The bidirectional RNN model used for sequence classification.

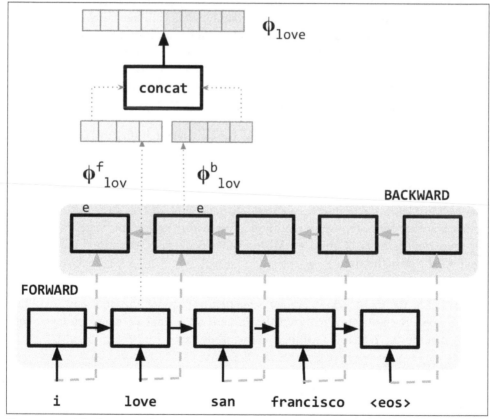

Figure 8-6. A bidirectional recurrent model for sequence labeling.

Capturing More from a Sequence: Attention

One problem with the S2S model formulation introduced in "Sequence-to-Sequence Models, Encoder–Decoder Models, and Conditioned Generation" on page 183 is that it crams ("encodes") the entire input sentence into a single vector, ϕ, and uses that encoding to generate the output, as illustrated in Figure 8-7. Although this might work with very short sentences, for long sentences such models fail to capture the information in the entire input.[5] This is a limitation of using just the final hidden state as the encoding. Another problem with long inputs is that the gradients vanish when back-propagating through time, making the training difficult.

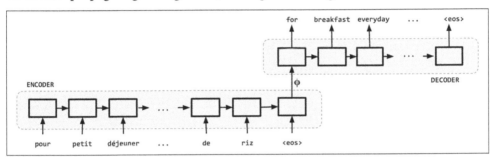

Figure 8-7. Translating a long French sentence to English with an encoder–decoder model. The final representation, ϕ, fails to capture long-range dependencies in the input and makes the training difficult.

This process of encode-first-then-decode might appear a little strange to bilingual/ multilingual readers who have ever attempted to translate. As humans, we don't usually distill the meaning of a sentence and generate the translation from the meaning. For the example in Figure 8-7, when we see the French word *pour* we know there will be a *for*; similarly, *breakfast* is on our mind when we see *petit-déjeuner*, and so on. In other words, our minds focus on the relevant parts of the input while producing output. This phenomenon is called *attention*. Attention has been widely studied in neuroscience and other allied fields, and it is what makes us quite successful despite having limited memories. Attention happens everywhere. In fact, it is happening right now to you, dear reader. Each. Word. You. Are. Reading. Now. Is. Being. Attended. To. Even if you have an exceptional memory, you're probably not reading this entire book as a string. When you read a word, you pay attention to the neighboring words, possibly the topic of the section and chapter, and so on.

In an analogous fashion, we would like our sequence generation models to incorporate attention to different parts of the input and not just the final summary of the entire input. This is called the *attention mechanism*. The first models to incorporate a

---

5 For example, see Bengio et al. (1994) and Le and Zuidema (2016).

notion of attention for natural language processing were, incidentally, machine translation models by Bahdanau et al. (2015). Since then, several kinds of attention mechanisms and several approaches to improving attention have been proposed. In this section, we review some of the basic attention mechanisms and introduce some terminology related to attention. Attention has proven extremely useful in improving the performance of deep learning systems with complex inputs and complex outputs. In fact, Bahdanau et al. show that the performance of a machine translation system, as measured by "BLEU score" (which we look at in "Evaluating Sequence Generation Models" on page 193), degrades without an attention mechanism as the inputs become longer, as demonstrated in Figure 8-8. Adding attention solves the problem.

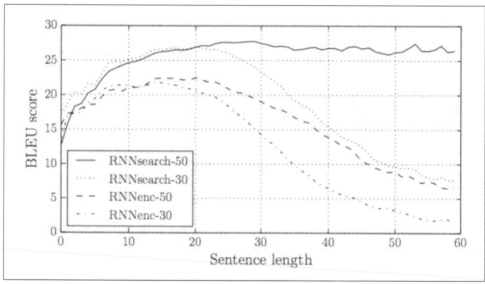

Figure 8-8. Why attention is needed. The chart shows the changes in BLEU scores of machine translation systems with (RNNsearch-30, RNNsearch-50) and without (RNNenc-30, RNNenc-50) attention. The RNN*-30 and RNN*-50 systems were trained with sentences with length up to 30 and 50 words, respectively. In machine translation systems, without attention, the performance of the system degrades as the length of the sentences increases. With attention, the translation for longer sentences improves but the stability of the machine translation performance is relative to the length of the sentences on which it is trained. (Figure courtesy of Bahdanau et al. [2015].)

Attention in Deep Neural Networks

Attention is a general mechanism and could be used with any of the models discussed earlier in the book. But we describe it here in the context of encoder–decoder models because these models are where attention mechanisms have really shone. Consider an S2S model. Recall that in a typical S2S model, each time step produces a hidden state representation, denoted as ϕ_w, specific to that time step in the encoder. (This is illustrated in Figure 8-6.) To incorporate attention, we consider not only the final hidden state of the encoder, but also the hidden states for each of the intermediate steps. These encoder hidden states are, somewhat uninformatively, called *values* (or in some situations, *keys*). Attention also depends on the previous hidden state of the decoder, called the *query*.[6] Figure 8-9 illustrates all of this for time step 0. The query vector for time step $t=0$ is a fixed hyperparameter. Attention is represented by a vector with the same dimension as the number of values it is attending to. This is called the *attention vector*, or *attention weights*, or sometimes *alignment*. The attention weights are combined with the encoder states ("values") to generate a *context vector* that's sometimes also known as a *glimpse*. This context vector becomes the input for the decoder instead of the full sentence encoding. The attention vector for the next time step is updated using a *compatibility function*. The exact nature of the compatibility function depends on the attention mechanism being used.

There are several ways to implement attention. The simplest and the most commonly used is the *content-aware* mechanism. You can see content-aware attention in action in "Example: Neural Machine Translation" on page 195. Another popular attention mechanism is *location-aware* attention, which depends only on the query vector and the key. The attention weights are typically floating-point values between 0 and 1. This is called *soft attention*. In contrast, it is possible to learn a binary 0/1 vector for attention. This is called *hard attention*.

The attention mechanism illustrated in Figure 8-9 depends on the encoder states for all the time steps in the input. This is also known as *global attention*. In contrast, for *local attention*, you could devise an attention mechanism that depended only on a window of the input around the current time step.

---

6 The terminology of *keys*, *values*, and *queries* can be quite confusing for the beginner, but we introduce it here anyway because these terms have now become a standard. It is worth reading this section a few times, until these concepts become clear. This terminology was introduced because attention was initially thought of as a search task. For an extended review of these concepts and attention in general, see Lilian Weng's article *"Attention? Attention!"* (*https://lilianweng.github.io/lil-log/2018/06/24/attention-attention.html*).

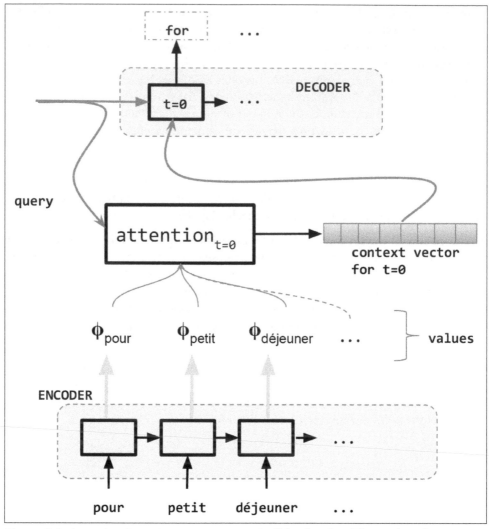

Figure 8-9. Attention in action at time step t=0 of the decoder. The predicted output is "for" and the attention block takes into account the hidden states of the encoder ϕ_w for all input words.

Sometimes, especially in machine translation, the alignment information could be explicitly provided as a part of the training data. In such situations, a *supervised attention* mechanism could be devised to learn the attention function using a separate neural network that's jointly trained. For large inputs such as documents, it is possible to design a coarse- to fine-grained (or *hierarchical*) attention mechanism, that not only focuses on the immediate input but also takes into account the structure of the document—paragraph, section, chapter, and so on.

The work on transformer networks by Vaswani et al. (2017) introduces *multiheaded attention*, in which multiple attention vectors are used to track different regions of the input. They also popularized the concept of *self-attention*, a mechanism whereby the model learns which regions of the input influence one another.

When the input is multimodal—for example, both image and speech—it is possible to design a *multimodal* attention mechanism. The literature on attention, although new, is already vast, indicating the importance of this topic. Covering each of the approaches in detail is beyond the scope of this book, and we direct you to Luong, Pham, and Manning (2015) and Vaswani et al. (2017) as a starting point.

Evaluating Sequence Generation Models

Classification metrics such as precision, recall, accuracy, and F1 do not help models when multiple valid answers are possible, as seen in the generation task—a single French sentence can have multiple English translations. Sequence models are evaluated against an expected output called a *reference output*. When comparing different models, we use scores that indicate "goodness"—that is, how close the model's output is to the reference. For example, in a task like machine translation, if a model is off by just one word, we might not want to penalize that model as much as another model that produces a completely unintelligible answer. It is possible to have multiple reference outputs for a single input example, as in the case of multiple valid English translations using slightly different words for a specific French sentence. There are two kinds of evaluation for sequence generation models: human evaluation and automatic evaluation.

Human evaluation for machine translation involves one or more human subjects either giving a "thumbs up" or "thumbs down" rating for the model output or making edits to correct the translation. This leads to a simple "error rate" that's very close to the final goal of the system's output being relevant to the human task. Human evaluation is important but is used sparingly because human annotators tend to be slow, expensive, and difficult to come by. It is also possible for humans to be inconsistent with one another, so, like any other gold standard, human evaluation is paired with an *inter-annotator agreement rate*. Measuring the inter-annotator agreement rate is another expensive proposition. One common human evaluation metric is the human-targeted translation error rate (HTER), a weighted edit distance computed by counting the number of insertions, deletions, and transpositions made by a human to "fix" the translation output to achieve a reasonable adequacy of meaning and fluency (see Figure 8-10).

Judge Sentence

You have already judged 14 of 3064 sentences, taking 86.4 seconds per sentence.

Source: les deux pays constituent plutôt un laboratoire nécessaire au fonctionnement interne de l'ue .

Reference: rather , the two countries form a laboratory needed for the internal working of the eu .

Translation	Adequacy	Fluency
both countries are rather a necessary laboratory the internal operation of the eu .	⬤ 1 2 3 4 5	⬤ 1 2 3 4 5
both countries are a necessary laboratory at internal functioning of the eu .	1 2 3 4 5	1 2 3 4 5
the two countries are rather a laboratory necessary for the internal workings of the eu .	1 2 3 4 5	1 2 3 4 5
the two countries are rather a laboratory for the internal workings of the eu .	1 2 3 4 5	1 2 3 4 5
the two countries are rather a necessary laboratory internal workings of the eu .	1 2 3 4 5	1 2 3 4 5
Annotator: Philipp Koehn **Task:** WMT06 French-English		Annotate
Instructions	5= All Meaning 4= Most Meaning 3= Much Meaning 2= Little Meaning 1= None	5= Flawless English 4= Good English 3= Non-native English 2= Disfluent English 1= Incomprehensible

Figure 8-10. Human evaluation in progress for a translation task (courtesy of Philipp Koehn).

Automatic evaluation, on the other hand, is easy and fast to execute. There are two kinds of metrics for automated evaluation of generated sequences: *n-gram overlap–based metrics* and *perplexity*. We again use machine translation as an example, but these metrics also apply to any task that involves generating sequences. *N*-gram overlap–based metrics tend to measure how close an output is with respect to a reference by computing a score using ngram overlap statistics. BLEU, ROUGE, and METEOR are examples of *n*-gram overlap–based metrics. Of these, BLEU (which stands for "BiLingual Evaluation Understudy") has stood the test of time as the metric of choice in machine translation literature.[7] We skip the exact formulation of BLEU here and recommend that you read Papineni et al. (2002). For practical purposes, we use a

---

7 So much that the original 2002 paper that proposed BLEU received a Test-of-Time award (*https://naacl2018.wordpress.com/2018/03/22/test-of-time-award-papers/*) in 2018.

package like NLTK[8] or SacreBLEU[9] to compute the scores. The computation of BLEU itself is quite fast and easy when reference data is available.

Perplexity is the other automatic evaluation metric based on information theory, and you can apply it to any situation in which you can measure the probability of the output sequence. For a sequence x, if $P(x)$ is the probability of the sequence, perplexity is defined as follows:

$$\text{Perplexity}(x) = 2^{-P(x)\log P(x)}$$

This gives us a simple way to compare different sequence generation models—measure the perplexity of the model for a held-out dataset. Although this is easy to compute, perplexity has many problems when used for sequence generation evaluation. First, it is an inflated metric. Notice that the expression for perplexity involves exponentiation. As a result, minor differences in model performance (likelihoods) can lead to large differences in perplexity, giving an illusion of significant progress. Second, changes to perplexity might not translate into corresponding changes in error rates of the models as observed via other metrics. Finally, like BLEU and other ngram-based metrics, improvements in perplexity might not translate to perceptible improvements as judged by humans.

In the next section, we follow up with a machine translation example and neatly tie these concepts together via a PyTorch implementation.

Example: Neural Machine Translation

In this section, we walk through an implementation of the most common use of S2S models: machine translation. As deep learning grew in popularity in the early 2010s, it became apparent that using word embeddings and RNNs was an extremely powerful methodology for translating between two languages—provided there was enough data. Machine translation models were further improved with the introduction of the attention mechanism described "Evaluating Sequence Generation Models" on page 193. In this section, we describe an implementation based on Luong, Pham, and Manning (2015), which simplified the attention approach in S2S models.

We begin by outlining the dataset and the special kinds of bookkeeping needed for neural machine translation. The dataset is a parallel corpus; it is composed of pairs of English sentences and their corresponding French translations. Because we are dealing with two sequences of potentially different lengths, we need to keep track of the

---

8 For an example, see *https://github.com/nltk/nltk/blob/develop/nltk/translate/bleu_score.py*.

9 SacreBLEU (*https://github.com/mjpost/sacreBLEU*) is the standard when it comes to machine translation evaluation.

maximum lengths and vocabularies of both the input sequence and the output sequence. For the most part, this example is a straightforward extension to what the thorough reader will have seen in previous chapters.

After covering the dataset and the bookkeeping data structures, we walk through the model and how it generates the target sequence by attending to different positions in the source sequence. The encoder in our model uses a bidirectional gated recurrent unit (bi-GRU) to compute vectors for each position in the source sequence that are informed by all parts of the sequence. To accomplish this, we use PyTorch's `PackedSe quence` data structure. We cover this in more depth in "Encoding and Decoding in the NMT Model" on page 201. The attention mechanism, discussed in "Capturing More from a Sequence: Attention" on page 189, is applied to the output of the bi-GRU and used to condition the target sequence generation. We discuss the results of the model and the ways it could be improved in "The Training Routine and Results" on page 212.

The Machine Translation Dataset

For this example, we use a dataset of English–French sentence pairs from the Tatoeba Project.[10] The data preprocessing begins by making all sentences lowercase and applying NLTK's English and French tokenizers to each of the sentence pairs. Next, we apply NLTK's language-specific word tokenizer to create a list of tokens. Even though we do further computations, which we describe next, this list of tokens is a preprocessed dataset.

In addition to the just-described standard preprocessing, we use a specified list of syntactic patterns to select a subset of the data in order to simplify the learning problem. In essence, this means that we are narrowing the scope of the data to be only a limited range of syntactic patterns. In turn, this means that during training, the model will see less variation and have higher performance in a shorter training time.

When building new models and experimenting with new architectures, you should aim for quicker iteration cycles between modeling choices and evaluating those choices.

The subset of the data we select consists of the English sentences that begin with "i am," "he is," "she is," "they are," "you are," or "we are."[11] This reduces the dataset

---

10 The dataset was retrieved from *http://www.manythings.org/anki/*.

11 We also include the cases in which these subject-verb pairs are contractions, such as "i'm," "we're," and "he's."

from 135,842 sentence pairs to just 13,062 sentence pairs, a factor of 10.[12] To finalize the learning setup, we split the remaining 13,062 sentence pairs into 70% training, 15% validation, and 15% test sets. The proportion of each sentence beginning with the just listed syntax is held constant by first grouping by sentence beginning, creating the splits from those groups, and then merging the splits from each group.

A Vectorization Pipeline for NMT

Vectorizing the source English and target French sentences requires a more complex pipeline than we have seen in previous chapters. There are two reasons for the increase in complexity. First, the source and target sequences have different roles in the model, belong to different languages, and are vectorized in two different ways. Second, as a prerequisite to use PyTorch's PackedSequences, we must sort each mini-batch by the length of the source sentences.[13] To prepare for these two complexities, the NMTVectorizer is instantiated with two separate SequenceVocabulary objects and two measurements of max sequence length, as shown in Example 8-1.

Example 8-1. Constructing the NMTVectorizer

```
class NMTVectorizer(object):
    """ The Vectorizer which coordinates the Vocabularies and puts them to use"""
    def __init__(self, source_vocab, target_vocab, max_source_length,
                 max_target_length):
        """
        Args:
            source_vocab (SequenceVocabulary): maps source words to integers
            target_vocab (SequenceVocabulary): maps target words to integers
            max_source_length (int): the longest sequence in the source dataset
            max_target_length (int): the longest sequence in the target dataset
        """
        self.source_vocab = source_vocab
        self.target_vocab = target_vocab

        self.max_source_length = max_source_length
        self.max_target_length = max_target_length

    @classmethod
    def from_dataframe(cls, bitext_df):
        """Instantiate the vectorizer from the dataset dataframe

        Args:
```

---

12 This simply means that the model will be able to see the entire dataset 10 times faster. It doesn't exactly follow that the convergence will happen in one-tenth the time, because it could be that the model needs to see this dataset for a smaller number of epochs, or some other confounding factor.

13 Sorting the sequences in order takes advantage of a low-level CUDA primitive for RNNs.

```
        bitext_df (pandas.DataFrame): the parallel text dataset
    Returns:
        an instance of the NMTVectorizer
    """
    source_vocab = SequenceVocabulary()
    target_vocab = SequenceVocabulary()
    max_source_length, max_target_length = 0, 0

    for _, row in bitext_df.iterrows():
        source_tokens = row["source_language"].split(" ")
        if len(source_tokens) > max_source_length:
            max_source_length = len(source_tokens)
        for token in source_tokens:
            source_vocab.add_token(token)

        target_tokens = row["target_language"].split(" ")
        if len(target_tokens) > max_target_length:
            max_target_length = len(target_tokens)
        for token in target_tokens:
            target_vocab.add_token(token)

    return cls(source_vocab, target_vocab, max_source_length,
               max_target_length)
```

The first increase in complexity is in the different ways in which the source and target sequences are handled. The source sequence is vectorized with the BEGIN-OF-SEQUENCE token inserted at the beginning and the END-OF-SEQUENCE token added to the end. The model uses a bi-GRU to create summary vectors for each token in the source sentence, and these summary vectors greatly benefit from having an indication of sentence boundaries. In contrast, the target sequence is vectorized as two copies offset by one token: the first copy needs the BEGIN-OF-SEQUENCE token and the second copy needs the END-OF-SEQUENCE token. If you recall from Chapter 7, sequence prediction tasks require observations of the input token and output token at every time step. The decoder in an S2S model is performing this task, but with the added availability of the encoder context. To address this complexity, we make the core vectorization method, _vectorize(), indifferent to whether it is the source or target indices. Then, two methods are written to handle the source and target indices separately. Finally, these sets of indices are coordinated by using the NMTVector izer.vectorize method, which is the method invoked by the dataset. Example 8-2 shows the code.

Example 8-2. The vectorization functions in the NMTVectorizer

```
class NMTVectorizer(object):
    """ The Vectorizer which coordinates the Vocabularies and puts them to use"""
    def _vectorize(self, indices, vector_length=-1, mask_index=0):
        """Vectorize the provided indices
```

```
    Args:
        indices (list): a list of integers that represent a sequence
        vector_length (int): forces the length of the index vector
        mask_index (int): the mask_index to use; almost always 0
    """
    if vector_length < 0:
        vector_length = len(indices)
    vector = np.zeros(vector_length, dtype=np.int64)
    vector[:len(indices)] = indices
    vector[len(indices):] = mask_index
    return vector

def _get_source_indices(self, text):
    """Return the vectorized source text

    Args:
        text (str): the source text; tokens should be separated by spaces
    Returns:
        indices (list): list of integers representing the text
    """
    indices = [self.source_vocab.begin_seq_index]
    indices.extend(self.source_vocab.lookup_token(token)
                for token in text.split(" "))
    indices.append(self.source_vocab.end_seq_index)
    return indices

def _get_target_indices(self, text):
    """Return the vectorized source text

    Args:
        text (str): the source text; tokens should be separated by spaces
    Returns:
        a tuple: (x_indices, y_indices)
            x_indices (list): list of ints; observations in target decoder
            y_indices (list): list of ints; predictions in target decoder
    """
    indices = [self.target_vocab.lookup_token(token)
                for token in text.split(" ")]
    x_indices = [self.target_vocab.begin_seq_index] + indices
    y_indices = indices + [self.target_vocab.end_seq_index]
    return x_indices, y_indices

def vectorize(self, source_text, target_text, use_dataset_max_lengths=True):
    """Return the vectorized source and target text

    Args:
        source_text (str): text from the source language
        target_text (str): text from the target language
        use_dataset_max_lengths (bool): whether to use the max vector lengths
    Returns:
        The vectorized data point as a dictionary with the keys:
```

```
            source_vector, target_x_vector, target_y_vector, source_length
    """
    source_vector_length = -1
    target_vector_length = -1

    if use_dataset_max_lengths:
        source_vector_length = self.max_source_length + 2
        target_vector_length = self.max_target_length + 1

    source_indices = self._get_source_indices(source_text)
    source_vector = self._vectorize(source_indices,
                                    vector_length=source_vector_length,
                                    mask_index=self.source_vocab.mask_index)

    target_x_indices, target_y_indices = self._get_target_indices
    (target_text)
    target_x_vector = self._vectorize(target_x_indices,
                                    vector_length=target_vector_length,
                                    mask_index=self.target_vocab.mask_index)
    target_y_vector = self._vectorize(target_y_indices,
                                    vector_length=target_vector_length,
                                    mask_index=self.target_vocab.mask_index)
    return {"source_vector": source_vector,
            "target_x_vector": target_x_vector,
            "target_y_vector": target_y_vector,
            "source_length": len(source_indices)}
```

The second increase in complexity arises again from the source sequence. To encode the source sequence using a bi-GRU, we use PyTorch's PackedSequence data structure. Normally, a minibatch of variable-length sequences is represented numerically as rows in a matrix of integers in which each sequence is left aligned and zero-padded to accommodate the variable lengths. The PackedSequence data structure represents variable-length sequences as an array by concatenating the data for the sequences at each time step, one after another, and knowing the number of sequences at each time step, as shown in Figure 8-11.

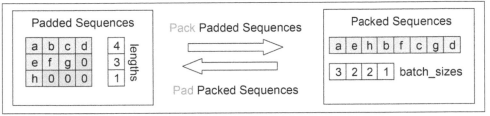

Figure 8-11. A matrix of padded sequences and its lengths are shown on the left. The padded matrix is the standard way of representing variable-length sequences, by right-padding them with zeroes and stacking them as row vectors. In PyTorch, we can pack the padded sequences into a terser representation, the PackedSequence, shown on the right along with the batch sizes. This representation allows the GPU to step through the sequence by keeping track of how many sequences are in each time step (the batch sizes).

There are two prerequisites for creating a `PackedSequence`: knowing the length of each sequence, and sorting the sequences in descending order by the length of the source sequence. To reflect this newly sorted matrix, the remaining tensors in the minibatch are sorted in the same order so that they stay aligned with the source sequence encoding. In Example 8-3, the `generate_batches()` function is modified to become the `generate_nmt_batches()` function.

Example 8-3. Generating minibatches for the NMT example

```
def generate_nmt_batches(dataset, batch_size, shuffle=True,
                         drop_last=True, device="cpu"):
    """A generator function which wraps the PyTorch DataLoader; NMT version """
    dataloader = DataLoader(dataset=dataset, batch_size=batch_size,
                            shuffle=shuffle, drop_last=drop_last)

    for data_dict in dataloader:
        lengths = data_dict['x_source_length'].numpy()
        sorted_length_indices = lengths.argsort()[::-1].tolist()

        out_data_dict = {}
        for name, tensor in data_dict.items():
            out_data_dict[name] = data_dict[name][sorted_length_indices].to(device)
        yield out_data_dict
```

Encoding and Decoding in the NMT Model

In this example, we start with a source sequence—an English sentence—and we produce a target sequence—the corresponding French translation. The standard approach is to use the encoder–decoder models as described in "Sequence-to-Sequence Models, Encoder–Decoder Models, and Conditioned Generation" on page

183. In the model presented in Example 8-4 and Example 8-5, the encoder first maps each source sequence to a sequence of vector states with a bi-GRU (see "Capturing More from a Sequence: Bidirectional Recurrent Models" on page 187). Then, the decoder starts with the encoder's hidden states as its initial hidden state and uses an attention mechanism (see "Capturing More from a Sequence: Attention" on page 189) to select different information in the source sequence to generate an output sequence. In the remainder of this section, we explain this process in more detail.

Example 8-4. The NMTModel encapsulates and coordinates the encoder and decoder in a single forward() method

```python
class NMTModel(nn.Module):
    """ A Neural Machine Translation Model """
    def __init__(self, source_vocab_size, source_embedding_size,
                 target_vocab_size, target_embedding_size, encoding_size,
                 target_bos_index):
        """
        Args:
            source_vocab_size (int): number of unique words in source language
            source_embedding_size (int): size of the source embedding vectors
            target_vocab_size (int): number of unique words in target language
            target_embedding_size (int): size of the target embedding vectors
            encoding_size (int): size of the encoder RNN
            target_bos_index (int): index for BEGIN-OF-SEQUENCE token
        """
        super(NMTModel, self).__init__()
        self.encoder = NMTEncoder(num_embeddings=source_vocab_size,
                                  embedding_size=source_embedding_size,
                                  rnn_hidden_size=encoding_size)
        decoding_size = encoding_size * 2
        self.decoder = NMTDecoder(num_embeddings=target_vocab_size,
                                  embedding_size=target_embedding_size,
                                  rnn_hidden_size=decoding_size,
                                  bos_index=target_bos_index)

    def forward(self, x_source, x_source_lengths, target_sequence):
        """The forward pass of the model

        Args:
            x_source (torch.Tensor): the source text data tensor
                x_source.shape should be (batch, vectorizer.max_source_length)
            x_source_lengths torch.Tensor): the length of the sequences in x_source
            target_sequence (torch.Tensor): the target text data tensor
        Returns:
            decoded_states (torch.Tensor): prediction vectors at each output step
        """
        encoder_state, final_hidden_states = self.encoder(x_source,
                                                          x_source_lengths)
        decoded_states = self.decoder(encoder_state=encoder_state,
                                      initial_hidden_state=final_hidden_states,
```

```
                              target_sequence=target_sequence)
        return decoded_states
```

Example 8-5. The encoder embeds the source words and extracts features with a bi-GRU

```
class NMTEncoder(nn.Module):
    def __init__(self, num_embeddings, embedding_size, rnn_hidden_size):
        """
        Args:
            num_embeddings (int): size of source vocabulary
            embedding_size (int): size of the embedding vectors
            rnn_hidden_size (int): size of the RNN hidden state vectors
        """
        super(NMTEncoder, self).__init__()

        self.source_embedding = nn.Embedding(num_embeddings, embedding_size,
                                             padding_idx=0)
        self.birnn = nn.GRU(embedding_size, rnn_hidden_size, bidirectional=True,
                            batch_first=True)

    def forward(self, x_source, x_lengths):
        """The forward pass of the model

        Args:
            x_source (torch.Tensor): the input data tensor
                x_source.shape is (batch, seq_size)
            x_lengths (torch.Tensor): vector of lengths for each item in batch
        Returns:
            a tuple: x_unpacked (torch.Tensor), x_birnn_h (torch.Tensor)
                x_unpacked.shape = (batch, seq_size, rnn_hidden_size * 2)
                x_birnn_h.shape = (batch, rnn_hidden_size * 2)
        """
        x_embedded = self.source_embedding(x_source)
        # create PackedSequence; x_packed.data.shape=(number_items,
        #              embedding_size)
        x_lengths = x_lengths.detach().cpu().numpy()
        x_packed = pack_padded_sequence(x_embedded, x_lengths, batch_first=True)

        # x_birnn_h.shape = (num_rnn, batch_size, feature_size)
        x_birnn_out, x_birnn_h  = self.birnn(x_packed)
        # permute to (batch_size, num_rnn, feature_size)
        x_birnn_h = x_birnn_h.permute(1, 0, 2)

        # flatten features; reshape to (batch_size, num_rnn * feature_size)
        #  (recall: -1 takes the remaining positions,
        #           flattening the two RNN hidden vectors into 1)
        x_birnn_h = x_birnn_h.contiguous().view(x_birnn_h.size(0), -1)

        x_unpacked, _ = pad_packed_sequence(x_birnn_out, batch_first=True)
        return x_unpacked, x_birnn_h
```

In general, the encoder takes as input a sequence of integers and creates a feature vector for each position. The output of the encoder in this example is these vectors and the final hidden state of the bi-GRU that is used to make the feature vectors. This hidden state is used to initialize the hidden state of the decoder in the next section.

Diving deeper into the encoder, we first embed the input sequence using an embedding layer. Usually, just by setting the `padding_idx` flag on the embedding layer, we enable the model to handle variable-length sequences because any position that equals `padding_idx` is given a zero-valued vector, which does not update during optimization. Recall that this is called the *mask*. However, in this encoder–decoder model, masked positions need to be handled differently because we use a bi-GRU to encode the source sequence. The primary reason is that the backward component can be influenced by the masked positions, with a factor proportional to the number of masked positions it encounters before it starts on the sequence.[14]

To handle the masked positions of variable-length sequences in the bi-GRU, we use PyTorch's `PackedSequence` data structure. `PackedSequences` are derived from how CUDA allows for the handling of variable-length sequences in a batched format. Any zero-padded sequence, such as the embedded source sequence in the encoder presented in Example 8-6, can be converted to a `PackedSequence` if two conditions are met: the length of each sequence is provided, and the minibatch is sorted according to the length of those sequences. This was shown visually in Figure 8-11, and because it is a complex topic, we demonstrate it again in Example 8-6 and its output.[15]

Example 8-6. A simple demonstration of packed_padded_sequences and pad_packed_sequences

```
Input[0]    abcd_padded = torch.tensor([1, 2, 3, 4], dtype=torch.float32)
            efg_padded = torch.tensor([5, 6, 7, 0], dtype=torch.float32)
            h_padded = torch.tensor([8, 0, 0, 0], dtype=torch.float32)

            padded_tensor = torch.stack([abcd_padded, efg_padded, h_padded])

            describe(padded_tensor)
```

---

14 You should try to convince yourself of this by either visualizing the computations or drawing them out. As a hint, consider the single recurrent step: the input and last hidden state are weighted and added together with the bias. If the input is all 0's, what effect does the bias have on the output?

15 We utilize the `describe()` function shown in "Creating Tensors" on page 13.

```
Output[0]    Type: torch.FloatTensor
             Shape/size: torch.Size([3, 4])
             Values:
             tensor([[ 1.,   2.,   3.,   4.],
                     [ 5.,   6.,   7.,   0.],
                     [ 8.,   0.,   0.,   0.]])
```

```
Input[1]     lengths = [4, 3, 1]
             packed_tensor = pack_padded_sequence(padded_tensor, lengths,
                                                  batch_first=True)

             packed_tensor
```

```
Output[1]    PackedSequence(data=tensor([ 1.,   5.,   8.,   2.,   6.,   3.,   7.,   4.]),
                            batch_sizes=tensor([ 3,   2,   2,   1]))
```

```
Input[2]     unpacked_tensor, unpacked_lengths = \
                 pad_packed_sequence(packed_tensor, batch_first=True)

             describe(unpacked_tensor)
             describe(unpacked_lengths)
```

```
Output[2]    Type: torch.FloatTensor
             Shape/size: torch.Size([3, 4])
             Values:
             tensor([[ 1.,   2.,   3.,   4.],
                     [ 5.,   6.,   7.,   0.],
                     [ 8.,   0.,   0.,   0.]])
             Type: torch.LongTensor
             Shape/size: torch.Size([3])
             Values:
             tensor([ 4,   3,   1])
```

We handle the sorting when generating each minibatch as described in the previous section. Then, as shown in Example 8-7, PyTorch's `pack_padded_sequence()` function is evoked by passing the embedded sequences, the lengths of the sequences, and a Boolean flag indicating that the 1st dimension is the batch dimension. The output of this function is a `PackedSequence`. The resulting `PackedSequence` is input into the bi-GRU to create state vectors for the downstream decoder. The output of the bi-GRU is unpacked into a full tensor using another Boolean flag indicating that batch is on the first dimension. The unpacking operation, as illustrated in Figure 8-11, sets each masked position[16] to be a zero-valued vector, preserving the integrity of downstream computations.

---

16 Starting from left to right on the sequence dimension, any position past the known length of the sequence is assumed to be masked.

Example 8-7. The NMTDecoder constructs a target sentence from the encoded source sentence

```python
class NMTDecoder(nn.Module):
    def __init__(self, num_embeddings, embedding_size, rnn_hidden_size, bos_index):
        """
        Args:
            num_embeddings (int): number of embeddings; also the number of
                unique words in the target vocabulary
            embedding_size (int): size of the embedding vector
            rnn_hidden_size (int): size of the hidden RNN state
            bos_index(int): BEGIN-OF-SEQUENCE index
        """
        super(NMTDecoder, self).__init__()
        self._rnn_hidden_size = rnn_hidden_size
        self.target_embedding = nn.Embedding(num_embeddings=num_embeddings,
                                             embedding_dim=embedding_size,
                                             padding_idx=0)
        self.gru_cell = nn.GRUCell(embedding_size + rnn_hidden_size,
                                   rnn_hidden_size)
        self.hidden_map = nn.Linear(rnn_hidden_size, rnn_hidden_size)
        self.classifier = nn.Linear(rnn_hidden_size * 2, num_embeddings)
        self.bos_index = bos_index

    def _init_indices(self, batch_size):
        """ return the BEGIN-OF-SEQUENCE index vector """
        return torch.ones(batch_size, dtype=torch.int64) * self.bos_index

    def _init_context_vectors(self, batch_size):
        """ return a zeros vector for initializing the context """
        return torch.zeros(batch_size, self._rnn_hidden_size)

    def forward(self, encoder_state, initial_hidden_state, target_sequence):
        """The forward pass of the model

        Args:
            encoder_state (torch.Tensor): output of the NMTEncoder
            initial_hidden_state (torch.Tensor): last hidden state in the NMTEncoder
            target_sequence (torch.Tensor): target text data tensor
            sample_probability (float): schedule sampling parameter
                probability of using model's predictions at each decoder step
        Returns:
            output_vectors (torch.Tensor): prediction vectors at each output step
        """
        # We are making an assumption here: batch is on 1st dimension
        # The input is (Batch, Seq)
        # We want to iterate over the sequence so we permute it to (S, B)
        target_sequence = target_sequence.permute(1, 0)

        # use the provided encoder hidden state as the initial hidden state
        h_t = self.hidden_map(initial_hidden_state)
```

```python
batch_size = encoder_state.size(0)
# initialize context vectors to zeros
context_vectors = self._init_context_vectors(batch_size)
# initialize first y_t word as BOS
y_t_index = self._init_indices(batch_size)

h_t = h_t.to(encoder_state.device)
y_t_index = y_t_index.to(encoder_state.device)
context_vectors = context_vectors.to(encoder_state.device)

output_vectors = []
# All cached tensors are moved from the GPU and stored for analysis
self._cached_p_attn = []
self._cached_ht = []
self._cached_decoder_state = encoder_state.cpu().detach().numpy()

output_sequence_size = target_sequence.size(0)
for i in range(output_sequence_size):

    # Step 1: Embed word and concat with previous context
    y_input_vector = self.target_embedding(target_sequence[i])
    rnn_input = torch.cat([y_input_vector, context_vectors], dim=1)

    # Step 2: Make a GRU step, getting a new hidden vector
    h_t = self.gru_cell(rnn_input, h_t)
    self._cached_ht.append(h_t.cpu().data.numpy())

    # Step 3: Use current hidden vector to attend to encoder state
    context_vectors, p_attn, _ = \
        verbose_attention(encoder_state_vectors=encoder_state,
                          query_vector=h_t)

    # auxiliary: cache the attention probabilities for visualization
    self._cached_p_attn.append(p_attn.cpu().detach().numpy())

    # Step 4: Use current hidden and context vectors
    #         to make a prediction for the next word
    prediction_vector = torch.cat((context_vectors, h_t), dim=1)
    score_for_y_t_index = self.classifier(prediction_vector)

    # auxiliary: collect the prediction scores
    output_vectors.append(score_for_y_t_index)
```

After the encoder creates the state vectors with its bi-GRU and packing-unpacking coordination, the decoder iterates over the time steps to generate an output sequence. Functionally, this loop should seem very similar to the generation loop in Chapter 7, but with a few differences that are distinctly the methodological choices of Luong, Pham, and Manning's (2015) style of attention. First, a target sequence is provided as observations at each time step.[17] Hidden states are computed by using a GRUCell. The initial hidden state is computed by applying a Linear layer to the concatenated final hidden states of the encoder bi-GRU.[18] The input to the decoder GRU at each time step is a concatenated vector of an embedded input token and the last time step's context vector. The context vector is intended to capture information that's useful for that time step and acts to condition the output of the model. For the first time step, the context vector is all 0s to represent no context and mathematically allow only the input to contribute to the GRU computation.

Using the new hidden state as a query vector, a new set of context vectors are created using the attention mechanism for the current time step. These context vectors are concatenated with the hidden state to create a vector representing the decoding information at that time step. This decoding information state vector is used in a classifier (in this case, a simple Linear layer) to create a prediction vector, score_for_y_t_index. These prediction vectors can be turned into probability distributions over the output vocabulary using the softmax function, or they can be used with cross-entropy loss to optimize for ground truth targets. Before we turn to how the prediction vector is used in the training routine, we first examine the attention computation itself.

A closer look at attention

It is important to understand how the attention mechanism is working in this example. Recall from "Attention in Deep Neural Networks" on page 190 that the attention mechanism can be described using *queries*, *keys*, and *values*. A score function takes as input the *query* vector and the *key* vectors to compute a set of weights that select among the *value* vectors. In this example, we use the dot-product scoring function, but it is not the only one.[19] In this example, the decoder's hidden state is used as the *query* vector, and the set of encoder state vectors are both the *key* and *value* vectors.

The dot product of the decoder's hidden state with the vectors in the encoder state creates a scalar for each item in the encoded sequence. Upon using the softmax function, these scalars become a probability distribution over the vectors in the encoder state.[20] These probabilities are used to weight the encoder state vectors before they are added together to result in a single vector for each batch item. To summarize, the

---

17 The Vectorizer prepends the BEGIN-OF-SEQUENCE token to the sequence, so the first observation is always a special token indicating the boundary.

18 See section 7.3 of Neubig (2007) for a discussion on connecting encoders and decoders in neural machine translation.

19 We refer you to Luong, Pham, and Manning (2015), in which they outline three different scoring functions.

20 Each batch item is a sequence and the probabilities for each sequence sum to 1.

---

decoder hidden state is allowed to preferentially weight the encoder state at each time step. This is like a spotlight, giving the model the ability to learn how to highlight the information it needs to generate an output sequence. We demonstrate this version of the attention mechanism in Example 8-8. The first function tries to verbosely spell out the operations. Additionally, it uses the `view()` operation to insert dimensions with size 1 so that the tensor can be broadcast against another tensor.[21] In the `terse_attention()` version, the `view()` operation is replaced with the more commonly accepted practice, `unsqueeze()`. In addition, rather than multiplying element-wise and summing, the more efficient `matmul()` operation is used.

Example 8-8. Attention mechanism that does element-wise multiplication and summing more explicitly

```
def verbose_attention(encoder_state_vectors, query_vector):
    """
    encoder_state_vectors: 3dim tensor from bi-GRU in encoder
    query_vector: hidden state in decoder GRU
    """
    batch_size, num_vectors, vector_size = encoder_state_vectors.size()
    vector_scores = \
        torch.sum(encoder_state_vectors * query_vector.view(batch_size, 1,
                                                            vector_size),
                    dim=2)
    vector_probabilities = F.softmax(vector_scores, dim=1)
    weighted_vectors = \
        encoder_state_vectors * vector_probabilities.view(batch_size,
                                                        num_vectors, 1)
    context_vectors = torch.sum(weighted_vectors, dim=1)
    return context_vectors, vector_probabilities

def terse_attention(encoder_state_vectors, query_vector):
    """
    encoder_state_vectors: 3dim tensor from bi-GRU in encoder
    query_vector: hidden state
    """
    vector_scores = torch.matmul(encoder_state_vectors,
                                query_vector.unsqueeze(dim=2)).squeeze()
    vector_probabilities = F.softmax(vector_scores, dim=-1)
    context_vectors = torch.matmul(encoder_state_vectors.transpose(-2, -1),
```

---

21 Broadcasting happens when a tensor has a dimension of size 1. Let this tensor be called *Tensor A*. When Tensor A is used in an element-wise mathematical operation (such as addition or subtraction) with another tensor called *Tensor B*, its shape (the number of elements on each dimension) should be identical except for the dimension with size 1. The operation of Tensor A on Tensor B is repeated for each position in Tensor B. If Tensor A has shape (10, 1, 10) and Tensor B has shape (10, 5, 10), A+B will repeat the addition of Tensor A for each of the five positions in Tensor B.

```
                          vector_probabilities.unsqueeze(dim=2)).squeeze()
        return context_vectors, vector_probabilities
```

Learning to search and scheduled sampling

The way it is currently written, the model assumes that the target sequence is provided and will be used as the input at each time step in the decoder. At test time, this assumption is violated because the model cannot cheat and know the sequence it is trying to generate. To accommodate this fact, one technique is to allow the model to use its own predictions during training. This is a technique explored in the literature as "learning to search" and "scheduled sampling."[22] One intuitive way to understand this technique is to think of the prediction problem as a search problem. At each time step, the model has many paths from which to choose (the number of choices is the size of the target vocabulary) and the data is observations of correct paths. At test time, the model is finally allowed to go "off path" because it is not provided the correct path from which it should be computing probability distributions. Thus, the technique of letting the model sample its own path provides a way in which you can optimize the model for having better probability distributions when it deviates from target sequences in the dataset.

There are three primary modifications to the code to have the model sample its own predictions during training. First, the initial indices are made more explicit as the BEGIN-OF-SEQUENCE token indices. Second, a random sample is drawn for each step in the generation loop, and if the random sample is smaller than the sample probability, it uses the model's predictions during that iteration.[23] Finally, the actual sampling itself is done under the conditional if use_sample. In Example 8-9, a commented line shows how you could use the maximum prediction, whereas the uncommented line shows how to actually sample indices at rates proportional to their probability.

Example 8-9. The decoder with a sampling procedure (in bold) built into the forward pass

```
class NMTDecoder(nn.Module):
    def __init__(self, num_embeddings, embedding_size, rnn_size, bos_index):
        super(NMTDecoder, self).__init__()
        # ... other init code here ...

        # arbitrarily set; any small constant will be fine
        self._sampling_temperature = 3

    def forward(self, encoder_state, initial_hidden_state, target_sequence,
```

---

[22] For details, we refer you to Daumé, Langford, and Marcu (2009) and Bengio et al. (2015).

[23] If you're familiar with Monte Carlo sampling for optimization techniques such as Markov chain Monte Carlo, you will recognize this pattern.

```
            sample_probability=0.0):
if target_sequence is None:
    sample_probability = 1.0
else:
    # We are making an assumption here: batch is on 1st dimension
    # The input is (Batch, Seq)
    # We want to iterate over the sequence so we permute it to (S, B)
    target_sequence = target_sequence.permute(1, 0)
    output_sequence_size = target_sequence.size(0)

# ... nothing changes from the other implementation

output_sequence_size = target_sequence.size(0)
for i in range(output_sequence_size):
    # new: a helper Boolean and the teacher y_t_index
    use_sample = np.random.random() < sample_probability
    if not use_sample:
        y_t_index = target_sequence[i]

    # Step 1: Embed word and concat with previous context
    # ... code omitted for space
    # Step 2: Make a GRU step, getting a new hidden vector
    # ... code omitted for space
    # Step 3: Use current hidden vector to attend to the encoder state
    # ... code omitted for space
    # Step 4: Use current hidden and context vectors
    #         to make a prediction about the next word
    prediction_vector = torch.cat((context_vectors, h_t), dim=1)
    score_for_y_t_index = self.classifier(prediction_vector)
    # new: sampling if Boolean is true
    if use_sample:
        # sampling temperature forces a peakier distribution
        p_y_t_index = F.softmax(score_for_y_t_index *
                                self._sampling_temperature, dim=1)
        # method 1: choose most likely word
        # _, y_t_index = torch.max(p_y_t_index, 1)
        # method 2: sample from the distribution
        y_t_index = torch.multinomial(p_y_t_index, 1).squeeze()

    # auxiliary: collect the prediction scores
    output_vectors.append(score_for_y_t_index)

output_vectors = torch.stack(output_vectors).permute(1, 0, 2)

return output_vectors
```

The Training Routine and Results

The training routine for this example is nearly identical to the training routines seen in previous chapters.[24] For a fixed number of epochs, we iterate over the dataset in chunks called minibatches. However, each minibatch here is composed of four tensors: a matrix of integers for the source sequence, two matrices of integers for the target sequence, and a vector of integers for the source sequence lengths. The two target sequence matrices are the target sequence offset by one and padded with either `BEGIN-OF-SEQUENCE` tokens to act as target sequence observations or `END-OF-SEQUENCE` tokens to act as target sequence prediction labels. The model takes as input the source sequence and the target sequence observations to produce target sequence predictions. The target sequence prediction labels are used in the loss function to compute the cross-entropy loss, which is then backpropagated to each model parameter so that it knows its gradient. The optimizer is then invoked and updates each model parameter by some amount proportional to the gradient.

In addition to the loop over the training portion of the dataset, there is a loop over the validation portion. The validation score serves as a less-biased metric of model improvement. The procedure is identical to the training routine except that the model is put into eval mode and is not updated relative to the validation data.

After training the model, measuring the performance becomes an important and nontrivial problem. Several sequence generation evaluation metrics were described in "Evaluating Sequence Generation Models" on page 193, but metrics such as BLEU which measure the *n*-gram overlap between predicted sentences and reference sentences have become a standard for the machine translation field. The evaluation code that aggregates the results has been omitted, but you can find it in this book's GitHub repo (*https://nlproc.info/PyTorchNLPBook/repo/*). In the code, the model's outputs are aggregated with the source sentence, the reference target sentence, and the attention probability matrix for that example. Finally, BLEU-4 is computed for each pair of source and generated sentences.

To qualitatively assess how well the model is working, we visualize the attention probability matrix as alignments between the source and generated text. It is important to note, however, that recent research has shown attention-based alignments are not exactly the same as they are in classical machine translation. Instead of the alignments between words and phrases being indicative of translation synonymy, attention-based alignment scores could indicate useful information for the decoder, such as attending to the sentence's subject when generating the output verb (Koehn and Knowles, 2017).

---

24 Primarily, this is because gradient descent and automatic differentiation is an elegant abstraction between model definitions and their optimization.

The two versions of our model differ by how they interact with the target sentence. The first version uses the provided target sequences as the inputs at each time step in the decoder. The second version uses scheduled sampling to allow the model to see its own predictions as inputs in the decoder. This has the benefit of forcing the model to optimize against its own errors. Table 8-1 shows the BLEU scores. It is important to remember that, for ease of training, we chose a simplified version of the standard NMT task, which is why the scores seem higher than what you would normally find in research literature. Although the second model, the model with scheduled sampling, has a higher BLEU score, the scores are fairly close. But what does do these scores mean, exactly? To investigate this question, we need to inspect the model qualitatively.

Table 8-1. The BLEU scores for the two models shown earlier; BLEU is computed as the simple average of the 1-, 2-, 3-, and 4-gram overlap

Model name	Bleu score
Model without Scheduled Sampling	46.8
Model with Scheduled Sampling	48.1

For our deeper inspection, we plot the attention scores to see whether they provide any sort of alignment information between the source and target sentences. We find a stark contrast between the two models during this inspection.[25] Figure 8-12 shows the attention probability distribution for each decoder time step for the model with scheduled sampling. In this model, the attention weights line up fairly well for a sentence sampled from the validation portion of the dataset.

---

25 We omit a plot for the first model because it attended to only the final state in the encoder RNN. As noted by Koehn and Knowles (2017), the attention weights are endemic of many different situations. We suspect the attention weights in the first model did not need to rely on attention as much because the information it needed was already encoded in the states of the encoder GRU.

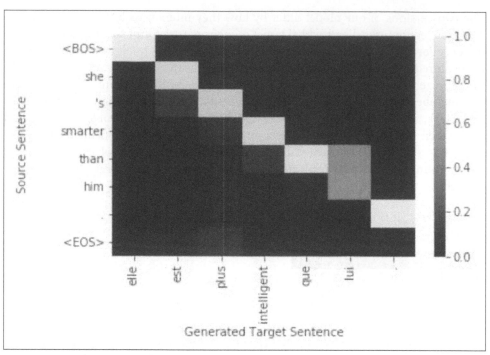

Figure 8-12. The matrix of attention weights for the model with scheduled sampling is plotted as a qualitative assessment of the model performance.

Summary

This chapter focused on producing sequence outputs given a conditioning context with the so-called conditioned generation models. When the conditioning context is itself derived from another sequence, we refer to it as a sequence-to-sequence (S2S) model. We also discussed how S2S models are a special case of encoder–decoder models. To get the most out of a sequence, we discussed structural variants of the sequence models discussed in Chapters 6 and 7—specifically, the bidirectional models. We also learned how the attention mechanism could be incorporated to capture longer-range contexts efficiently. Finally, we discussed how to evaluate sequence-to-sequence models and demonstrated with an end-to-end machine translation example. So far, we have dedicated each chapter of the book to a specific network architecture. In the next chapter, we tie all the previous chapters together and see examples of how you can build many real-world systems using a synthesis of the various model architectures.

References

1. Bengio, Yoshua, Patrice Simard, and Paolo Frasconi. (1994). "Learning Long-Term Dependencies with Gradient Descent is Difficult." *IEEE Transactions on Neural Networks* 5.

2. Bahdanau, Dzmitry, Kyunghyun Cho, and Yoshua Bengio. (2015). "Neural Machine Translation by Jointly Learning to Align and Translate." *Proceedings of the International Conference on Learning Representations.*

3. Papineni, Kishore, et al. (2002). "BLEU: A Method for Automatic Evaluation of Machine Translation." *Proceedings of the 40th Annual Meeting of the ACL.*

4. Daumé III, Hal, John Langford, and Daniel Marcu. (2009). "Search-Based Structured Prediction." *Machine Learning Journal.*

5. Bengio, Samy et al. (2015). "Scheduled Sampling for Sequence Prediction with Recurrent Neural Networks." *Proceedings of NIPS.*

6. Luong, Minh-Thang, Hieu Pham, and Christopher D. Manning. (2015). "Effective Approaches to Attention-Based Neural Machine Translation." *Proceedings of EMNLP.*

7. Le, Phong, and Willem Zuidema. (2016). "Quantifying the Vanishing Gradient and Long Distance Dependency Problem in Recursive Neural Networks and Recursive LSTMs." *Proceedings of the 1st Workshop on Representation Learning for NLP.*

8. Koehn, Philipp and Rebecca Knowles. (2017). "Six Challenges for Neural Machine Translation." *Proceedings of the 1st Workshop on Neural Machine Translation.*

9. Neubig, Graham. (2017). "Neural Machine Translation and Sequence-to-Sequence Models: A Tutorial." arXiv:1703.01619.

10. Vaswani, Ashish et al. (2017). "Attention is all you need." *Proceedings of NIPS.*

Classics, Frontiers, and Next Steps

In this chapter, we review the previous chapters from the perspective of the entire book and see how the seemingly independent topics discussed in the book are interdependent, and how researchers can mix and match these ideas to solve the problem at hand. We also summarize some classical topics in natural language processing that we could not discuss in depth between these covers. Finally, we point to the frontiers in the field, as of 2018. In fast-moving fields like empirical NLP and deep learning, it is important for us to learn new ideas and keep ourselves up-to-date. We dedicate some space for learning how to learn about new topics in NLP.

What Have We Learned so Far?

We began with the supervised learning paradigm and how we could use the computational graph abstraction to encode complex ideas as a model that could be trained via backpropagation. PyTorch was introduced as our computational framework of choice. There is a risk in writing an NLP book that uses deep learning in treating the text input as "data" to be fed to black boxes. In Chapter 2, we introduced some basic concepts from NLP and linguistics to set the stage for rest of the book. The foundational concepts discussed in Chapter 3 like activation functions, loss functions, gradient-based optimization for supervised learning, and the training-eval loop came in handy for the rest of the chapters. We studied two examples of feed-forward networks—the Multilayer Perceptron and convolutional networks. We saw how to use regularization mechanisms like the L1 and L2 norm and dropout to make the networks more robust. The MLPs were able to capture ngram-like relationships in their hidden layers, but they do that inefficiently. The convolutional networks, on the other hand, learn this substructure in a computationally efficient manner using an idea called "parameter sharing."

In Chapter 6, we saw how recurrent networks are also able to capture long-range dependencies across time, with few parameters. You could say convolutional networks share parameters across space and recurrent networks share parameters across time. We saw three variants of the recurrent networks, starting with the Elman RNN and moving on to the gated variants like long short-term memory networks (LSTMs) and gated recurrent units (GRUs). We also saw how you could use the recurrent networks in a prediction or sequence labeling setting, where an output is predicted at each time step of the input. Finally, we introduced a class of models called the encoder–decoder models and studied the sequence-to-sequence (S2S) model as an example of that to solve conditioned generation problems like machine translation. We worked through end-to-end examples in PyTorch for many of these topics.

Timeless Topics in NLP

There is more to NLP than what can be covered within the bounds of a single book, and this book is no exception. In Chapter 2, we identified some core terminology and tasks in NLP. We covered many NLP tasks in the remaining chapters, but here we briefly mention some important topics that we could not address either in part or whole, due to limiting our scope to an initial expository book.

Dialogue and Interactive Systems

Seamless dialogue between computers and humans is considered a holy grail of computing and has inspired the Turing test and the Loebner Prize. Since the early days of artificial intelligence, NLP has been associated with dialogue systems and popularized in pop culture by fictional systems like the main computer on board the *USS Enterprise* in *Star Trek* and HAL 9000 in the film *2001: A Space Odyssey*.[1] Dialogue and the broader area of designing interactive systems is a fertile area of research, as evidenced by the success of recent products like Amazon's Alexa, Apple's Siri, and Google's Assistant. Dialogue systems can be open domain (ask me anything) or closed domain (e.g., flight booking, car navigation). Some important research topics in this area include the following: How do we model the dialogue acts, the dialogue context (see Figure 9-1), and the dialogue state? How do we build multimodal dialogue systems (say, with speech and vision or text and vision inputs)? How can a system recognize user intents? How can we model the user's preferences and generate responses tailored to the user? How can the responses be more human-sounding? For example, recent production dialogue systems have begun to incorporate disfluencies like "umm" and "uh" into the responses to make the systems appear less robotic.

---

1 HAL was more than a dialogue system with emotions and self-awareness, but we're referring to the dialogue component here. We refer you to season 2, episode 9 of *Star Trek: The Next Generation* for an exploration into bot sentience.

Figure 9-1. A dialogue system in action (using Apple's Siri). Notice how the system maintains the context to answer the follow-up question; that is, it knows to map "they" to Barack Obama's daughters.

Discourse

Discourse involves understanding the part-whole nature of textual documents. The task of discourse parsing, for example, involves understanding how two sentences are related to each other in the context. Table 9-1 gives some examples from the Penn Discourse Treebank (PDTB) to illustrate the task.

Table 9-1. Examples from the CoNLL 2015 Shallow Discourse Processing task

Example	Discourse relation
GM officials want to get their strategy to reduce capacity and the workforce in place before those talks begin.	Temporal.Asynchronous.Precedence
But that ghost wouldn't settle for words, he wanted money and people—lots. So Mr. Carter formed three new Army divisions and gave them to a new bureaucracy in Tampa called the Rapid Deployment Force.	Contingency.Cause.Result
The Arabs had merely oil. Implicit=while These farmers may have a grip on the world's very heart	Comparison.Contrast

Understanding discourse also involves solving other problems like *anaphora resolution* and *metonymy detection*. In anaphora resolution, we want to resolve occurrences of pronouns to the entities to which they refer. This can become a complicated problem, as Figure 9-2 illustrates.[2]

```
(a) The dog chewed the bone. It was delicious.

(b) The dog chewed the bone. It was a hot day.

(c) Nia drank a tall glass of beer. It was chipped.

(d) Nia drank a tall glass of beer. It was bubbly.
```

Figure 9-2. Some issues with anaphora resolution. In example (a), does "It" refer to the dog or the bone? In example (b), "It" refers to neither of them. In examples (c) and (d), "It" refers to the glass and the beer, respectively. Knowing beer is more likely to be bubbly is critical in resolving such referents (selectional preferences).

Referents can also be metonyms, as illustrated in this example:

> <u>Beijing</u> *imposed trade tariffs in response to tariffs on Chinese goods.*

Here, Beijing refers to not a location but to the Chinese government. Sometimes, successfully resolving referents might require working with a knowledge base.

Information Extraction and Text Mining

One of the common categories of problems encountered in the industry pertains to information extraction. How do we extract entities (person names, product names, etc.), events, and relations from text? How do we map the entity mentions in text to the entries in a knowledge base (aka entity discovery, entity linking, slot-filling)?[3] How do we build and maintain that knowledge base in the first place (knowledge base population)? These are a few of the questions routinely answered in information extraction research in different contexts.

Document Analysis and Retrieval

Another common category of industry NLP problems includes making sense of large collections of documents. How do we extract topics from a document (topic modeling)? How can we index and search documents more intelligently? How can we

---

2 For a broader discussion of such problems, we refer the reader to the *Winograd Schema Challenge* (*https://cs.nyu.edu/faculty/davise/papers/WinogradSchemas/WS.html*).

3 For more details about these tasks see, for example, *https://tac.nist.gov/2018/SM-KBP/*.

understand search queries (query parsing)? How can we generate summaries for large collections?

The scope and applicability of NLP techniques is wide, and in fact, NLP techniques can be applied anywhere unstructured or semi-structured data is present. As an example, we refer you to Dill et al. (2007), in which they apply natural-language parsing techniques to explain protein folding.

Frontiers in NLP

It seems like a fool's errand to write a section titled "Frontiers in NLP" when the field is undergoing rapid innovation. However, we would like to leave you with a glimpse of what the latest trends appear to be as of the fall 2018:

Bringing classical NLP literature into the differentiable learning paradigm
> The field of NLP is several decades old, although the field of deep learning is just a few years young. A lot of the innovation appears to be examining traditional approaches and tasks under the new deep learning (differentiable learning) paradigm. A good question to ask when reading classic NLP papers (and we recommend reading them!) is what the authors are trying to learn. What are the input/output representations? How can you simplify that with techniques learned in the previous chapters?

Compositionality of models
> In this book, we discussed different kinds of deep learning architectures for NLP: MLPs, CNNs, sequence models, sequence-to-sequence models, and attention-based models. It is important to note that although we discussed each of these models in isolation, this was purely for pedagogical reasons. One trend that's seen in literature is to compose different architectures to get a job done. For instance, you could write a convolutional network over characters of the word, followed by an LSTM over that representation, and have the final classification of the LSTM's encoding be done via an MLP. Being able to combine different architectures compositionally based on the task needs is one of the most powerful ideas of deep learning that help make it successful.

Convolution for sequences
> One recent trend we see in sequence modeling is to model the sequence entirely using convolution operations. As an example of an entirely convolutional machine translation model, see Gehring et al. (2018). The decoding step uses the deconvolution operation. This is advantageous because the training can be significantly sped up using an all-convolution model.

Attention is all you need
> Another recent trend is to replace convolutions with the attention mechanism (Vaswani et al., 2017). Using the attention mechanism, particularly variants

known as self-attention and multiheaded attention, you can essentially capture long-range dependencies that are typically modeled by using RNNs and CNNs.

Transfer learning

Transfer learning is the task of learning representations for one task and using those representations to improve the learning of another task. In the recent resurgence of neural networks and deep learning in NLP, transfer learning techniques using pretrained word vectors have become ubiquitous. More recent works (Radford et al., 2018; Peters et al., 2018) demonstrate how unsupervised representations learned for the language modeling task can be helpful in a variety of NLP tasks, such as question answering, classification, sentence similarity, and natural language inference.

In addition, the field of *reinforcement learning* has enjoyed some recent success in dialogue-related tasks, and modeling with memory and knowledge bases for complex natural-language reasoning tasks seem to be of high interest among researchers in industry and academia alike. In the next section, we switch from the classics and frontiers to something more immediate—developing a systems thinking behind designing production NLP systems.

Design Patterns for Production NLP Systems

Production NLP systems can be complex. When building an NLP system, it is important to remember that the system you are building is solving a task and is simply a means to that end. During system building, the engineers, researchers, designers, and product managers have several choices to make. Although our book has focused mostly on techniques or foundational building blocks, putting those building blocks together to come up with complex structures to suit your needs will require some pattern thinking and a language to describe the patterns.[4] This is popular in many disciplines (Alexander, 1979), including software engineering. In this section, we describe a few common design and deployment patterns of production NLP systems. These are choices or trade-offs that teams often need to make to align the product development with technical, business, strategic, and operational goals. We examine these design choices under six axes:

Online versus offline systems

Online systems are those in which the model predictions need to be made in real time or near real time. Some tasks, such as fighting spam and content moderation, by their very nature require an online system. Offline systems, on the other hand, don't need to run in real time. We can build them to run efficiently on a

---

4 A pattern language (*https://en.wikipedia.org/wiki/Pattern_language*) is a "method of describing good design practices or patterns of useful organization within a field of expertise."

batch of inputs at once and can take advantage of approaches like *transductive learning*. Some online systems can be reactive and can even do the learning in an online fashion (aka *online learning*), but many online systems are built and deployed with a periodic offline model build that is pushed to production. Systems that are built using online learning should be especially sensitive to adversarial environments. A recent example of this was the (in)famous Twitter chatbot Tay (*https://en.wikipedia.org/wiki/Tay_(bot)*), which went astray and started learning from online trolls. As hindsight wisdom expected, Tay soon began responding with offensive tweets and its parent company, Microsoft, had to shut down the service less than a day after its launch.

A typical trajectory in system building is to first build an "offline" system, make it an "online" system with a lot of engineering effort, and then make it an "online learning" system by adding a feedback loop and possibly changing the learning method. Although such a path is organic in terms of complexity added to the code base, it can introduce blind spots like handling adversaries and so on. Figure 9-3 shows the "Facebook Immune System" as an example of an online system that detects spam (caveat: circa 2012; not a reflection of current Facebook infrastructure). Notice how an online system requires a lot more engineering than a similar offline system.

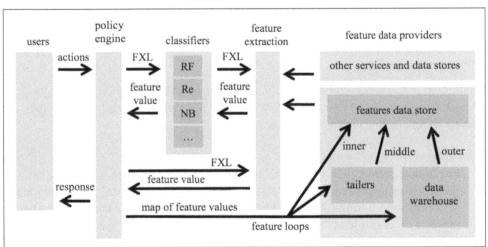

Figure 9-3. Facebook Immune System: an example of an online system, deployed to fight spam and abuse (Stein et al., 2012).

Interactive versus noninteractive systems

Most natural language systems are noninteractive, in the sense that the predictions come solely from a model. In fact, many production NLP models are deeply embedded in the Transform step of an Extract, Transform, and Load (ETL) data processing pipeline. In some situations, it might be helpful for a human to be involved in the loop of making predictions. Figure 9-4 shows an example of an interactive machine translation interface from Lilt Inc., in which models and humans are jointly involved in prediction making in the so-called "mixed-initiative models" (Green, 2014). Interactive systems are difficult to engineer but can achieve very high accuracies by bringing a human into the loop.

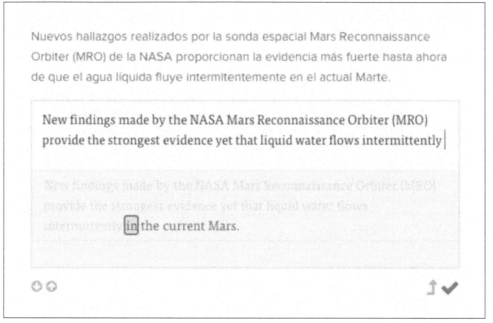

Figure 9-4. A human-in-the-loop machine translation model in action, allowing a human to correct or rephrase suggestions from the MT system to produce very high-quality translations (courtesy of Lilt Inc.).

Unimodal versus multimodal systems

In many situations, it might be helpful to incorporate more than one modality in the learning and prediction process. For instance, it is helpful for a news transcription system to not just use the audio stream but also use the video frames as input. For example, a recent work from Google, dubbed "Looking to Listen" (Ephrat et al., 2018), uses multimodal inputs to the solve the difficult problem of speaker source separation (aka the Cocktail Party problem). Multimodal systems are expensive to build and to deploy, but for difficult problems combining inputs from more than one modality provides signals that would be otherwise impossible to achieve with any single modality alone. We see examples of this in NLP, too. For example, in multimodal translation, we can improve translation quality by incorporating inputs from multiple source languages when available. When generating topics for web pages (topic modeling), you could incorporate features extracted from the images contained therein in addition to the text on the web page, as illustrated in Figure 9-5.

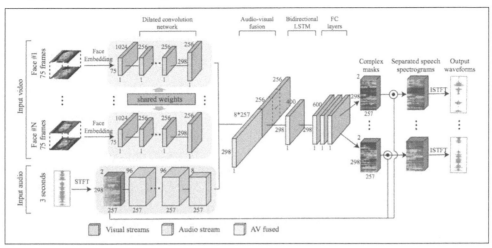

Figure 9-5. A multimodal system that utilizes both audio and video features jointly to solve a difficult problem like the Cocktail Party problem (courtesy of Ephrat et al., 2018).

End-to-end systems versus piecewise systems

Since the advent of deep learning, another choice point available to researchers and engineers is to build a complex NLP system either as a pipeline of different units or as a monolithic end-to-end system. An end-to-end design is appealing in many areas (like machine translation, summarization, and speech recognition) for which carefully designed end-to-end systems can significantly decrease the implementation and deployment complexity, and certainly cut down the number of lines of code. Piecewise systems (Figure 9-6) break down a complex NLP task into subtasks, each of which is optimized separately, independent of the final task objective. Subtasks in the piecewise system make it very modular and easy to "patch" a specific issue in production but usually come with some technical debt.

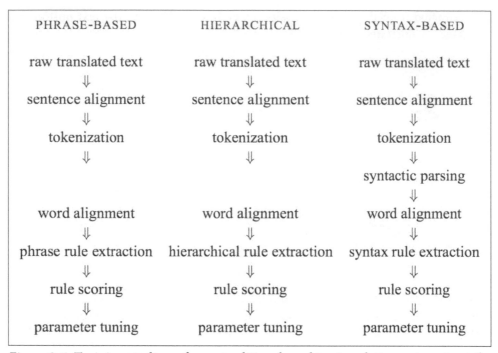

PHRASE-BASED	HIERARCHICAL	SYNTAX-BASED
raw translated text	raw translated text	raw translated text
⇓	⇓	⇓
sentence alignment	sentence alignment	sentence alignment
⇓	⇓	⇓
tokenization	tokenization	tokenization
⇓	⇓	⇓
		syntactic parsing
		⇓
word alignment	word alignment	word alignment
⇓	⇓	⇓
phrase rule extraction	hierarchical rule extraction	syntax rule extraction
⇓	⇓	⇓
rule scoring	rule scoring	rule scoring
⇓	⇓	⇓
parameter tuning	parameter tuning	parameter tuning

Figure 9-6. Training pipelines of some traditional machine translation systems treat the task as a sequence of subtasks, each with its own model. Compare this with the neural machine translation model discussed in "Example: Neural Machine Translation" on page 195 (courtesy of Hoang et al., 2009).

Closed-domain versus open-domain systems

A closed-domain system is optimized explicitly for a singular purpose: to perform well in that domain. For example, a machine translation system could be optimized explicitly to work with biomedical journals—this would involve more than just training on a biomedical parallel corpus. Open-domain systems, on the other hand, are intended for general-purpose use (e.g., Google Translate). For another example, consider a document labeling system. If the system predicts only one of a number of predefined classes (the typical case), it will result in a closed-domain system. But if the system is engineered to discover new classes as it is running, it is an open-domain system. In the context of translation and speech recognition systems, closed-domain systems are also referred to as "limited vocabulary" systems.

Monolingual versus multilingual systems

NLP systems built to work with a single language are called *monolingual systems*. It is easy to build and optimize a monolingual system. *Multilingual systems*, in contrast, are equipped to handle multiple languages. They are expected to work out of the box when trained on a dataset for a different language. Although building a multilingual system is attractive, focusing on a monolingual version has its advantages. Researchers and engineers can take advantage of widely available resources and domain expertise in that language to produce high-quality systems, achieving results that would not be possible with a general multilingual system. For this reason, we often find multilingual products implemented as a collection of individually optimized monolingual systems with a language identification component dispatching the inputs to them.

Where Next?

Working with an upcoming framework like PyTorch and a fast-changing field like deep learning feels like building a mansion on shifting ground. In this section, we point to some resources related to deep learning, PyTorch, and NLP to help our readers continue strengthening the foundation we've built in this book.

We did not cover every single feature of PyTorch. We recommend that you follow the excellent PyTorch documentation and participate in the PyTorch forums to continue with your PyTorch practice:

- PyTorch documentation (*https://pytorch.org/docs*)
- PyTorch forums (*https://discuss.pytorch.org/*)

The field of deep learning itself is seeing a profusion of activity from industry and academia alike. Most deep learning works appear on arXiv under different categories:

- Machine learning (*https://arxiv.org/list/cs.LG/recent*)
- Language and computation (*https://arxiv.org/list/cs.CL/recent*)
- Artificial intelligence (*https://arxiv.org/list/cs.AI/recent*)

The best way to catch up on new works in NLP is to follow academic conferences such as the following:

- Association of Computational Linguistics (ACL)
- Empirical Methods in Natural Language Processing (EMNLP)
- North American Association for Computational Linguistics (NAACL)
- European chapter of ACL (EACL)
- Conference on Computational Natural Language Learning (CoNLL)

We recommend *aclweb.org* (*https://www.aclweb.org/*) to keep up-to-date with proceedings of these and other conferences, workshops, and other important NLP news.

As you prepare to move beyond the basics, you might find yourself having to read research papers. Reading papers is an acquired art. You can find some helpful hints for reading NLP papers in this article by Jason Eisner (*https://www.cs.jhu.edu/~jason/advice/how-to-read-a-paper.html*).

Finally, we will continue offering more educational materials to supplement the contents of this book in our GitHub repo (*https://nlproc.info/PyTorchNLPBook/repo/*).

References

1. Alexander, Christopher. (1979). *The Timeless Way of Building*. Oxford University Press.

2. Dill, Ken A. et al. (2007). "Computational linguistics: A New Tool for Exploring Biopolymer Structures and Statistical Mechanics." *Polymer* 48.

3. Hoang, Hieu, Philipp Koehn, and Adam Lopez. (2009). "A Unified Framework for Phrase-Based, Hierarchical, and Syntax-Based Statistical Machine Translation." *Proceedings of IWSLT*.

4. Stein, Tao, Erdong Chen, and Karan Mangla. (2011). "Facebook Immune System." SNS.

5. Green, Spence. (2014). "Mixed-Initiative Language Translation." PhD thesis, Stanford University.

6. Vaswani, Ashish, et al. (2017). "Attention Is All You Need." *Proceedings of NIPS*.

7. Ephrat, Ariel et al. (2018). "Looking to Listen: A Speaker-Independent Audio-Visual Model for Speech Separation." SIGGRAPH.

8. Peters, Matthew E., et al. (2018). "Deep Contextualized Word Representations." *Proceedings of NAACL-HLT*.

Index

Symbols

1x1 convolutions, 118
@handles, 31
^ (hat) notation, 3
_ (underscore), 14
__getitem__ method, 60, 91
__len__ method, 60, 91

A

accuracy, definition of, 53
activation functions
    definition of, 41
    in perceptrons, 40
    ReLU, 43, 86
    sigmoid, 42
    softmax, 44, 88, 94
    tanh, 42
Adagrad, 51
Adam optimizer, 51, 70, 179
adaptive optimizers, 51
.add() function, 17
add_token, 62, 92
advanced sequence modeling
    attention mechanism, 189-193
    bidirectional recurrent models, 187
    conditioned generation models, 184
    evaluating sequence generation models, 193
    neural machine translation example, 195-213
    sequence-to-sequence (S2S) models, 183
    use cases for, 183
affine transforms, 40
AG News dataset, 137
agglutinative languages, 30

Alexa, 218
alignment, 191
analogy task, 127
anaphora resolution, 220
annoy package, 125
apply_softmax argument, 89, 97
approximate nearest-neighbor package, 125
args object, 69, 95
attention mechanism, 189-193, 208, 221
attention vector, 191
attention weights, 191
automatic evaluation, 194
average pooling, 116

B

Backpropagation Through Time (BPTT), 151
backpropagation, definition of term, 4
backward pass, definition of term, 4
backward() function, 23, 52
batch normalization (BatchNorm), 117
batches, 52
batch_dict, 96
batch_first flag, 155
batch_generator, 73
BCEWithLogitsLoss, 70
BEGIN-SEQUENCE token, 138, 169, 198
bidirectional recurrent models, 187
bigrams, 32
bijection, 62
binary cross-entropy (BCE), 48, 70
BLEU (BiLingual Evaluation Understudy) score, 190, 194, 212
Boltzmann Distribution, 88

deep learning
    adoption of, 1
    as experimental discipline, ix
    attention mechanism in, 190-193
    computational graphs in, 10
    core of success, 121
    embedding techniques in, 146
    improving performance of, 190
    process of, 1
    PyTorch framework for, 11
    regularization in, 55
    role of ReLU in, 43
    sequence modeling in, 150
    smaller versions of datasets in, 57
    targets in, 49
    training routine for, 69
demographic information, 89
dense vectors, 121
dependency parsing, 36
describe(x) function, 13
device agnostic, 24
dialogue systems, 218
dilation, 106
discourse parsing, 219
discrete types, 121 (see also embeddings)
distributional representations, 122
documents
    categorizing, 34
    document analysis and retrieval, 220
    document classification using transfer
        learning, 137-145
drop probability, 99
dropout regularization, 99
dying ReLU problem, 44

E
early stopping, 54, 180
either-or (XOR) problems, 84
Elman RNN, 151, 153-155, 164, 170, 186
ELU module, 113
emails
    filtering spam, 34
    tagging, 34
embeddings
    approaches to learning, 124
    benefits of, 121
    challenges of, 129
    Continuous Bag of Words (CBOW) model,
        130-136

cultural gender bias in, 130, 146
    definition of term, 121
    document classification using, 137-145
    efficiency of, 123
    loading, 125
    pretrained word embeddings, 124
    relationships between word embeddings,
        126
    role in NLP, 122
    semantic and syntactic relationships, 128
    types of, 121
    word analogy task, 127
encodings
    encoder–decoder models, 183
    encoding and decoding in NMT model,
        201-210
    encoding gendered roles, 130, 146
    observation and target encoding, 5-10
    target encoding, 9
END-SEQUENCE token, 138, 169, 198
epochs, 52
error rate, 193
estimates, 3 (see also predictions)
eval() method, 73, 115
evaluation (see model evaluation)
evaluation error, 180
evaluation metrics, 53
example problems
    classic toy problem, 49-53
    classifying sentiment of restaurant reviews,
        56-76
    compliance with PyTorch versions, ix
    Continuous Bag of Words (CBOW) model,
        130-136
    document classification using transfer
        learning, 137-145
    neural machine translation, 195-213
    surname classification using character
        RNNs, 155-161
    surname classification using CNNs, 110-115
    surname classification with MLPs, 89-100
    surname generation with character RNNs,
        166-178
exploding gradients, 42, 165
Extract, Transform, and Load (ETL) pipeline,
    223

F
Facebook

in_channels argument, 103

K
k-fold cross validation, 54
kernels, 101, 152
kernel_size argument, 104
keys, 191, 208

L
L1 and L2 regularization, 56
language identification, 34
language modeling, 163
Language Modeling tasks, 124
Leaky ReLU, 44
learning rate, 51
learning to search, 210
learning-based embeddings, 121
lemmas, 33
lemmatization, 33
lexical resource projects, 37
lexicon, 32
Linear layers, 83
Linear() class, 41
linearly separable decision boundaries, 81, 83
local attention, 191
location-aware attention, 191
Long Short-Term Memory (LSTM), 166, 170, 179, 186
lookup_index, 62, 92
lookup_token, 62, 65, 92
loops
    improving speed of, 57
    in supervised learning, 52
    training loop, 71, 96
loss functions
    basics of, 45
    BCEWithLogitsLoss, 70
    binary cross-entropy (BCE), 48, 70
    categorical cross entropy, 46
    for classic toy problem, 50
    definition of term, 3
    gradient-based optimization of model
        parameters, 49
    mean absolute error (MAE) , 46
    mean squared error (MSE), 45
    role of in neural networks, 45-48
    root mean squared error (RMSE), 46
loss.backward() method, 73

M
machine learning, evolution of, 1
machine translation, 221 (see also neural
    machine translation)
MASK token, 138
masking, 152
mask_index, 174
matmul operation, 209
matrix, 12
max pooling, 116
maximum entropy (MaxEnt) Classifier, 88
mean absolute error (MAE) , 46
mean squared error (MSE), 45
metonymy detection, 220
minibatch SGD, 4
minibatches, 52
mixed-initiative models, 224
model evaluation
    evaluating on test data, 74
    for CBOW model, 136
    for document classification, 145
    for sequence generation models, 193
    for surname classification with CNNs, 115
    for surname classification with MLPs, 97
    generalization, 53
    inference and classifying new data, 75
    inspecting model weights, 76
    metrics for, 53
    splitting datasets for, 54
models, definition of term, 3
modified loss computation, 174
monolingual systems, 226
multiheaded attention, 193
multilayer perceptrons (MLPs) (see also per-
    ceptrons)
    basics of, 82, 89
    drawbacks of, 100
    implementation with dropout, 99
    implementing in PyTorch, 85
    versus perceptrons, 90
    surname classification with, 89-100
    visual representation of, 83
    XOR (either-or) example, 84
multilingual systems, 226
multimodal attention, 193
multimodal systems, 224
Multinomial Logistic Regression, 88

N

n-grams
  character n-grams, 33
  definition of, 32
  generating, 32
named entity recognition, 35, 163
natural language generation, 163
natural language processing (NLP)
  advanced sequence modeling for, 183-214
  categorizing sentences and documents, 34
  categorizing spans: chunking and named
    entity recognition, 35
  categorizing words: POS tagging, 34
  corpora, tokens, and types, 29-32, 121
  definition of, 1
  design patterns for production systems,
    222-227
  evaluation metrics, 53
  future of, 221
  goal of, 29
  important topics in, 218-221
  intermediate sequence modeling for,
    163-180
  lemmas and stems, 33
  overview of, 217
  resources for learning, 227
  sequence modeling for, 149-161
  structure of sentences, 36
  unigrams, bigrams, trigrams, …, n-grams,
    32
  word embedding, 121
  word senses and semantics, 37
nearest-neighbor package, 125
network-in-network (NiN) connections, 118
neural machine translation (NMT)
  dataset for, 196
  encoding and decoding, 201-210
  overview of, 195
  training routine and results, 212
  vectorization pipeline, 197
neural networks (see also convolutional neural
  networks)
  activation functions, 41-45
  classifying sentiment of restaurant reviews,
    56-76
  impact of intermediate representations with
    specific properties, 83
  loss functions, 45-48
  perceptrons, 39-41

supervised training, 49-56
NewsClassifier class, 142
ngram overlap–based metric, 194
NLLLoss, 95
NLTK , 31, 131, 195
NMTVectorizer.vectorize method, 198
nn.Embedding module, 131
numerical optimization techniques, 1
numerical optimization theory, 55
num_channels hyperparameter, 113

O

observations
  definition of term, 2
  numerical representation of, 5
  one-hot representation, 6, 123
  Term-Frequency (TF) representation, 7
  Term-Frequency-Inverse-Document-
    Frequency (TF-IDF) representation, 8,
    34, 121
one-hot representation, 6, 7, 123
optimizer.step() method, 73
optimizer.zero_grad() method, 73
optimizers
  Adam optimizer, 51, 70, 179
  adaptive optimizers, 51
  for classic toy problem, 51
ordinal classification problem, 10
output vectors, 83
out_channels argument, 103
overfitting, 180

P

PackedSequences, 152, 197, 204
pack_padded_sequence function, 205
padding, 106
padding_idx argument, 134, 204
parameters
  definition of term, 3
  gradient-based optimization of, 49
Parametric ReLU (PReLU), 44
parsing, 36
patience, 55
Penn Discourse Treebank (PDTB), 219
perceptrons (see also multilayer perceptrons)
  activation function, 40
  biological model for, 39
  classic toy problem using, 50

classifying sentiment of restaurant reviews
using, 56-76
components of, 40
drawbacks of, 81
implementation using PyTorch, 40
inputs into, 40
perplexity, 194
phonemes, 149
pooling operations, 116
Porter's Stemmer, 34
POS (part-of-speech) tagging, 34, 163
prediction vectors, 88
prediction-based embeddings, 121
predictions
definition of term, 3
gradient-based optimization of model
parameters, 49
predict_nationality() function, 115
pretrained word embeddings, 124
PreTrainedEmbeddings class, 125
probabilistic graphical models, 150
probability distribution
attention mechanism and, 208, 213
discrete, 44
in RNNs, 166
optimizing, 47, 210
prediction vector and, 88, 134, 158, 175, 208
production NLP systems
closed-domain versus open-domain systems, 226
end-to-end systems versus piecewise systems, 225
interactive versus non-interactive systems,
223
monolingual versus multilingual systems,
226
online versus offline systems, 222
unimodal versus multimodal systems, 224
Project Gutenberg, 131
protected attributes, 89
Punkt tokenizer, 131
pure SGD, 4
PyTorch
CNN implementation using, 107
creating tensors, 13
CUDA tensors, 24
in-place operations, 14
indexing, slicing, and joining, 19
installing, 13

MLP implementation using, 85
perceptron implementation using, 40
tape-based automatic differentiation, 11
tensor manipulation in, 12
tensor operations, 17
tensor types and sizes, 16
tensors and computational graphs, 22
versions discussed, ix

Q

queries, 191, 208
query parsing, 221

R

Recurrent Neural Networks (RNNs)
Elman RNN drawbacks, 164
Elman RNN implementation, 153-155
overview of, 150-153
surname classification using character
RNNs, 155-161
reference output, 193
regularization, 55, 99
ReLU (rectified linear unit) activation function,
43, 86
representation learning, 121
representation vectors, 88
representations
as numerical vectors, 5
categorizing documents and sentences with,
34
definition of term, 1
distributional representations, 122
one-hot representation, 6, 123
Term-Frequency (TF) representation, 7
Term-Frequency-Inverse-Document-
Frequency (TF-IDF) representation, 8,
34, 121
understanding PyTorch's, 59
residual connections/residual block, 118
restaurant reviews (see sentiment analysis and
classification)
ReviewDataset class, 59
ReviewVectorizer class, 60, 92
RNNCell class, 153
root mean squared error (RMSE), 46
running mean formula, 73

S

About the Authors

Delip Rao is the founder of Joostware, a San Francisco–based consulting company specializing in machine learning and NLP research. He's also the cofounder of the Fake News Challenge, an initiative to bring hackers and AI researchers together to work on fact checking–related problems in the news media. Delip previously worked on NLP research and products at Twitter and Amazon (Alexa).

Brian McMahan is a research scientist at Wells Fargo focusing on NLP. Previously, he worked on NLP research at Joostware.

Colophon

The animal on the cover of *Natural Language Processing with PyTorch* is the flamecrest (*Regulus goodfellowi*), which lives in coniferous forests in the high mountains of Taiwan. It is the smallest of Taiwan's native birds. This bird is most closely related, by song as well as appearance and habits, to similar species of its genus on the Asian mainland. Its species name, *goodfellowi*, recognizes the British wildlife collector and ornithologist Walter Goodfellow, who first described it for science.

The flamecrest is an efficient insectivore: though only 3-5 inches long, and weighing only a quarter of an ounce, the birds remain in near-constant motion as they flutter through the trees, gleaning small insects as they hop from branch to branch. Flamecrests have a black stripe atop their heads, with an orange-yellow patch at the top; a white mask around the eye; yellow at the sides; and olive wings. On the male, the orange feather patch is larger, and when the bird is agitated because of territory or breeding disputes, these feathers rise to become the striking flame-colored tuft for which this bird is named. The flamecrest doesn't migrate, remaining on Taiwan year-round, only moving from one mountain elevation to another based on the season. Perhaps because of the remoteness of their mountain home, their breeding habits are considered to be poorly known and still due for study.

Though the flamecrest is common in its range, and not considered a threatened species, its range is restricted to the mountains of Taiwan, where it is protected by conservation laws. Protected areas in the mountains (Taiwan's national parks alone cover nearly 3,000 square miles) benefit not only birds such as the flamecrest, but also hikers and climbers.

Many of the animals on O'Reilly covers are endangered; all of them are important to the world. To learn more about how you can help, go to *animals.oreilly.com*.

The cover illustration is by Karen Montgomery, based on a black-and-white engraving from *British Birds*. The cover fonts are Gilroy and Guardian. The text font is

Adobe Minion Pro; the heading font is Adobe Myriad Condensed; and the code font is Dalton Maag's Ubuntu Mono.

O'REILLY®

There's much more where this came from.

Experience books, videos, live online training courses, and more from O'Reilly and our 200+ partners—all in one place.

Learn more at oreilly.com/online-learning